C-534 CAREER EXAMINATION SERIES

This is your
PASSBOOK for...

Nursing Assistant

Test Preparation Study Guide
Questions & Answers

COPYRIGHT NOTICE

This book is SOLELY intended for, is sold ONLY to, and its use is RESTRICTED to individual, bona fide applicants or candidates who qualify by virtue of having seriously filed applications for appropriate license, certificate, professional and/or promotional advancement, higher school matriculation, scholarship, or other legitimate requirements of education and/or governmental authorities.

This book is NOT intended for use, class instruction, tutoring, training, duplication, copying, reprinting, excerption, or adaptation, etc., by:

1) Other publishers
2) Proprietors and/or Instructors of "Coaching" and/or Preparatory Courses
3) Personnel and/or Training Divisions of commercial, industrial, and governmental organizations
4) Schools, colleges, or universities and/or their departments and staffs, including teachers and other personnel
5) Testing Agencies or Bureaus
6) Study groups which seek by the purchase of a single volume to copy and/or duplicate and/or adapt this material for use by the group as a whole without having purchased individual volumes for each of the members of the group
7) Et al.

Such persons would be in violation of appropriate Federal and State statutes.

PROVISION OF LICENSING AGREEMENTS – Recognized educational, commercial, industrial, and governmental institutions and organizations, and others legitimately engaged in educational pursuits, including training, testing, and measurement activities, may address request for a licensing agreement to the copyright owners, who will determine whether, and under what conditions, including fees and charges, the materials in this book may be used them. In other words, a licensing facility exists for the legitimate use of the material in this book on other than an individual basis. However, it is asseverated and affirmed here that the material in this book CANNOT be used without the receipt of the express permission of such a licensing agreement from the Publishers. Inquiries re licensing should be addressed to the company, attention rights and permissions department.

All rights reserved, including the right of reproduction in whole or in part, in any form or by any means, electronic or mechanical, including photocopying, recording, or by any information storage and retrieval system, without permission in writing from the Publisher.

Copyright © 2025 by
National Learning Corporation

212 Michael Drive, Syosset, NY 11791
(516) 921-8888 • www.passbooks.com
E-mail: info@passbooks.com

PASSBOOK® SERIES

THE *PASSBOOK® SERIES* has been created to prepare applicants and candidates for the ultimate academic battlefield – the examination room.

At some time in our lives, each and every one of us may be required to take an examination – for validation, matriculation, admission, qualification, registration, certification, or licensure.

Based on the assumption that every applicant or candidate has met the basic formal educational standards, has taken the required number of courses, and read the necessary texts, the *PASSBOOK® SERIES* furnishes the one special preparation which may assure passing with confidence, instead of failing with insecurity. Examination questions – together with answers – are furnished as the basic vehicle for study so that the mysteries of the examination and its compounding difficulties may be eliminated or diminished by a sure method.

This book is meant to help you pass your examination provided that you qualify and are serious in your objective.

The entire field is reviewed through the huge store of content information which is succinctly presented through a provocative and challenging approach – the question-and-answer method.

A climate of success is established by furnishing the correct answers at the end of each test.

You soon learn to recognize types of questions, forms of questions, and patterns of questioning. You may even begin to anticipate expected outcomes.

You perceive that many questions are repeated or adapted so that you can gain acute insights, which may enable you to score many sure points.

You learn how to confront new questions, or types of questions, and to attack them confidently and work out the correct answers.

You note objectives and emphases, and recognize pitfalls and dangers, so that you may make positive educational adjustments.

Moreover, you are kept fully informed in relation to new concepts, methods, practices, and directions in the field.

You discover that you are actually taking the examination all the time: you are preparing for the examination by "taking" an examination, not by reading extraneous and/or supererogatory textbooks.

In short, this PASSBOOK®, used directedly, should be an important factor in helping you to pass your test.

NURSING ASSISTANT

GENERAL STATEMENT OF DUTIES:
Performs routine non-professional tasks in support of nursing service, including tasks involving minor personal services for patients and/or residents at a hospital, nursing home, or health related facility; does related work as required.

TYPICAL WORK ACTIVITIES:
- Assists in walking, feeding, bathing, and related restorative and rehabilitation care activities for patients and/or residents and aids in caring for their personal needs and comfort;
- Assists nurses in lifting and turning patients and/or residents, in restraining disoriented patients and/or residents, in holding patients and/or residents and may assist in preparing them for surgery;
- Helps regulate number of visitors and gives information to visitors in accordance with instructions from the nurse in charge;
- Assists professional nursing personnel in carrying out assigned range of motion, promotion, or self-help and independence activities and reality orientation;
- Assembles information concerning the patients and/or residents condition and enters reports on the patient and/or residents records;
- Clean and sterilizes equipment;
- Labels and stores patients and/or residents clothes and turns over valuables to person designated by the facility;
- May assist with care and moving of room furniture, fixtures, and supplies to help keep patients and/or residents safe and comfortable.

SCOPE OF THE EXAMINATION:
The test will assess basic nursing and health information, and the candidate's ability to develop skills in the performance of routine hospital techniques such as bathing, feeding, lifting and transporting patients, making beds, and caring for patients' clothing and other property, assisting medically trained personnel, communicating at the level required for successful job performance, keeping simple records, following oral and written directions, analyzing situations accurately and participating in an appropriate course of action.

HOW TO TAKE A TEST

I. YOU MUST PASS AN EXAMINATION

A. WHAT EVERY CANDIDATE SHOULD KNOW

Examination applicants often ask us for help in preparing for the written test. What can I study in advance? What kinds of questions will be asked? How will the test be given? How will the papers be graded?

As an applicant for a civil service examination, you may be wondering about some of these things. Our purpose here is to suggest effective methods of advance study and to describe civil service examinations.

Your chances for success on this examination can be increased if you know how to prepare. Those "pre-examination jitters" can be reduced if you know what to expect. You can even experience an adventure in good citizenship if you know why civil service exams are given.

B. WHY ARE CIVIL SERVICE EXAMINATIONS GIVEN?

Civil service examinations are important to you in two ways. As a citizen, you want public jobs filled by employees who know how to do their work. As a job seeker, you want a fair chance to compete for that job on an equal footing with other candidates. The best-known means of accomplishing this two-fold goal is the competitive examination.

Exams are widely publicized throughout the nation. They may be administered for jobs in federal, state, city, municipal, town or village governments or agencies.

Any citizen may apply, with some limitations, such as the age or residence of applicants. Your experience and education may be reviewed to see whether you meet the requirements for the particular examination. When these requirements exist, they are reasonable and applied consistently to all applicants. Thus, a competitive examination may cause you some uneasiness now, but it is your privilege and safeguard.

C. HOW ARE CIVIL SERVICE EXAMS DEVELOPED?

Examinations are carefully written by trained technicians who are specialists in the field known as "psychological measurement," in consultation with recognized authorities in the field of work that the test will cover. These experts recommend the subject matter areas or skills to be tested; only those knowledges or skills important to your success on the job are included. The most reliable books and source materials available are used as references. Together, the experts and technicians judge the difficulty level of the questions.

Test technicians know how to phrase questions so that the problem is clearly stated. Their ethics do not permit "trick" or "catch" questions. Questions may have been tried out on sample groups, or subjected to statistical analysis, to determine their usefulness.

Written tests are often used in combination with performance tests, ratings of training and experience, and oral interviews. All of these measures combine to form the best-known means of finding the right person for the right job.

II. HOW TO PASS THE WRITTEN TEST

A. NATURE OF THE EXAMINATION

To prepare intelligently for civil service examinations, you should know how they differ from school examinations you have taken. In school you were assigned certain definite pages to read or subjects to cover. The examination questions were quite detailed and usually emphasized memory. Civil service exams, on the other hand, try to discover your present ability to perform the duties of a position, plus your potentiality to learn these duties. In other words, a civil service exam attempts to predict how successful you will be. Questions cover such a broad area that they cannot be as minute and detailed as school exam questions.

In the public service similar kinds of work, or positions, are grouped together in one "class." This process is known as *position-classification*. All the positions in a class are paid according to the salary range for that class. One class title covers all of these positions, and they are all tested by the same examination.

B. FOUR BASIC STEPS

1) Study the announcement

How, then, can you know what subjects to study? Our best answer is: "Learn as much as possible about the class of positions for which you've applied." The exam will test the knowledge, skills and abilities needed to do the work.

Your most valuable source of information about the position you want is the official exam announcement. This announcement lists the training and experience qualifications. Check these standards and apply only if you come reasonably close to meeting them.

The brief description of the position in the examination announcement offers some clues to the subjects which will be tested. Think about the job itself. Review the duties in your mind. Can you perform them, or are there some in which you are rusty? Fill in the blank spots in your preparation.

Many jurisdictions preview the written test in the exam announcement by including a section called "Knowledge and Abilities Required," "Scope of the Examination," or some similar heading. Here you will find out specifically what fields will be tested.

2) Review your own background

Once you learn in general what the position is all about, and what you need to know to do the work, ask yourself which subjects you already know fairly well and which need improvement. You may wonder whether to concentrate on improving your strong areas or on building some background in your fields of weakness. When the announcement has specified "some knowledge" or "considerable knowledge," or has used adjectives like "beginning principles of…" or "advanced … methods," you can get a clue as to the number and difficulty of questions to be asked in any given field. More questions, and hence broader coverage, would be included for those subjects which are more important in the work. Now weigh your strengths and weaknesses against the job requirements and prepare accordingly.

3) Determine the level of the position

Another way to tell how intensively you should prepare is to understand the level of the job for which you are applying. Is it the entering level? In other words, is this the position in which beginners in a field of work are hired? Or is it an intermediate or advanced level? Sometimes this is indicated by such words as "Junior" or "Senior" in the class title. Other jurisdictions use Roman numerals to designate the level – Clerk I, Clerk II, for example. The word "Supervisor" sometimes appears in the title. If the level is not indicated by the title, check the description of duties. Will you be working under very close supervision, or will you have responsibility for independent decisions in this work?

4) Choose appropriate study materials

Now that you know the subjects to be examined and the relative amount of each subject to be covered, you can choose suitable study materials. For beginning level jobs, or even advanced ones, if you have a pronounced weakness in some aspect of your training, read a modern, standard textbook in that field. Be sure it is up to date and has general coverage. Such books are normally available at your library, and the librarian will be glad to help you locate one. For entry-level positions, questions of appropriate difficulty are chosen – neither highly advanced questions, nor those too simple. Such questions require careful thought but not advanced training.

If the position for which you are applying is technical or advanced, you will read more advanced, specialized material. If you are already familiar with the basic principles of your field, elementary textbooks would waste your time. Concentrate on advanced textbooks and technical periodicals. Think through the concepts and review difficult problems in your field.

These are all general sources. You can get more ideas on your own initiative, following these leads. For example, training manuals and publications of the government agency which employs workers in your field can be useful, particularly for technical and professional positions. A letter or visit to the government department involved may result in more specific study suggestions, and certainly will provide you with a more definite idea of the exact nature of the position you are seeking.

III. KINDS OF TESTS

Tests are used for purposes other than measuring knowledge and ability to perform specified duties. For some positions, it is equally important to test ability to make adjustments to new situations or to profit from training. In others, basic mental abilities not dependent on information are essential. Questions which test these things may not appear as pertinent to the duties of the position as those which test for knowledge and information. Yet they are often highly important parts of a fair examination. For very general questions, it is almost impossible to help you direct your study efforts. What we can do is to point out some of the more common of these general abilities needed in public service positions and describe some typical questions.

1) General information

Broad, general information has been found useful for predicting job success in some kinds of work. This is tested in a variety of ways, from vocabulary lists to questions about current events. Basic background in some field of work, such as sociology or economics, may be sampled in a group of questions. Often these are principles which have become familiar to most persons through exposure rather than through formal training. It is difficult to advise you how to study for these questions; being alert to the world around you is our best suggestion.

2) Verbal ability

An example of an ability needed in many positions is verbal or language ability. Verbal ability is, in brief, the ability to use and understand words. Vocabulary and grammar tests are typical measures of this ability. Reading comprehension or paragraph interpretation questions are common in many kinds of civil service tests. You are given a paragraph of written material and asked to find its central meaning.

3) **Numerical ability**
Number skills can be tested by the familiar arithmetic problem, by checking paired lists of numbers to see which are alike and which are different, or by interpreting charts and graphs. In the latter test, a graph may be printed in the test booklet which you are asked to use as the basis for answering questions.

4) **Observation**
A popular test for law-enforcement positions is the observation test. A picture is shown to you for several minutes, then taken away. Questions about the picture test your ability to observe both details and larger elements.

5) **Following directions**
In many positions in the public service, the employee must be able to carry out written instructions dependably and accurately. You may be given a chart with several columns, each column listing a variety of information. The questions require you to carry out directions involving the information given in the chart.

6) **Skills and aptitudes**
Performance tests effectively measure some manual skills and aptitudes. When the skill is one in which you are trained, such as typing or shorthand, you can practice. These tests are often very much like those given in business school or high school courses. For many of the other skills and aptitudes, however, no short-time preparation can be made. Skills and abilities natural to you or that you have developed throughout your lifetime are being tested.

Many of the general questions just described provide all the data needed to answer the questions and ask you to use your reasoning ability to find the answers. Your best preparation for these tests, as well as for tests of facts and ideas, is to be at your physical and mental best. You, no doubt, have your own methods of getting into an exam-taking mood and keeping "in shape." The next section lists some ideas on this subject.

IV. KINDS OF QUESTIONS

Only rarely is the "essay" question, which you answer in narrative form, used in civil service tests. Civil service tests are usually of the short-answer type. Full instructions for answering these questions will be given to you at the examination. But in case this is your first experience with short-answer questions and separate answer sheets, here is what you need to know:

1) Multiple-choice Questions
Most popular of the short-answer questions is the "multiple choice" or "best answer" question. It can be used, for example, to test for factual knowledge, ability to solve problems or judgment in meeting situations found at work.

A multiple-choice question is normally one of three types—
- It can begin with an incomplete statement followed by several possible endings. You are to find the one ending which *best* completes the statement, although some of the others may not be entirely wrong.
- It can also be a complete statement in the form of a question which is answered by choosing one of the statements listed.

- It can be in the form of a problem – again you select the best answer.

Here is an example of a multiple-choice question with a discussion which should give you some clues as to the method for choosing the right answer:

When an employee has a complaint about his assignment, the action which will *best* help him overcome his difficulty is to
- A. discuss his difficulty with his coworkers
- B. take the problem to the head of the organization
- C. take the problem to the person who gave him the assignment
- D. say nothing to anyone about his complaint

In answering this question, you should study each of the choices to find which is best. Consider choice "A" – Certainly an employee may discuss his complaint with fellow employees, but no change or improvement can result, and the complaint remains unresolved. Choice "B" is a poor choice since the head of the organization probably does not know what assignment you have been given, and taking your problem to him is known as "going over the head" of the supervisor. The supervisor, or person who made the assignment, is the person who can clarify it or correct any injustice. Choice "C" is, therefore, correct. To say nothing, as in choice "D," is unwise. Supervisors have and interest in knowing the problems employees are facing, and the employee is seeking a solution to his problem.

2) True/False Questions

The "true/false" or "right/wrong" form of question is sometimes used. Here a complete statement is given. Your job is to decide whether the statement is right or wrong.

SAMPLE: A roaming cell-phone call to a nearby city costs less than a non-roaming call to a distant city.

This statement is wrong, or false, since roaming calls are more expensive.

This is not a complete list of all possible question forms, although most of the others are variations of these common types. You will always get complete directions for answering questions. Be sure you understand *how* to mark your answers – ask questions until you do.

V. RECORDING YOUR ANSWERS

Computer terminals are used more and more today for many different kinds of exams.
For an examination with very few applicants, you may be told to record your answers in the test booklet itself. Separate answer sheets are much more common. If this separate answer sheet is to be scored by machine – and this is often the case – it is highly important that you mark your answers correctly in order to get credit.
An electronic scoring machine is often used in civil service offices because of the speed with which papers can be scored. Machine-scored answer sheets must be marked with a pencil, which will be given to you. This pencil has a high graphite content which responds to the electronic scoring machine. As a matter of fact, stray dots may register as answers, so do not let your pencil rest on the answer sheet while you are pondering the correct answer. Also, if your pencil lead breaks or is otherwise defective, ask for another.

Since the answer sheet will be dropped in a slot in the scoring machine, be careful not to bend the corners or get the paper crumpled.

The answer sheet normally has five vertical columns of numbers, with 30 numbers to a column. These numbers correspond to the question numbers in your test booklet. After each number, going across the page are four or five pairs of dotted lines. These short dotted lines have small letters or numbers above them. The first two pairs may also have a "T" or "F" above the letters. This indicates that the first two pairs only are to be used if the questions are of the true-false type. If the questions are multiple choice, disregard the "T" and "F" and pay attention only to the small letters or numbers.

Answer your questions in the manner of the sample that follows:

32. The largest city in the United States is
    A. Washington, D.C.
    B. New York City
    C. Chicago
    D. Detroit
    E. San Francisco

1) Choose the answer you think is best. (New York City is the largest, so "B" is correct.)
2) Find the row of dotted lines numbered the same as the question you are answering. (Find row number 32)
3) Find the pair of dotted lines corresponding to the answer. (Find the pair of lines under the mark "B.")
4) Make a solid black mark between the dotted lines.

VI. BEFORE THE TEST

Common sense will help you find procedures to follow to get ready for an examination. Too many of us, however, overlook these sensible measures. Indeed, nervousness and fatigue have been found to be the most serious reasons why applicants fail to do their best on civil service tests. Here is a list of reminders:

- Begin your preparation early – Don't wait until the last minute to go scurrying around for books and materials or to find out what the position is all about.
- Prepare continuously – An hour a night for a week is better than an all-night cram session. This has been definitely established. What is more, a night a week for a month will return better dividends than crowding your study into a shorter period of time.
- Locate the place of the exam – You have been sent a notice telling you when and where to report for the examination. If the location is in a different town or otherwise unfamiliar to you, it would be well to inquire the best route and learn something about the building.
- Relax the night before the test – Allow your mind to rest. Do not study at all that night. Plan some mild recreation or diversion; then go to bed early and get a good night's sleep.
- Get up early enough to make a leisurely trip to the place for the test – This way unforeseen events, traffic snarls, unfamiliar buildings, etc. will not upset you.
- Dress comfortably – A written test is not a fashion show. You will be known by number and not by name, so wear something comfortable.

- Leave excess paraphernalia at home – Shopping bags and odd bundles will get in your way. You need bring only the items mentioned in the official notice you received; usually everything you need is provided. Do not bring reference books to the exam. They will only confuse those last minutes and be taken away from you when in the test room.
- Arrive somewhat ahead of time – If because of transportation schedules you must get there very early, bring a newspaper or magazine to take your mind off yourself while waiting.
- Locate the examination room – When you have found the proper room, you will be directed to the seat or part of the room where you will sit. Sometimes you are given a sheet of instructions to read while you are waiting. Do not fill out any forms until you are told to do so; just read them and be prepared.
- Relax and prepare to listen to the instructions
- If you have any physical problem that may keep you from doing your best, be sure to tell the test administrator. If you are sick or in poor health, you really cannot do your best on the exam. You can come back and take the test some other time.

VII. AT THE TEST

The day of the test is here and you have the test booklet in your hand. The temptation to get going is very strong. Caution! There is more to success than knowing the right answers. You must know how to identify your papers and understand variations in the type of short-answer question used in this particular examination. Follow these suggestions for maximum results from your efforts:

1) Cooperate with the monitor

The test administrator has a duty to create a situation in which you can be as much at ease as possible. He will give instructions, tell you when to begin, check to see that you are marking your answer sheet correctly, and so on. He is not there to guard you, although he will see that your competitors do not take unfair advantage. He wants to help you do your best.

2) Listen to all instructions

Don't jump the gun! Wait until you understand all directions. In most civil service tests you get more time than you need to answer the questions. So don't be in a hurry. Read each word of instructions until you clearly understand the meaning. Study the examples, listen to all announcements and follow directions. Ask questions if you do not understand what to do.

3) Identify your papers

Civil service exams are usually identified by number only. You will be assigned a number; you must not put your name on your test papers. Be sure to copy your number correctly. Since more than one exam may be given, copy your exact examination title.

4) Plan your time

Unless you are told that a test is a "speed" or "rate of work" test, speed itself is usually not important. Time enough to answer all the questions will be provided, but this does not mean that you have all day. An overall time limit has been set. Divide the total time (in minutes) by the number of questions to determine the approximate time you have for each question.

5) Do not linger over difficult questions

If you come across a difficult question, mark it with a paper clip (useful to have along) and come back to it when you have been through the booklet. One caution if you do this – be sure to skip a number on your answer sheet as well. Check often to be sure that you have not lost your place and that you are marking in the row numbered the same as the question you are answering.

6) Read the questions

Be sure you know what the question asks! Many capable people are unsuccessful because they failed to *read* the questions correctly.

7) Answer all questions

Unless you have been instructed that a penalty will be deducted for incorrect answers, it is better to guess than to omit a question.

8) Speed tests

It is often better NOT to guess on speed tests. It has been found that on timed tests people are tempted to spend the last few seconds before time is called in marking answers at random – without even reading them – in the hope of picking up a few extra points. To discourage this practice, the instructions may warn you that your score will be "corrected" for guessing. That is, a penalty will be applied. The incorrect answers will be deducted from the correct ones, or some other penalty formula will be used.

9) Review your answers

If you finish before time is called, go back to the questions you guessed or omitted to give them further thought. Review other answers if you have time.

10) Return your test materials

If you are ready to leave before others have finished or time is called, take ALL your materials to the monitor and leave quietly. Never take any test material with you. The monitor can discover whose papers are not complete, and taking a test booklet may be grounds for disqualification.

VIII. EXAMINATION TECHNIQUES

1) Read the general instructions carefully. These are usually printed on the first page of the exam booklet. As a rule, these instructions refer to the timing of the examination; the fact that you should not start work until the signal and must stop work at a signal, etc. If there are any *special* instructions, such as a choice of questions to be answered, make sure that you note this instruction carefully.

2) When you are ready to start work on the examination, that is as soon as the signal has been given, read the instructions to each question booklet, underline any key words or phrases, such as *least, best, outline, describe* and the like. In this way you will tend to answer as requested rather than discover on reviewing your paper that you *listed without describing*, that you selected the *worst* choice rather than the *best* choice, etc.

3) If the examination is of the objective or multiple-choice type – that is, each question will also give a series of possible answers: A, B, C or D, and you are called upon to select the best answer and write the letter next to that answer on your answer paper – it is advisable to start answering each question in turn. There may be anywhere from 50 to 100 such questions in the three or four hours allotted and you can see how much time would be taken if you read through all the questions before beginning to answer any. Furthermore, if you come across a question or group of questions which you know would be difficult to answer, it would undoubtedly affect your handling of all the other questions.

4) If the examination is of the essay type and contains but a few questions, it is a moot point as to whether you should read all the questions before starting to answer any one. Of course, if you are given a choice – say five out of seven and the like – then it is essential to read all the questions so you can eliminate the two that are most difficult. If, however, you are asked to answer all the questions, there may be danger in trying to answer the easiest one first because you may find that you will spend too much time on it. The best technique is to answer the first question, then proceed to the second, etc.

5) Time your answers. Before the exam begins, write down the time it started, then add the time allowed for the examination and write down the time it must be completed, then divide the time available somewhat as follows:
    - If 3-1/2 hours are allowed, that would be 210 minutes. If you have 80 objective-type questions, that would be an average of 2-1/2 minutes per question. Allow yourself no more than 2 minutes per question, or a total of 160 minutes, which will permit about 50 minutes to review.
    - If for the time allotment of 210 minutes there are 7 essay questions to answer, that would average about 30 minutes a question. Give yourself only 25 minutes per question so that you have about 35 minutes to review.

6) The most important instruction is to *read each question* and make sure you know what is wanted. The second most important instruction is to *time yourself properly* so that you answer every question. The third most important instruction is to *answer every question*. Guess if you have to but include something for each question. Remember that you will receive no credit for a blank and will probably receive some credit if you write something in answer to an essay question. If you guess a letter – say "B" for a multiple-choice question – you may have guessed right. If you leave a blank as an answer to a multiple-choice question, the examiners may respect your feelings but it will not add a point to your score. Some exams may penalize you for wrong answers, so in such cases *only*, you may not want to guess unless you have some basis for your answer.

7) Suggestions
    a. Objective-type questions
        1. Examine the question booklet for proper sequence of pages and questions
        2. Read all instructions carefully
        3. Skip any question which seems too difficult; return to it after all other questions have been answered
        4. Apportion your time properly; do not spend too much time on any single question or group of questions

5. Note and underline key words – *all, most, fewest, least, best, worst, same, opposite*, etc.
6. Pay particular attention to negatives
7. Note unusual option, e.g., unduly long, short, complex, different or similar in content to the body of the question
8. Observe the use of "hedging" words – *probably, may, most likely*, etc.
9. Make sure that your answer is put next to the same number as the question
10. Do not second-guess unless you have good reason to believe the second answer is definitely more correct
11. Cross out original answer if you decide another answer is more accurate; do not erase until you are ready to hand your paper in
12. Answer all questions; guess unless instructed otherwise
13. Leave time for review

   b. Essay questions
   1. Read each question carefully
   2. Determine exactly what is wanted. Underline key words or phrases.
   3. Decide on outline or paragraph answer
   4. Include many different points and elements unless asked to develop any one or two points or elements
   5. Show impartiality by giving pros and cons unless directed to select one side only
   6. Make and write down any assumptions you find necessary to answer the questions
   7. Watch your English, grammar, punctuation and choice of words
   8. Time your answers; don't crowd material

8) Answering the essay question

Most essay questions can be answered by framing the specific response around several key words or ideas. Here are a few such key words or ideas:

M's: manpower, materials, methods, money, management
P's: purpose, program, policy, plan, procedure, practice, problems, pitfalls, personnel, public relations

   a. Six basic steps in handling problems:
   1. Preliminary plan and background development
   2. Collect information, data and facts
   3. Analyze and interpret information, data and facts
   4. Analyze and develop solutions as well as make recommendations
   5. Prepare report and sell recommendations
   6. Install recommendations and follow up effectiveness

   b. Pitfalls to avoid
   1. *Taking things for granted* – A statement of the situation does not necessarily imply that each of the elements is necessarily true; for example, a complaint may be invalid and biased so that all that can be taken for granted is that a complaint has been registered

2. *Considering only one side of a situation* – Wherever possible, indicate several alternatives and then point out the reasons you selected the best one
3. *Failing to indicate follow up* – Whenever your answer indicates action on your part, make certain that you will take proper follow-up action to see how successful your recommendations, procedures or actions turn out to be
4. *Taking too long in answering any single question* – Remember to time your answers properly

IX. AFTER THE TEST

Scoring procedures differ in detail among civil service jurisdictions although the general principles are the same. Whether the papers are hand-scored or graded by machine we have described, they are nearly always graded by number. That is, the person who marks the paper knows only the number – never the name – of the applicant. Not until all the papers have been graded will they be matched with names. If other tests, such as training and experience or oral interview ratings have been given, scores will be combined. Different parts of the examination usually have different weights. For example, the written test might count 60 percent of the final grade, and a rating of training and experience 40 percent. In many jurisdictions, veterans will have a certain number of points added to their grades.

After the final grade has been determined, the names are placed in grade order and an eligible list is established. There are various methods for resolving ties between those who get the same final grade – probably the most common is to place first the name of the person whose application was received first. Job offers are made from the eligible list in the order the names appear on it. You will be notified of your grade and your rank as soon as all these computations have been made. This will be done as rapidly as possible.

People who are found to meet the requirements in the announcement are called "eligibles." Their names are put on a list of eligible candidates. An eligible's chances of getting a job depend on how high he stands on this list and how fast agencies are filling jobs from the list.

When a job is to be filled from a list of eligibles, the agency asks for the names of people on the list of eligibles for that job. When the civil service commission receives this request, it sends to the agency the names of the three people highest on this list. Or, if the job to be filled has specialized requirements, the office sends the agency the names of the top three persons who meet these requirements from the general list.

The appointing officer makes a choice from among the three people whose names were sent to him. If the selected person accepts the appointment, the names of the others are put back on the list to be considered for future openings.

That is the rule in hiring from all kinds of eligible lists, whether they are for typist, carpenter, chemist, or something else. For every vacancy, the appointing officer has his choice of any one of the top three eligibles on the list. This explains why the person whose name is on top of the list sometimes does not get an appointment when some of the persons lower on the list do. If the appointing officer chooses the second or third eligible, the No. 1 eligible does not get a job at once, but stays on the list until he is appointed or the list is terminated.

X. HOW TO PASS THE INTERVIEW TEST

The examination for which you applied requires an oral interview test. You have already taken the written test and you are now being called for the interview test – the final part of the formal examination.

You may think that it is not possible to prepare for an interview test and that there are no procedures to follow during an interview. Our purpose is to point out some things you can do in advance that will help you and some good rules to follow and pitfalls to avoid while you are being interviewed.

What is an interview supposed to test?

The written examination is designed to test the technical knowledge and competence of the candidate; the oral is designed to evaluate intangible qualities, not readily measured otherwise, and to establish a list showing the relative fitness of each candidate – as measured against his competitors – for the position sought. Scoring is not on the basis of "right" and "wrong," but on a sliding scale of values ranging from "not passable" to "outstanding." As a matter of fact, it is possible to achieve a relatively low score without a single "incorrect" answer because of evident weakness in the qualities being measured.

Occasionally, an examination may consist entirely of an oral test – either an individual or a group oral. In such cases, information is sought concerning the technical knowledges and abilities of the candidate, since there has been no written examination for this purpose. More commonly, however, an oral test is used to supplement a written examination.

Who conducts interviews?

The composition of oral boards varies among different jurisdictions. In nearly all, a representative of the personnel department serves as chairman. One of the members of the board may be a representative of the department in which the candidate would work. In some cases, "outside experts" are used, and, frequently, a businessman or some other representative of the general public is asked to serve. Labor and management or other special groups may be represented. The aim is to secure the services of experts in the appropriate field.

However the board is composed, it is a good idea (and not at all improper or unethical) to ascertain in advance of the interview who the members are and what groups they represent. When you are introduced to them, you will have some idea of their backgrounds and interests, and at least you will not stutter and stammer over their names.

What should be done before the interview?

While knowledge about the board members is useful and takes some of the surprise element out of the interview, there is other preparation which is more substantive. It *is* possible to prepare for an oral interview – in several ways:

1) Keep a copy of your application and review it carefully before the interview

This may be the only document before the oral board, and the starting point of the interview. Know what education and experience you have listed there, and the sequence and dates of all of it. Sometimes the board will ask you to review the highlights of your experience for them; you should not have to hem and haw doing it.

2) Study the class specification and the examination announcement

Usually, the oral board has one or both of these to guide them. The qualities, characteristics or knowledges required by the position sought are stated in these documents. They offer valuable clues as to the nature of the oral interview. For example, if the job involves supervisory responsibilities, the announcement will usually indicate that knowledge of modern supervisory methods and the qualifications of the candidate as a supervisor will be tested. If so, you can expect such questions, frequently in the form of a hypothetical situation which you are expected to solve. NEVER go into an oral without knowledge of the duties and responsibilities of the job you seek.

3) Think through each qualification required

Try to visualize the kind of questions you would ask if you were a board member. How well could you answer them? Try especially to appraise your own knowledge and background in each area, *measured against the job sought*, and identify any areas in which you are weak. Be critical and realistic – do not flatter yourself.

4) Do some general reading in areas in which you feel you may be weak

For example, if the job involves supervision and your past experience has NOT, some general reading in supervisory methods and practices, particularly in the field of human relations, might be useful. Do NOT study agency procedures or detailed manuals. The oral board will be testing your understanding and capacity, not your memory.

5) Get a good night's sleep and watch your general health and mental attitude

You will want a clear head at the interview. Take care of a cold or any other minor ailment, and of course, no hangovers.

What should be done on the day of the interview?

Now comes the day of the interview itself. Give yourself plenty of time to get there. Plan to arrive somewhat ahead of the scheduled time, particularly if your appointment is in the fore part of the day. If a previous candidate fails to appear, the board might be ready for you a bit early. By early afternoon an oral board is almost invariably behind schedule if there are many candidates, and you may have to wait. Take along a book or magazine to read, or your application to review, but leave any extraneous material in the waiting room when you go in for your interview. In any event, relax and compose yourself.

The matter of dress is important. The board is forming impressions about you – from your experience, your manners, your attitude, and your appearance. Give your personal appearance careful attention. Dress your best, but not your flashiest. Choose conservative, appropriate clothing, and be sure it is immaculate. This is a business interview, and your appearance should indicate that you regard it as such. Besides, being well groomed and properly dressed will help boost your confidence.

Sooner or later, someone will call your name and escort you into the interview room. *This is it.* From here on you are on your own. It is too late for any more preparation. But remember, you asked for this opportunity to prove your fitness, and you are here because your request was granted.

What happens when you go in?

The usual sequence of events will be as follows: The clerk (who is often the board stenographer) will introduce you to the chairman of the oral board, who will introduce you to the other members of the board. Acknowledge the introductions before you sit down. Do not be surprised if you find a microphone facing you or a stenotypist sitting by. Oral interviews are usually recorded in the event of an appeal or other review.

Usually the chairman of the board will open the interview by reviewing the highlights of your education and work experience from your application – primarily for the benefit of the other members of the board, as well as to get the material into the record. Do not interrupt or comment unless there is an error or significant misinterpretation; if that is the case, do not hesitate. But do not quibble about insignificant matters. Also, he will usually ask you some question about your education, experience or your present job – partly to get you to start talking and to establish the interviewing "rapport." He may start the actual questioning, or turn it over to one of the other members. Frequently, each member undertakes the questioning on a particular area, one in which he is perhaps most competent, so you can expect each member to participate in the examination. Because time is limited, you may also expect some rather abrupt switches in the direction the questioning takes, so do not be upset by it. Normally, a board member will not pursue a single line of questioning unless he discovers a particular strength or weakness.

After each member has participated, the chairman will usually ask whether any member has any further questions, then will ask you if you have anything you wish to add. Unless you are expecting this question, it may floor you. Worse, it may start you off on an extended, extemporaneous speech. The board is not usually seeking more information. The question is principally to offer you a last opportunity to present further qualifications or to indicate that you have nothing to add. So, if you feel that a significant qualification or characteristic has been overlooked, it is proper to point it out in a sentence or so. Do not compliment the board on the thoroughness of their examination – they have been sketchy, and you know it. If you wish, merely say, "No thank you, I have nothing further to add." This is a point where you can "talk yourself out" of a good impression or fail to present an important bit of information. Remember, *you close the interview yourself*.

The chairman will then say, "That is all, Mr. _____, thank you." Do not be startled; the interview is over, and quicker than you think. Thank him, gather your belongings and take your leave. Save your sigh of relief for the other side of the door.

How to put your best foot forward

Throughout this entire process, you may feel that the board individually and collectively is trying to pierce your defenses, seek out your hidden weaknesses and embarrass and confuse you. Actually, this is not true. They are obliged to make an appraisal of your qualifications for the job you are seeking, and they want to see you in your best light. Remember, they must interview all candidates and a non-cooperative candidate may become a failure in spite of their best efforts to bring out his qualifications. Here are 15 suggestions that will help you:

1) **Be natural – Keep your attitude confident, not cocky**

If you are not confident that you can do the job, do not expect the board to be. Do not apologize for your weaknesses, try to bring out your strong points. The board is interested in a positive, not negative, presentation. Cockiness will antagonize any board member and make him wonder if you are covering up a weakness by a false show of strength.

2) **Get comfortable, but don't lounge or sprawl**

Sit erectly but not stiffly. A careless posture may lead the board to conclude that you are careless in other things, or at least that you are not impressed by the importance of the occasion. Either conclusion is natural, even if incorrect. Do not fuss with your clothing, a pencil or an ashtray. Your hands may occasionally be useful to emphasize a point; do not let them become a point of distraction.

3) **Do not wisecrack or make small talk**

This is a serious situation, and your attitude should show that you consider it as such. Further, the time of the board is limited – they do not want to waste it, and neither should you.

4) Do not exaggerate your experience or abilities
In the first place, from information in the application or other interviews and sources, the board may know more about you than you think. Secondly, you probably will not get away with it. An experienced board is rather adept at spotting such a situation, so do not take the chance.

5) If you know a board member, do not make a point of it, yet do not hide it
Certainly you are not fooling him, and probably not the other members of the board. Do not try to take advantage of your acquaintanceship – it will probably do you little good.

6) Do not dominate the interview
Let the board do that. They will give you the clues – do not assume that you have to do all the talking. Realize that the board has a number of questions to ask you, and do not try to take up all the interview time by showing off your extensive knowledge of the answer to the first one.

7) Be attentive
You only have 20 minutes or so, and you should keep your attention at its sharpest throughout. When a member is addressing a problem or question to you, give him your undivided attention. Address your reply principally to him, but do not exclude the other board members.

8) Do not interrupt
A board member may be stating a problem for you to analyze. He will ask you a question when the time comes. Let him state the problem, and wait for the question.

9) Make sure you understand the question
Do not try to answer until you are sure what the question is. If it is not clear, restate it in your own words or ask the board member to clarify it for you. However, do not haggle about minor elements.

10) Reply promptly but not hastily
A common entry on oral board rating sheets is "candidate responded readily," or "candidate hesitated in replies." Respond as promptly and quickly as you can, but do not jump to a hasty, ill-considered answer.

11) Do not be peremptory in your answers
A brief answer is proper – but do not fire your answer back. That is a losing game from your point of view. The board member can probably ask questions much faster than you can answer them.

12) Do not try to create the answer you think the board member wants
He is interested in what kind of mind you have and how it works – not in playing games. Furthermore, he can usually spot this practice and will actually grade you down on it.

13) Do not switch sides in your reply merely to agree with a board member
Frequently, a member will take a contrary position merely to draw you out and to see if you are willing and able to defend your point of view. Do not start a debate, yet do not surrender a good position. If a position is worth taking, it is worth defending.

14) Do not be afraid to admit an error in judgment if you are shown to be wrong

The board knows that you are forced to reply without any opportunity for careful consideration. Your answer may be demonstrably wrong. If so, admit it and get on with the interview.

15) Do not dwell at length on your present job

The opening question may relate to your present assignment. Answer the question but do not go into an extended discussion. You are being examined for a *new* job, not your present one. As a matter of fact, try to phrase ALL your answers in terms of the job for which you are being examined.

Basis of Rating

Probably you will forget most of these "do's" and "don'ts" when you walk into the oral interview room. Even remembering them all will not ensure you a passing grade. Perhaps you did not have the qualifications in the first place. But remembering them will help you to put your best foot forward, without treading on the toes of the board members.

Rumor and popular opinion to the contrary notwithstanding, an oral board wants you to make the best appearance possible. They know you are under pressure – but they also want to see how you respond to it as a guide to what your reaction would be under the pressures of the job you seek. They will be influenced by the degree of poise you display, the personal traits you show and the manner in which you respond.

ABOUT THIS BOOK

This book contains tests divided into Examination Sections. Go through each test, answering every question in the margin. We have also attached a sample answer sheet at the back of the book that can be removed and used. At the end of each test look at the answer key and check your answers. On the ones you got wrong, look at the right answer choice and learn. Do not fill in the answers first. Do not memorize the questions and answers, but understand the answer and principles involved. On your test, the questions will likely be different from the samples. Questions are changed and new ones added. If you understand these past questions you should have success with any changes that arise. Tests may consist of several types of questions. We have additional books on each subject should more study be advisable or necessary for you. Finally, the more you study, the better prepared you will be. This book is intended to be the last thing you study before you walk into the examination room. Prior study of relevant texts is also recommended. NLC publishes some of these in our Fundamental Series. Knowledge and good sense are important factors in passing your exam. Good luck also helps. So now study this Passbook, absorb the material contained within and take that knowledge into the examination. Then do your best to pass that exam.

EXAMINATION SECTION

EXAMINATION SECTION
TEST 1

DIRECTIONS: Each question or incomplete statement is followed by several suggested answers or completions. Select the one that BEST answers the question or completes the statement. *PRINT THE LETTER OF THE CORRECT ANSWER IN THE SPACE AT THE RIGHT.*

1. Of the following, the one which is NOT considered to be a duty of the assistant is to

    A. interview the patients
    B. administer local anaesthesia to a patient
    C. take the temperature of patients
    D. aid the patient in preparing for a medical examination

1.____

2. Assume that a patient appears at your clinic at 11:00 on a busy day while you are on duty in the reception room. He says that he missed his 9:00 appointment and that he must return to work within an hour.
The one of the following which is the MOST acceptable course of action for you to take FIRST is to

    A. ask the others who are waiting if they will allow this patient to precede them
    B. immediately schedule another appointment for the patient for the same day in the following week
    C. take the patient to the examining room to see the doctor immediately
    D. explain to the patient that others are waiting and ask him to wait his turn

2.____

3. As an assistant, you will be required to follow certain instructions of the doctor or nurse in the administration of the clinic. Suppose that you have been given some instructions by the doctor which you do not completely understand.
The one of the following which is the MOST advisable course of conduct for you to follow is to

    A. carry out the instructions to the best of your ability
    B. ask another employee in the clinic to interpret the order to you
    C. ask the doctor to repeat the instructions or to clarify them
    D. disregard the instructions and wait until the doctor speaks to you again

3.____

4. As the assistant assigned to a district health center, you are required to interview new patients briefly to determine which clinics they are to go to. There are a number of patients waiting to talk to you. The person whom you are interviewing is Italian and speaks English so poorly that it is almost impossible for you to understand her. She is also very upset and excited. You know that one of the clerks in the eye clinic speaks Italian.
For you to call that clerk and ask him to act as interpreter is

    A. *inadvisable;* the information you must get is confidential and should not be known to the clerk
    B. *advisable* ; the person you are interviewing will be more comfortable in her own language and the interview will, therefore, be completed more quickly
    C. *inadvisable;* the clerk you wish to call may not want to act as interpreter
    D. *advisable;* you will not be responsible for any misunderstanding in this situation if someone else did the interviewing

4.____

1

5. You are assigned to a chest clinic. One Saturday morning, you are alone in the clinic. The doctor has telephoned that he will be delayed and the nurse has not yet reported. One of the regular clinic patients begins coughing while she is talking to you and has a severe hemorrhage.
The BEST procedure for you to follow in this situation is to

   A. give the patient a stimulant and apply a cold compress to the back of the neck
   B. look in the other clinics to see if there is anyone else on duty
   C. do nothing until the doctor comes in
   D. call the police for an ambulance

6. Suppose that you are assigned to interviewing incoming patients for certain routine information in a busy dental clinic. You learn that some patients go to the eye clinic after you have interviewed them where another assistant interviews them for the same information. The two sets of information are to be kept in permanent card files, in two separate clinic offices.
Of the following suggestions which you might make to your supervisor, the one which would prove to be MOST helpful in simplifying this procedure would be for you to

   A. continue to record the information separately so that you can check your records with those of the other assistant for possible errors
   B. send the patient to the other clinic first since they may need more information than you do
   C. fill out two record cards and forward one card to the other clinic
   D. send your record card to the other clinic with the patient after he has been examined by the doctor

7. Suppose that a visitor calls at your clinic and requests information concerning the medical history of a patient. Of the following, the MOST acceptable action for you to take is to

   A. ask him why he wants the information so that you may determine if there is sufficient reason for you to give him the information
   B. give him the information readily as this will foster favorable public relations
   C. refer him to the doctor who examined the patient as he is in a better position to know the patient's medical history
   D. explain that you cannot give out such information as it is strictly confidential and suggest that he write to the department for the information

8. To equip a corner of the outer office of a health center with toys is

   A. *advisable;* the children will be occupied while waiting and, therefore, will be more manageable during the doctor's examination and treatment
   B. *inadvisable;* the child may become too absorbed in play to submit to examination
   C. *advisable;* the children will be so absorbed in play that they will not be aware of whatever discomfort is caused by treatment
   D. *inadvisable;* playing may overstimulate the child and thus cause inaccurate results in the examination

9. While working in a clinic, you discover some obvious inconsistencies in the filing system as a whole. You also have in mind a corrective measure which you would like to see put into practice.
   The one of the following which is the MOST acceptable procedure for you to follow is to

   A. try out your new system for a few days to determine its success before discussing it with your supervisor
   B. explain the probable advantages of your proposed plan to your supervisor and secure his approval before making any changes
   C. continue working under the old procedure until the inconsistencies become apparent to the rest of the staff
   D. collect sufficient evidence to prove the obvious inconsistencies in the present filing system in order to convince your supervisor that the system is unsatisfactory

9.____

10. Assume that you are in charge of the patients' files in the health center to which you are assigned. The record cards of the individual patients are filed alphabetically according to the name of the patient. You want to make it easier to pick out the cards of those patients who are under treatment for any one of five indicated diseases. Of the following, the procedure which would be MOST helpful for this purpose would be to

    A. insert the card of each patient having one of the five diseases into a special folder
    B. use a different size card for each of the five diseases
    C. use a different color card for each of the five diseases
    D. underline the name of the disease on each card in the file

10.____

11. Assume that you are assigned to the chest clinic where you are responsible for the patients' x-ray records. The doctor in charge tells you that in an old group of about 250 disarranged pictures, he thinks there may be several instances in which more than one record exists for the same patient. He asks you to pick out any such records and give them to him.
    Of the following, the BEST procedure for you to follow FIRST is to

    A. look at each record in turn, number it, and make a list of the numbers and corresponding names
    B. go through the records quickly and pick out those names which you remember
    C. arrange the records in alphabetical order according to the names of the patients
    D. list the names of all the patients whose records appear in the group

11.____

12. As an assistant, one of your principal duties is the proper maintenance of the supply cabinet of the clinic to which you are assigned. Upon inspecting the cabinet, you find several large containers with identical labels. However, these contain pills of different color and shapes. Of the following, the MOST acceptable course of conduct for you to follow is to

    A. attempt to sort the pills and relabel them on the basis of your own knowledge
    B. throw all of the pills away to make certain they will not be misused
    C. inform the doctor that you have relabeled the containers after sorting the pills
    D. inform the doctor of the situation so that he may decide what is to be done

12.____

13. Assume that a patient arrives at the clinic and demands an immediate appointment at a time when the doctor is busy.
    Of the following, the action which is MOST acceptable for you to take is to

    A. give the patient a sedative to quiet his nerves and guide him to an unoccupied examination room to rest
    B. explain to the patient that the doctor is busy and ask him to be seated in the waiting room
    C. ask the doctor to examine the patient immediately
    D. talk to the patient until the doctor is ready

14. One of your duties in the clinic is the weighing and measurement of adult patients.
    Of the following, the procedure which is NOT necessary to secure accurate weighing of patients is

    A. daily testing and adjustment of the scale for accurate balance
    B. instructing the patient to stand firmly in the center of the scale
    C. noting what type of clothing the patient is wearing
    D. placing a clean paper towel on the scale before each patient is weighed

15. Suppose that a patient in the clinic is in immediate need of first aid for shock.
    The MOST important thing to do first when both the doctor and nurse are absent is to

    A. make the patient as comfortable as possible and administer a sedative
    B. keep the patient on his feet and moving about in order to activate blood circulation throughout the body
    C. keep the patient as warm as possible
    D. try to locate the doctor before attempting any independent action

16. A patient reports for her scheduled appointment in the pre-natal clinic and tells you, while she is waiting to be examined, that she has a very severe pain in her back. Of the following, the MOST acceptable action for you to take is to

    A. express sympathy and tell her that you yourself once had a severe backache for which it was difficult to get any relief
    B. tell her politely not to take up your time with her ailments as you have other things to do
    C. recommend a liniment which you have used and found to be very helpful in such cases
    D. suggest that she speak to the doctor about it when he examines her

17. A *ticketer system* in a health center may be used as a

    A. follow-up procedure for the recall of patients
    B. method of charting blood pressure recordings at each visit
    C. standard procedure for recording information to be included in memoranda to the doctors
    D. series of tests of nervous reactions

18. When papers are filed according to the date of their receipt, they are said to be filed

    A. numerically   B. geographically
    C. chronologically   D. alphabetically

19. The one of the following which is the MOST important requirement of a good filing system is that   19.____

   A. the expense of installation and operation be low
   B. papers be found easily when needed
   C. the system be capable of any amount of expansion which may be necessary in the future
   D. the filing system have a cross-reference index

Questions 20-24.

DIRECTIONS: Questions 20 through 24 consist of a group of names which are to be arranged in alphabetical order for filing.

20. Of the following, the name which should be filed FIRST is   20.____

   A. Joseph J. Meadeen   B. Gerard L. Meader
   C. John F. Madcar   D. Philip F. Malder

21. Of the following, the name which should be filed LAST is   21.____

   A. Stephen Fischer   B. Benjamin Fitchmann
   C. Thomas Fishman   D. Augustus S. Fisher

22. The name which should be filed SECOND is   22.____

   A. Yeatman, Frances   B. Yeaton, C.S.
   C. Yeatman, R.M.   D. Yeats, John

23. The name which should be filed THIRD is   23.____

   A. Hauser, Ann   B. Hauptmann, Jane
   C. Hauster, Mary   D. Hauprich, Julia

24. The name which should be filed SECOND is   24.____

   A. Flora McDougall   B. Fred E. MacDowell
   C. Juanita Mendez   D. James A. Madden

25. The *initial* contact is of great importance in setting a pattern for future relations.   25.____
    The word *initial,* as used in this sentence, means MOST NEARLY

   A. first   B. written   C. direct   D. hidden

26. The doctor prescribed a diet which was *adequate* for the patient's needs.   26.____
    The word *adequate,* as used in this sentence, means MOST NEARLY

   A. insufficient   B. unusual
   C. required   D. enough

27. The child was reported to be suffering from a vitamin *deficiency.*   27.____
    The word *deficiency,* as used in this sentence, means MOST NEARLY

   A. surplus   B. infection   C. shortage   D. injury

28. In obtaining medical case data, a medical record librarian should discourage the patient from giving *irrelevant* information.
The word *irrelevant*, as used in this sentence means MOST NEARLY

   A. too detailed
   B. pertaining to relatives
   C. insufficient
   D. inappropriate

29. The doctor requested that a *tentative* appointment be made for the patient.
The word *tentative*, as used in this sentence, means MOST NEARLY

   A. definite
   B. subject to change
   C. later
   D. of short duration

30. The black plague resulted in an usually high *mortality rate* in the population of Europe.
The term *mortality rate*, as used in this sentence, means MOST NEARLY

   A. future immunity of the people
   B. death rate
   C. general weakening of the health of the people
   D. sickness rate

31. The public health assistant was asked to file a number of *identical* reports on the case.
The word *identical*, as used in this sentence, means MOST NEARLY

   A. accurate   B. detailed   C. same   D. different

32. The nurse assisted in the *biopsy* of the patient.
The word *biopsy*, as used in this sentence, means MOST NEARLY

   A. autopsy
   B. excision and diagnostic study of tissue
   C. biography and health history
   D. administering of anesthesia

33. The assistant noted that the swelling on the patient's face had *subsided*.
The word *subsided*, as used in this sentence, means MOST NEARLY

   A. become aggravated
   B. increased
   C. vanished
   D. abated

34. The patient was given food *intravenously*.
The word *intravenously*, as used in this sentence, means MOST NEARLY

   A. orally
   B. against his will
   C. through the veins
   D. without condiment

Questions 35-40.

DIRECTIONS: Questions 35 through 40 are to be answered on the basis of the chart below.

SEMI-ANNUAL REPORT OF EXPENDITURES FOR SUPPLIES AND EQUIPMENT
Health Center X - January to June

MONTH	BABY	CHEST	DENTAL	PRE-NATAL	X-RAY	TOTAL
January	$ 456.32	$ 204.28	$723.22	$ 436.29	$ 153.25	$ 1,973.36
February	425.59	225.27	743.33	452.51	174.42	2,021.12
March	631.93	226.35	716.29	429.33	173.37	2,177.27
April	587.27	321.42	729.37	397.27	185.28	2,220.61
May	535.22	275.52	750.54	335.23	184.97	2,081.48
June	539.20	226.80	755.67	394.25	181.08	2,097.00
Total	$3,175.53	$1,479.64	$4,418.42	$2,444.88	$1,052.37	$12,570.84

35. On the basis of the above chart, the TOTAL expenses of the dental clinic exceed the total expenses of the baby clinic for the six-month period by

    A. $1,242.89   B. $1,243.79   C. $1,342.79   D. $1,343.89

36. The total expenses for the month of January for Health Center X EXCEED the total expenses of the chest clinic for the six-month period by

    A. $473.82   B. $483.72   C. $484.72   D. $493.72

37. The expenditures for the entire Health Center were HIGHEST during the month of

    A. February   B. March   C. April   D. June

38. If the total number of patients treated at the Health Center during February was 632, the APPROXIMATE cost per patient for the month of February is

    A. $3.20   B. $12.50   C. $21.00   D. $31.90

39. The TOTAL expenditure for the dental clinic for the six-month period is

    A. *more* than double the total expenses of the Health Center for March
    B. *less* than one-fourth the total expenses of the Health Center for the six-month period
    C. *more* than double the total expenses of the Health Center for April
    D. *less* than the combined totals for the six-month period of expenses for the baby and x-ray clinics

40. The TOTAL expenditure for the first three months for the baby clinic is

    A. *greater* than the total expenses for the baby clinic for the last three months
    B. *less* than the total expenses for the chest clinic for the entire six-month period
    C. *less* than the total expenses for the baby clinic for the last three months
    D. *greater* than the total expenses for the pre-natal clinic for the entire six-month period

KEY (CORRECT ANSWERS)

1.	B	11.	C	21.	B	31.	C
2.	A	12.	D	22.	C	32.	B
3.	C	13.	B	23.	A	33.	D
4.	B	14.	D	24.	D	34.	C
5.	D	15.	C	25.	A	35.	A
6.	C	16.	D	26.	D	36.	D
7.	D	17.	A	27.	C	37.	C
8.	A	18.	C	28.	D	38.	A
9.	B	19.	B	29.	B	39.	A
10.	C	20.	C	30.	B	40.	C

TEST 2

DIRECTIONS: Each question or incomplete statement is followed by several suggested answers or completions. Select the one that BEST answers the question or completes the statement. *PRINT THE LETTER OF THE CORRECT ANSWER IN THE SPACE AT THE RIGHT.*

1. For an employee to address callers at the clinic by name is   1.____

    A. *advisable;* this is a courtesy that everyone appreciates
    B. *inadvisable;* it would be very embarrassing if she greeted a patient by the wrong name
    C. *advisable;* this assures the patient that the assistant is concentrating on her work
    D. *inadvisable;* patients will tend to take advantage of this display of familiarity

2. One of your duties is to get certain preliminary information from a new patient before giving him or her an appointment with the doctor for a later day. The data are to be entered on a permanent record card. Assume that you are interviewing a woman who speaks very broken English and asks if she can talk to you in Spanish. You speak some Spanish and are able to get most of the information from her, but are unable to understand a few of her answers.   2.____
The one of the following which is the BEST action for you to take is to

    A. tell the woman you can't understand her and ask her to come back with an interpreter
    B. fill in on the card all the necessary data as best you can
    C. fill in the information you are certain to have understood correctly, and, at the time of the next appointment, point out to the doctor the omissions
    D. write out for the woman the questions you have not answered on the card and ask her to bring back the answers in writing, in English, the next time she comes

3. Assume that the doctor who is to take charge of the morning session of your clinic has been unavoidably detained and arrives an hour late, at 10 A.M.   3.____
The one of the following which is the BEST action for you to take is to

    A. ask the patients who have arrived for the appointment between 9 and 10:00 to come back at another time
    B. ask all patients if they can wait; if not, give them appointments for another time
    C. say nothing to any of the patients
    D. ask the patients who had appointments for the last hour of the session to come back at another time

4. Assume that you are put in charge of a medicine supply cabinet and you note two identical bottles, one containing a harmless liquid, the other a poisonous substance. You should   4.____

    A. make certain that both bottles are clearly labeled at all times
    B. make certain that the bottle containing the poisonous substance is clearly labeled at all times
    C. pour the liquids over into different shaped bottles
    D. keep the bottles on two different shelves

5. Assume that a patient with a painful shoulder comes in during the doctor's absence and asks you to give him a treatment such as the doctor had prescribed for him some months earlier.
   You should

   A. comply with the request since the difficulty is obviously a relapse
   B. give the patient a sedative and suggest that he call for a future appointment if the pain does not subside
   C. ask him to return later when the doctor will be in
   D. explain that, since you are not a registered nurse, you are not qualified to give treatment

6. A patient telephones the clinic before the doctor arrives and says that the medicine the doctor prescribed for her makes her nauseous. She wants to know whether she should continue taking it.
   The one of the following steps which you should take FIRST is to

   A. advise her to stop taking the medication if it is not effective
   B. suggest that she continue taking the medicine for another week to see if the nausea stops
   C. say that you will inform the doctor and call her back
   D. recommend that she check the accuracy of the prescription with the pharmacist

7. Assume that one of the medicines in your supply cabinet is one which deteriorates within a certain period of time, and becomes ineffective after that time. According to instructions, you reorder the medicine periodically, so that when the old supply becomes ineffective a fresh supply is on hand. You find, however, that only a small quantity from each bottle is being used, and the major portion has to be thrown away.
   The one of the following which is the BEST procedure for you to follow is to

   A. continue to order as before, since you cannot prevent the medicine from spoiling
   B. wait with the fresh order until the old supply has been used up
   C. order periodically as before, but in smaller quantities
   D. order periodically, but at greater intervals, so that more of the medicine will be used up

8. Assume that you are charged with the weekly weighing of a certain group of children attending your clinic. Your doctor instructs you to fill out a certain card form for any child whose weight differs by 5% or more from the previous week's reading. One morning, you weigh five of these children. Child A weighs 63 lbs., B, 54 lbs., C, 47 1/2 lbs., D, 57 lbs., and E, 61 lbs. The previous week's readings were: A, 65 lbs.; B, 51 lbs.; C, 50 lbs.; D, 59 1/2 lbs.; E, 56 1/2 lbs.
   The children for whom you will make out cards will be

   A. A, B, and C   B. B and E
   C. A, C, D, and E   D. B, C, and E

9. A mother comes to the health center with an infant who appears to be ill. As she comes in, she tells you she believes the child may have caught the measles from a neighbor's child who is just recovering from the disease. The BEST of the following actions for you to take is to

   A. tell the mother to take a seat and wait her turn to see the doctor

B. ask the mother if she wants to take a chance on a cancelled appointment, as the doctor's schedule is filled for the day
C. scold the mother for coming in without an appointment and arrange for an appointment on the next clinic day
D. take the mother and child into a vacant examination room and inform the doctor at once

10. Assume that you notice that one of the drugs in your supply cabinet has changed color. It is not on the list of drugs which deteriorate and which must be reordered periodically. The one of the following which is the BEST action for you to take is to

    A. order a new supply of the drug immediately
    B. report the matter to the doctor immediately
    C. ignore the change in the drug, as it is not caused by deterioration
    D. point out the change to the doctor the next time he asks for the drug

10.____

11. To use screw caps on medicine bottles in preference to glass stoppers is

    A. *wise*; screw caps are more attractive
    B. *unwise*; glass stoppers are less expensive
    C. *wise*; screw caps afford more protection to the lip of the bottle
    D. *unwise*; glass stoppers are often interchangeable for several bottles

11.____

12. The one of the following which is the LEAST important precaution to take in connection with the pouring of a dose of medicine from a bottle into a glass is to

    A. wear sterile rubber gloves while pouring
    B. hold the label on the bottle uppermost while pouring
    C. clean the rim of the bottle after pouring
    D. make certain the medicine isn't left around for any time in an unmarked glass

12.____

13. To cover a typed label on a medicine bottle with shellac is

    A. *inadvisable*; the shellac may have a chemical reaction on the drug
    B. *advisable*; the label will become waterproof and the printing on it remain legible
    C. *inadvisable*; the shellac will cause the printing on the label to become illegible
    D. *advisable*; the shellac will prevent the bottle from breaking in case it is dropped

13.____

14. The one of the following which is the MOST valid reason for a patient's needing a prescription in order to obtain a certain drug is that the drug is

    A. poisonous   B. habit-forming
    C. expensive   D. potent

14.____

15. While a growing health consciousness is apparent here and in many other countries, our knowledge of how to prevent and control disease far exceeds its application. This statement means MOST NEARLY that

    A. much of our knowledge of how to improve public health is not put into practice
    B. there has been little increase in our knowledge of disease prevention and control
    C. some of our knowledge on control of diseases is impossible to put into practice
    D. there has been no improvement in the prevention and control of disease

15.____

16. Developments in the field of nutrition have been an important part of medical progress. Not only have dietary cures been discovered for true nutritional diseases but, in almost every branch of medicine and surgery, therapy has been improved by more scientific methods of feeding. The one of the following which is the MOST accurate statement on the basis of the above paragraph is that

    A. nutrition plays a minor role in medicine
    B. dietary cures have therapeutic values only in cases of nutritional diseases
    C. proper nutrition is important in the cure of diseases in almost every branch of medicine
    D. nutritional diseases can be cured only by special diets

17. An individual may be wholly immune to one disease and ultra-susceptible to another; and such immunity, which may be born with the individual or acquired, has absolutely no relation to physique, robustness, or great vitality. The one of the following which is the MOST accurate statement on the basis of this paragraph is that

    A. an adult who is immune to a disease must have been immune to that disease as a child
    B. a person who is susceptible to one disease has a tendency to be susceptible to all diseases
    C. a person of poor physique and low vitality may nevertheless be immune to certain diseases
    D. persons of low vitality are more susceptible to diseases than persons of great vitality

18. If the doctor is in <u>consultation</u> with another doctor, he should not be disturbed.
    As used in this sentence, the word *consultation* means MOST NEARLY

    A. conference   B. operation   C. agreement   D. argument

19. A nurse should not <u>prescribe</u> for patients without the doctor's instructions.
    As used in this sentence, the word *prescribe* means MOST NEARLY

    A. explain the cuases of illness
    B. ascertain the case history
    C. determine the appointment time
    D. recommend treatment

20. The doctor has the right to <u>refer</u> patients to the hospital. As used in this sentence, the word *refer* means MOST NEARLY

    A. accept   B. admit   C. direct   D. accompany

21. An <u>antidote</u> is an agent which

    A. allays pain
    B. counteracts the effects of a poison
    C. reduces acidity
    D. stimulates the heart

22. Physical <u>therapy</u> has an important place in medicine. As used in this sentence, the word *therapy* means MOST NEARLY

    A. massage   B. treatment   C. exercise   D. examination

23. Doctors must not advertise or in any way solicit patients. As used in this sentence, the word *solicit* means MOST NEARLY   23._____

   A. actively seek
   B. greet
   C. exploit
   D. deliberately hurt

24. After examining the patient, the doctor indicated the prognosis of the illness. As used in this sentence, the word *prognosis* means MOST NEARLY   24._____

   A. probable course
   B. cause
   C. treatment
   D. past history

25. A doctor practicing *obstetrics* deals with   25._____

   A. glandular disorders
   B. deformities of the bones
   C. pregnancy
   D. children's diseases

26. The patient's condition was aggravated by a severe case of phobia. The word *phobia* means MOST NEARLY   26._____

   A. fever
   B. apathy
   C. indigestion
   D. fear

27. Neglect of immediate treatment may cause an illness to become chronic. The word *chronic* means MOST NEARLY   27._____

   A. incurable
   B. painful
   C. prolonged
   D. contagious

28. The one of the following which is NOT generally used to alleviate pain is   28._____

   A. aspirin   B. morphine   C. cocaine   D. quinine

29. The administration of a drug subcutaneously means administration by   29._____

   A. mouth
   B. injection beneath the skin
   C. application on the surface of the skin
   D. rectum

30. The one of the following which is NOT a disinfectant is   30._____

   A. boiling water
   B. iodine
   C. formaldehyde
   D. novocain

31. The one of the following which is LEAST related to the pulse rate of an individual is his   31._____

   A. blood pressure
   B. temperature
   C. weight
   D. emotional state

32. The one of the following which denotes normal vision is   32._____

   A. 20/10   B. 20/20   C. 20/30   D. 20/40

33. Of the following, the temperature which is MOST desirable for a babies' weighing room in a health center is _____ °F.   33._____

   A. 60-62   B. 65-68   C. 75-77   D. 85-88

34. Of the following, it is MOST advisable for the operator to wear dark glasses during treatments by

    A. x-ray
    B. infrared radiation
    C. diathermy
    D. ultraviolet radiation

35. Of the following, the BEST method of sterilizing glassware for surgical purposes is by means of

    A. immersion in boiling water
    B. steaming under pressure
    C. cold sterilization
    D. washing thoroughly with soap and water

36. The apparatus used for sterilizing medical equipment by means of steam under pressure is the

    A. autoclave   B. manometer   C. catheter   D. reamer

37. After each use of a thermometer, it should be

    A. held under hot water for several minutes
    B. disinfected in a chemical solution
    C. rinsed in cold water
    D. wiped clean with cotton

38. The LEAST desirable action to take in administering first aid to a person suffering from shock is to

    A. give the patient some aromatic spirits of ammonia
    B. place the patient in a reclining position and elevate his legs
    C. loosen any tight clothing and place a pillow under his head
    D. place a hot water bottle near the patient's feet

39. Of the following symptoms, the one which does NOT generally accompany a fainting spell is

    A. a flushed face
    B. perspiration of the forehead
    C. shallow breathing
    D. a slow pulse

40. Assume that a six-year-old boy is brought to the clinic, bleeding profusely from a scalp wound. The doctor has not as yet arrived.
    Of the following, the MOST effective action for you to take is to

    A. wash the wound thoroughly with soap and water to prevent infection; apply pressure on the bleeding point; then treat for shock
    B. place the boy in a comfortable position; apply tincture of iodine to the wound to prevent infection; then treat for shock
    C. give the patient a stimulant; then attempt to stop the bleeding by applying digital pressure
    D. make the boy comfortable; place a compress over the wound and bandage snugly; then threat for shock

7 (#2)

41. Of the following, the MOST frequently used method for the diagnosis of pulmonary tuberculosis is the   41._____

   A. blood test
   B. x-ray
   C. metabolism test
   D. urinalysis

42. Of the following conditions, the one which may be infectious is   42._____

   A. diabetes
   B. tuberculosis
   C. appendicitis
   D. hypertension

43. Of the following, observation of deviations from normal body weight may aid LEAST in determining the presence of   43._____

   A. glandular disturbances
   B. malnutrition
   C. organic disturbances
   D. mental deficiency

44. Leukemia is a disease of the blood characterized by a   44._____

   A. moderate increase in the red cell count and decrease in the white cell count
   B. marked decrease in the red cell count and an increase in the white cell count
   C. marked increase in the hemoglobin content
   D. marked decrease in the white cell count

45. The one of the following which is MOST commonly used in the treatment of arthritis is   45._____

   A. radium
   B. an electrocardiogram
   C. a radiograph
   D. diathermy

46. The fluoroscope is used CHIEFLY to   46._____

   A. provide a permanent picture of the condition of internal organs at a given time
   B. make a chart of the action of the muscles of the heart
   C. observe the internal structure and functioning of the organs of the body at a given time
   D. produce heat in the tissues of the body

47. A stethoscope is an instrument used for   47._____

   A. determining the blood pressure
   B. taking the body temperature
   C. chest examination
   D. determining the amount of sugar in the blood

48. The Dick test is used to determine susceptibility to

    A. measles   B. scarlet fever
    C. diphtheria   D. chickenpox

49. The aorta is a(n)

    A. bone   B. artery   C. ligament   D. nerve

50. The esophagus is part of the

    A. alimentary canal   B. abdominal wall
    C. mucous membrane   D. circulatory system

51. Of the following, the one which is NOT a blood vessel is the

    A. vein   B. capillary   C. ganglion   D. artery

52. Vital statistics include data reflating to

    A. births, deaths, and marriages
    B. the cost of food, clothing, and shelter
    C. the number of children per family unit
    D. diseases and their comparative mortality rates

53. In filing letters by subject, you should be MOST concerned with the

    A. name of the sender
    B. main topic of the letter
    C. date of the correspondence
    D. alphabetic cross reference

54. When arranging the record cards of patients in alphabetical order, the one of the following which should be filed THIRD is

    A. Charles A. Clarke   B. James Clark
    C. Joan Carney   D. Mae Cohen

55. The one of the following names which should be filed FIRST is

    A. Benjamin Dermody   B. Frank Davidson
    C. Matthew Davids   D. Seymour Diana

Questions 56-60.

DIRECTIONS: Questions 56 through 60 are to be answered on the basis of the chart below.

ATTENDANCE OF PATIENTS AT Y HEALTH CENTER
FOR WEEK OF APRIL 10

Clinic	Number Summoned for				Number Reported to			
	Baby	Chest	Eye	V.D.	Baby	Chest	Eye	V.D.
Monday	30	42	36	38	29	40	33	35
Tuesday	33	29	34	37	30	29	31	36
Wednesday	38	31	45	42	35	30	40	40
Thursday	41	48	41	32	36	45	39	28
Friday	35	37	39	36	33	35	37	32

56. On the basis of the above chart, it is CORRECT to say that   56._____

    A. more patients were summoned to the baby clinic than to the chest clinic during the week
    B. the same number of patients were absent from the eye clinic and the baby clinic during the week
    C. more patients reported to the eye clinic than to the chest clinic during the week
    D. more patients were summoned to the V.D. clinic than to the eye clinic during the week

57. On the basis of the above chart, the daily average number of patients summoned to the   57._____
    eye clinic exceeds the daily average reporting to the eye clinic by

    A. 3   B. 7   C. 11   D. 15

58. The percentage of all patients summoned to Y Health Center on Thursday who failed to   58._____
    report for their appointments is

    A. *less* than 5%
    B. *more* than 5% but less than 10%
    C. *more* than 10% but less than 15%
    D. *more* than 15%

59. The number of patients summoned for the entire week to the eye clinic exceeds the num- 59._____
    ber of patients summoned to the baby clinic by

    A. 6   B. 9   C. 13   D. 18

60. The total number of patients who reported to Y Health Center for the week is   60._____

    A. 683   B. 693   C. 724   D. 744

Questions 61-80.

DIRECTIONS: Column I below lists words used in medical practice. Column II lists phrases which describe the words in Column I. In the space at the right, place the letter preceding the phrase in Column II which BEST describes the word in Column I.

COLUMN I	COLUMN II
61. Abrasion	A. A disturbance of digestion
62. Aseptic	B. Destroying the germs of disease
63. Cardiac	C. A general poisoning of the blood
64. Catarrh	D. An instrument used for injecting fluids
65. Contamination	E. A scraping off of the skin
66. Dermatology	F. Free from disease germs
67. Disinfectant	G. An apparatus for viewing internal organs by means of x-rays
68. Dyspepsia	H. An instrument for assisting the eye in observing minute objects
69. Epidemic	I. An inoculable immunizing agent
70. Epidermis	J. The extensive prevalence in a community of a disease
71. Incubation	K. Chemical product of an organ
72. Microscope	L. Preceding birth
73. Pediatrics	M. Fever
74. Plasma	N. The branch of medical science that relates to the skin and its diseases
75. Prenatal	O. Fluid part of the blood
76. Retina	P. The science of the hygienic care of children
77. Syphilis	Q. Infection by contact
78. Syringe	R. Relating to the heart
79. Toxemia	S. Inner structure of the eye
80. Vaccine	T. Outer portion of the skin
	U. Pertaining to the ductless gland
	V. An infectious venereal disease
	W. Pertaining to the hip
	X. The development of an infectious disease from the period of infection to that of the appearance of the first symptoms
	Y. Simple inflammation of a mucous membrane
	Z. An instrument for measuring blood pressure

61. ____
62. ____
63. ____
64. ____
65. ____
66. ____
67. ____
68. ____
69. ____
70. ____
71. ____
72. ____
73. ____
74. ____
75. ____
76. ____
77. ____
78. ____
79. ____
80. ____

KEY (CORRECT ANSWERS)

1. A	16. C	31. C	46. C	61. E	76. S
2. D	17. C	32. B	47. C	62. F	77. V
3. B	18. A	33. C	48. B	63. R	78. D
4. A	19. D	34. D	49. B	64. Y	79. C
5. C	20. C	35. B	50. A	65. Q	80. I
6. C	21. B	36. A	51. C	66. N	
7. C	22. B	37. B	52. A	67. B	
8. D	23. A	38. C	53. B	68. A	
9. D	24. A	39. A	54. A	69. J	
10. B	25. C	40. D	55. C	70. T	
11. C	26. D	41. B	56. C	71. X	
12. A	27. C	42. B	57. A	72. H	
13. B	28. D	43. D	58. B	73. P	
14. B	29. B	44. B	59. D	74. O	
15. A	30. D	45. D	60. B	75. L	

EXAMINATION SECTION
TEST 1

DIRECTIONS: Each question or incomplete statement is followed by several suggested answers or completions. Select the one that BEST answers the question or completes the statement. *PRINT THE LETTER OF THE CORRECT ANSWER IN THE SPACE AT THE RIGHT.*

1. Penicillin is effective in the treatment of several diseases because it

    A. builds up bodily resistance to the disease
    B. builds an immunity to the organisms causing the disease
    C. halts the growth of disease-producing organisms
    D. kills the organisms which cause the disease

2. The HIGHEST incidence of tuberculosis occurs during the ages of

    A. 1-9 B. 10-14 C. 15-30 D. 31-45

3. The MOST infectious stage of measles is the

    A. febrile B. convalescent C. eruptive D. coryzal

4. When caring for a child ill with measles, you should

    A. select a room which is light and airy, but should protect the child's eyes from direct light
    B. regulate the temperature of the room to about 72-75° F
    C. keep the child in a darkened room to protect its eyes
    D. have the child wear woolen clothing for warmth

5. Ringworm on the skin is caused by a

    A. bacterium B. fungus C. protozoan D. worm

6. Body temperature taken by rectum is _____ body temperature taken orally.

    A. 1° lower than
    B. the same as
    C. 1° higher than
    D. 2° higher than

7. The dishes used by a patient ill with a communicable disease should be.

    A. scraped and rinsed, then washed
    B. soaked overnight in a strong disinfectant solution
    C. boiled for twenty minutes
    D. kept separate and washed with soap and hot water

8. Cold applications tend to

    A. decrease the supply of blood in the area to which they are applied
    B. dilate the blood vessels
    C. bring a greater supply of blood to the area to which they are applied
    D. increase the pressure on the nerve endings

9. A bed cradle is a useful device for

   A. elevating an extremity
   B. keeping the weight of the upper bed covers off the patient
   C. helping to keep a restless patient in bed
   D. allowing for the free circulation of air

10. If a patient shows signs of a pressure sore at the base of the spine, the nurse should

    A. try a sitting position for the patient
    B. use small cotton rings on the pressure spot
    C. apply an ointment to the sore
    D. place an air-ring under the patient's buttocks

11. If a patient lying on her side is uncomfortable, the nurse may give her a(n)

    A. extra top cover
    B. back rest
    C. snug abdominal bandage
    D. pillow to support the lumbar region

12. The diet for a patient with gallstones MAY include

    A. grapefruit juice   B. liver
    C. cream   D. peas

13. A rich source of vitamin K is

    A. butter   B. spinach   C. oranges   D. milk

14. Flaxseed meal is prescribed for making an application of moist heat because of its

    A. medicinal properties   B. mucilaginous ingredients
    C. lightness   D. ability to retain heat

15. Of the following, the substance that is NOT commonly used as an emetic is

    A. bicarbonate of soda   B. mustard powder
    C. syrup of ipecac   D. table salt

16. Supervised practice periods are USEFUL to

    A. insure continued practice on part of students
    B. prevent wrong bonds from becoming fixed through practice
    C. supplement class instruction
    D. teach children to study

17. The science of human behavior is called

    A. psychiatry   B. mental hygiene
    C. psychology   D. psychoanalysis

18. The microscopical examination of bacteria is used to determine

    A. best conditions for growth
    B. their virulency
    C. their size, shape, etc.
    D. their relation toward certain foods

19. A disease that confers active immunity is 19.____

    A. scarlet fever B. erysipelas
    C. pneumonia D. common colds

20. A SERIOUS infection of the eyes is 20.____

    A. trachoma B. myopia
    C. astigmatism D. amblyopia

21. A substance that inhibits the growth of bacteria but does NOT destroy them is called 21.____

    A. germicide B. disinfectant
    C. antiseptic D. sterilizer

22. Organisms which cause diseases of the intestinal tract are 22.____

    A. colon bacillus B. diphtheria bacillus
    C. typhoid bacillus D. cholera spirillum

23. Proved protection has been discovered against 23.____

    A. smallpox B. mumps
    C. common colds D. measles

24. Strabismus is COMMONLY known as 24.____

    A. near-sightedness B. far-sightedness
    C. cross-eyes D. pink eyes

25. The country that has the HIGHEST death rate of mothers in childbirth is 25.____

    A. England   B. Italy   C. China   D. United States

KEY (CORRECT ANSWERS)

1.	C	11.	D
2.	C	12.	A
3.	D	13.	B
4.	A	14.	D
5.	B	15.	A
6.	C	16.	C
7.	C	17.	C
8.	A	18.	C
9.	B	19.	A
10.	D	20.	A

21. B
22. C
23. A
24. C
25. C

———

TEST 2

DIRECTIONS: Each question or incomplete statement is followed by several suggested answers or completions. Select the one that BEST answers the question or completes the statement. *PRINT THE LETTER OF THE CORRECT ANSWER IN THE SPACE AT THE RIGHT.*

1. The one of the following which is NOT generally used to alleviate pain is 1.____

    A. aspirin   B. morphine   C. cocaine   D. quinine

2. The administration of a drug subcutaneously means administration by 2.____

    A. mouth
    B. injection beneath the skin
    C. application on the surface of the skin
    D. rectum

3. The one of the following which is NOT a disinfectant is 3.____

    A. boiling water   B. iodine
    C. formaldehyde   D. novocain

4. The one of the following which is LEAST related to the pulse rate of an individual is his 4.____

    A. blood pressure   B. temperature
    C. weight   D. emotional state

5. The one of the following which denotes normal vision is 5.____

    A. 20/10   B. 20/20   C. 20/30   D. 20/40

6. Of the following, the temperature which is MOST desirable for a babies' weighing room in a health center is 6.____

    A. 60-62° F   B. 65-68° F   C. 75-77° F   D. 85-88° F

7. Of the following, it is MOST advisable for the operator to wear dark glasses during treatments by 7.____

    A. x-ray   B. infra-red radiation
    C. diathermy   D. ultra-violet radiation

8. Of the following, the BEST method of sterilizing glassware for surgical purposes is by means of 8.____

    A. immersion in boiling water
    B. steaming under pressure
    C. cold sterilization
    D. washing thoroughly with soap and water

9. The apparatus used for sterilizing medical equipment by means of steam under pressure is the 9.____

    A. autoclave   B. manometer   C. catheter   D. reamer

25

10. After each use of a thermometer, it should be

    A. held under hot water for several minutes
    B. disinfected in a chemical solution
    C. rinsed in cold water
    D. wiped clean with cotton

11. The LEAST desirable action to take in administering first aid to a person suffering from shock is to

    A. give the patient some aromatic spirits of ammonia
    B. place the patient in a reclining position and elevate his legs
    C. loosen any tight clothing and place a pillow under his head
    D. place a hot water bottle near the patient's feet

12. Of the following symptoms, the one which does NOT generally accompany a fainting spell is

    A. a flushed face
    B. perspiration of the forehead
    C. shallow breathing
    D. a slow pulse

13. Assume that a six-year-old boy is brought to the clinic bleeding profusely from a scalp wound. The doctor has not as yet arrived.
    Of the following, the MOST effective action for you to take is to

    A. wash the wound thoroughly with soap and water to prevent infection, apply pressure on the bleeding point, then treat for shock
    B. place the boy in a comfortable position, apply tincture of iodine to the wound to prevent infection, then treat for shock
    C. give the patient a stimulant, then attempt to stop the bleeding by applying digital pressure
    D. make the boy comfortable, place a compress over the wound and bandage snugly, then treat for shock

14. Of the following, the MOST frequently used method for the diagnosis of pulmonary tuberculosis is the

    A. blood test   B. x-ray
    C. metabolism test   D. urinalysis

15. Of the following conditions, the one which MAY be infectious is

    A. diabetes   B. tuberculosis
    C. appendicitis   D. hypertension

16. Of the following, observation of deviations from normal body weight may aid LEAST in determining the presence of

    A. glandular disturbances   B. malnutrition
    C. organic disturbances   D. mental deficiency

17. Leukemia is a disease of the blood characterized by a   17.____

    A. moderate increase in the red cell count and decrease in the white cell count
    B. marked decrease in the red cell count and an increase in the white cell count
    C. marked increase in the hemoglobin content
    D. marked decrease in the white cell count

18. The one of the following which is MOST commonly used in the treatment of arthritis is   18.____

    A. radium   B. an electrocardiogram
    C. a radiograph   D. diathermy

19. The fluoroscope is used CHIEFLY to   19.____

    A. provide a permanent picture of the condition of internal organs at a given time
    B. make a chart of the action of the muscles of the heart
    C. observe the internal structure and functioning of the organs of the body at a given time
    D. produce heat in the tissues of the body

20. A stethoscope is an instrument used for   20.____

    A. determining the blood pressure
    B. taking the body temperature
    C. chest examinations
    D. determining the amount of sugar in the blood

21. The Dick test is used to determine susceptibility to   21.____

    A. measles   B. scarlet fever
    C. diphtheria   D. chicken pox

22. The aorta is a(n)   22.____

    A. bone   B. artery   C. ligament   D. nerve

23. The esophagus is part of the   23.____

    A. alimentary canal   B. abdominal wall
    C. mucous membrane   D. circulatory system

24. Of the following, the one which is NOT a blood vessel is the   24.____

    A. vein   B. capillary   C. ganglion   D. artery

25. Vital statistics include data relating to   25.____

    A. births, deaths, and marriages
    B. the cost of food, clothing, and shelter
    C. the number of children per family unit
    D. diseases and their comparative mortality rates

KEY (CORRECT ANSWERS)

1. D
2. B
3. D
4. C
5. B
6. C
7. D
8. B
9. A
10. B

11. C
12. A
13. D
14. B
15. B
16. D
17. B
18. D
19. C
20. C

21. B
22. B
23. A
24. C
25. A

TEST 3

DIRECTIONS: Each question or incomplete statement is followed by several suggested answers or completions. Select the one that BEST answers the question or completes the statement. *PRINT THE LETTER OF THE CORRECT ANSWER IN THE SPACE AT THE RIGHT.*

1. The food rich in vitamin A is 1.____
   A. liver   B. butter   C. rice   D. soy beans

2. Vitamin B promotes 2.____
   A. clear vision
   B. good digestion
   C. good dentition
   D. resistance to respiratory diseases

3. When very rapid action of a drug is desired, it is USUALLY given 3.____
   A. in pill form
   B. in a capsule
   C. by hot applications
   D. hypodermic injection

4. Digestion takes place MOST extensively in the 4.____
   A. mouth
   B. large intestine
   C. stomach
   D. small intestine

5. Faulty posture MOST frequently results from 5.____
   A. a circulatory disorder
   B. anemia
   C. foot defects
   D. faulty nutrition

6. The chemical substances secreted by the endocrine glands are called 6.____
   A. body builders
   B. antibodies
   C. stimulants
   D. hormones

7. The master or *key* gland in the body is known as the 7.____
   A. thyroid   B. adrenal   C. thymus   D. pituitary

8. Hereditary susceptibility to disease means 8.____
   A. having the germ of a disease within us at birth
   B. inheriting a disease which may later develop
   C. inheriting some physical characteristic which might be a determining factor in developing the disease
   D. congenital contraction of a specific disease

9. The DIRECT cause of local infection is 9.____
   A. lowered resistance
   B. secondary anemia
   C. introduction of pathogenic organisms
   D. a break or tear in the skin

10. Sickroom visitors should be seated

    A. near the head of the bed out of sight of the patient but within hearing distance of the voice
    B. at the foot of the bed where the patient may see the visitor
    C. on a chair, at the side of the bed, within the patient's range of vision and hearing
    D. on a chair brought near enough to the bed so that the visitor may lean comfortably on the bed to see and hear the patient without difficulty

11. The incubation period is the

    A. time when the symptoms of illness appear
    B. period during which the disease-producing germ is developing in the body
    C. period during which the patient's excretions contain the disease-producing germs
    D. period when the patient is quarantined

12. The mouth care of a bed patient is

    A. given if the patient wants it
    B. given as part of the daily routine
    C. important only if the patient has a denture
    D. important only when the patient has fever

13. A device COMMONLY used to relieve pressure on the heels and elbows is

    A. an air cushion
    B. gauze and cotton rings
    C. a bed cradle
    D. a folded woolen blanket

14. The Schick test is given for determining susceptibility to

    A. scarlet fever
    B. diphtheria
    C. smallpox
    D. measles

15. A mustard footbath is USUALLY given to relieve

    A. convulsions
    B. nausea
    C. congestion in a distant area
    D. dizziness

16. The *mode of transmission* of a communicable disease is the

    A. medium by which the disease germ was carried to the patient
    B. point of attack
    C. source of the infectious agent
    D. incubation period

17. The foods that should be stressed in the diet for the prevention of constipation are:

    A. fruits, green vegetables, and whole grain cereals
    B. bran, and bran-filled cereals
    C. potatoes, meat, nuts, and white bread
    D. soups, bread, butter, and milk

18. Body temperature taken by rectum is 18.____

    A. 1° lower than oral B. the same as oral
    C. 1° higher than oral D. 2° higher than oral

19. The warm mustard footbath is prepared by 19.____

    A. mixing one cup of mustard and two quarts of water and boiling same
    B. soaking feet, rubbed with musterole, in hot water
    C. dissolving prepared mustard (one cup) in three quarts of hot water
    D. adding one tablespoon of mustard previously dissolved in cool water to four quarts of warm water

20. Medications given orally may be administered in the following form: 20.____

    A. Ampule   B. Injection   C. Inunction   D. Capsule

21. The dishes used by a patient ill with a communicable disease should be 21.____

    A. scraped and rinsed, then washed
    B. soaked overnight in a strong disinfectant solution
    C. boiled for twenty minutes
    D. kept separate and washed with soap and hot water

22. The temperature taken by mouth commonly accepted as normal is 22.____

    A. 99.6° F   B. 97.6° F   C. 98.6° F   D. 96.8° F

23. The nurse should administer medicine only when 23.____

    A. the patient feels ill
    B. recommended as safe by a licensed druggist
    C. ordered by the physician
    D. the symptoms indicate the need of medication

24. The MOST important duty of the nurse is to 24.____

    A. do everything herself
    B. protect the patient from visitors
    C. have full charge of carrying out orders and nursing procedures
    D. constantly reassure the patient

25. An infectious agent is 25.____

    A. a disease
    B. the organism that causes a disease
    C. the place where the germ is found
    D. the person who carries the disease

KEY (CORRECT ANSWERS)

1.	B	11.	B
2.	B	12.	B
3.	D	13.	B
4.	D	14.	B
5.	D	15.	C
6.	D	16.	A
7.	D	17.	A
8.	C	18.	C
9.	C	19.	D
10.	C	20.	D

21. C
22. C
23. C
24. C
25. B

TEST 4

DIRECTIONS: Each question or incomplete statement is followed by several suggested answers or completions. Select the one that BEST answers the question or completes the statement. *PRINT THE LETTER OF THE CORRECT ANSWER IN THE SPACE AT THE RIGHT.*

1. Vitamin A helps to prevent 1.____

    A. night blindness B. beri-beri
    C. sterility D. hemorrhage

2. When a simple enema has been ordered for the patient, the enema bag or can should be 2.____

    A. three feet above the level of the mattress
    B. six feet above the level of the mattress
    C. at a level to cause a moderate flow
    D. even with the head of the bed

3. Of the methods listed, the MOST satisfactory one for preventing the spread of the common cold is 3.____

    A. administering antitoxin
    B. administering sulpha drugs
    C. isolation of the patient
    D. avoiding crowded places

4. The germ theory of disease was formulated by 4.____

    A. Harvey B. Roentgen C. Pasteur D. Trudeau

5. The stomach is located in the _____ region. 5.____

    A. epigastric B. hypogastric
    C. right lumbar D. umbilical

6. Good dentition is BEST promoted by 6.____

    A. adequate diet
    B. brushing the teeth after eating
    C. routine visits to the dentist
    D. a quart of milk daily

7. Bacteria thrive BEST under conditions of 7.____

    A. light, moisture, and cold
    B. sunlight, moisture, and heat
    C. heat, moisture, and a food medium
    D. darkness, cold, and dryness

8. The test to measure food energy in the body is called _____ test. 8.____

    A. mechanical ingestion B. chemical ingestion
    C. basal metabolism D. endocrine balance

9. The hot water bottle is a GOOD medium for the application of

   A. dry heat
   B. moist heat
   C. a counter-irritant
   D. hydro-therapy

10. Cold applications tend to

    A. decrease the supply of blood in the area to which they are applied
    B. dilate the blood vessels
    C. bring a greater supply of blood to the area to which they are applied
    D. increase the pressure on the nerve endings

11. An acute ear infection is MOST often caused by

    A. a respiratory disease
    B. sitting in a draft
    C. poor nutrition
    D. lack of sleep

12. Red blood corpuscles which form the residue, after the serum has been removed for processing, are called

    A. gamma globulin
    B. antigen
    C. antitoxin
    D. plasma

13. Insulin shock therapy is COMMONLY used in the treatment of

    A. dementia praecox
    B. malaria
    C. neuroses
    D. diabetes

14. The test given to determine the individual's susceptibility to scarlet fever is the _____ test.

    A. Dick   B. Schick   C. Mantoux   D. Widal

15. Diabetes is a deficiency disease caused by the lack of an internal secretion manufactured in the

    A. adrenal cortex
    B. islands of Langerhans
    C. pineal gland
    D. ductless glands

16. Tuberculosis is classifed as a disease which is

    A. inherited
    B. environmental
    C. caused by diet deficiency
    D. non-communicable

17. The mineral known to be an important factor in the coagulation power of blood and the control of muscle contraction is

    A. iodine   B. calcium   C. phosphorus   D. iron

18. A carrier is a

    A. fly or other insect which may carry a disease-producing germ
    B. person who harbors the disease germs within his body but does not show symptoms of the disease
    C. person not immune to a disease
    D. disease-producing germ which may be carried from one person to another by some insect

19. A famous Belgian physician who wrote a book on human anatomy was   19.____

    A. Ehrlich   B. Lister   C. Domagk   D. Vesalius

20. Hemerolopia is   20.____

    A. night blindness   B. day blindness
    C. intestinal bleeding   D. dysmenorrhea

21. A bed cradle is a USEFUL device for   21.____

    A. elevating an extremity
    B. keeping the weight of the upper bed covers off the patient
    C. helping to keep a restless patient in bed
    D. allowing for the free circulation of air

22. At the termination of a communicable disease, the patient's room should be   22.____

    A. fumigated with sulphur
    B. disinfected with lysol
    C. allowed to remain unoccupied for 48 hours
    D. scrubbed thoroughly with soap and hot water and aired

23. Three ESSENTIALS of good ventilation are   23.____

    A. no drafts, humidity low, temperature high
    B. sufficient moisture, warmth, and fresh air
    C. humidity high, temperature low, air cool
    D. air in motion, correct temperature, and humidity

24. In order to guide the mental growth and normal development of the pre-school child, we should   24.____

    A. take advantage of his readiness to learn in a secure environment
    B. tell him exactly *what* to do and *how* to do the task
    C. guide him each step of the way
    D. correct him and reward him frequently

25. The technical term for vitamin B1 is   25.____

    A. nicotinic acid   B. thiamine chloride
    C. ascorbic acid   D. niacin

KEY (CORRECT ANSWERS)

1. A
2. C
3. C
4. C
5. A

6. A
7. C
8. C
9. A
10. A

11. A
12. A
13. A
14. A
15. B

16. B
17. B
18. B
19. D
20. B

21. B
22. D
23. D
24. A
25. B

EXAMINATION SECTION
TEST 1

DIRECTIONS: Each question or incomplete statement is followed by several suggested answers or completions. Select the one that BEST answers the question or completes the statement. *PRINT THE LETTER OF THE CORRECT ANSWER IN THE SPACE AT THE RIGHT.*

1. Those who are legally entitled to view a client's medical records without written consent include
    I. health care professionals who are caring for the client
    II. the client's insurer
    III. the client's son or daughter
    IV. the client's immediate nuclear family

    A. I only
    B. I and II
    C. I, II and III
    D. I, II, III and IV

2. For a nurse who provides community-based services in a senior center populated mostly by Asian-American clients, the most important preparatory skill or ability would be

    A. specialized knowledge in geriatric care
    B. mastery of how the health-care system works
    C. knowledge of the clients' culture
    D. knowledge of nutrition

3. Which of the following is an important source of insoluble dietary fiber?

    A. Whole grain foods
    B. Sweet potatoes
    C. Oats
    D. Soybeans

4. Factors that are known to contribute to heart disease include each of the following, EXCEPT

    A. sedentary lifestyle
    B. diabetes mellitus
    C. hyperlipidemia
    D. low triglycerides

5. _____ is a physiological process that affects oxygenation by limiting the amount of inspired oxygen that is delivered to the alveoli.

    A. Anemia
    B. Bradycardia
    C. Airway obstruction
    D. Fever

6. Which of the following types of data, collected during the assessment phase, would be considered subjective?

    A. The client's temperature is 98.
    B. The nurse observes that the client's face is flushed.
    C. The client states that he is nauseated and thirsty.
    D. The client's pulse is 100.

7. A nurse is designing a client teaching program that makes use of the humanistic model. The nurse's program is aimed at the client goal of

    A. becoming able to establish and maintain lifelong intimate relationships
    B. achieving her full potential
    C. gaining insight into her own behavior and being able to modify it
    D. becoming a productive member of society

8. Typically, a client's mental status is MOST effectively assessed by

    A. observing the client during the interview and examination
    B. having the client describe her mental status
    C. observing responses to a list of questions prepared in advance
    D. observing reactions to provocative questions

9. Nurses use critical thinking in the daily practice of nursing by

    A. anticipating likely medical diagnoses
    B. ensuring that there are adequate supplies on hand
    C. making conversions during medication dosage calculations
    D. setting priorities for the day

10. The oxygenation rate within body cells is regulated by the _____ gland.

    A. adrenal
    B. pineal
    C. thyroid
    D. apocrine

11. A nurse leads a group discussion on nutrition, and then asks the participants to decide on a topic of discussion for the next meeting. The nurse is representing the _____ leadership style.

    A. autocratic
    B. democratic
    C. exploitive
    D. laissez-faire

12. In order to be functional and appropriate for the situation, the nurse-client relationship must be

    A. established in an early stage by means of the nurse's statement of purpose
    B. developed from joint problem-solving work between nurse and client
    C. open-ended
    D. established by the client's willingness to accept the nurse's interventions

13. A client in a full arm cast expresses concern about preventing atrophy of the muscles in his upper arm. Assuming exercise is not contraindicated, the nurse should recommend _____ exercises.

    A. weightlifting
    B. kinetic
    C. aerobic
    D. isometric

14. An elderly client who lives at home has a history of glaucoma, for which she takes drops daily. She reports a loss of peripheral vision and an inability to adjust to darkness. Which of the following nursing diagnoses is most appropriate for her?

    A. High risk of injury related to sensory deficit
    B. High risk of injury related to impaired verbal communication
    C. High risk of injury related to lack of home safety precautions
    D. High risk for poisoning related to inadequate safeguards on medication

15. The presence of hyperemia represents the _____ stage of the inflammatory response.

    A. resolution
    B. granuloma
    C. acute vascular response
    D. chronic cellular response

16. During an assessment interview, the nurse should
    I. ask about the main problem first
    II. focus on the client, and not the signs or symptoms
    III. rely mostly on direct questions
    IV. try to avoid commentary unless it is absolutely necessary

    A. I and II
    B. I, II and IV
    C. II and III
    D. I, II, III and IV

17. Of the following clients, which would LEAST likely suffer from an imbalance in fluid, acid-base, or electrolytes?

    A. An adult with impaired cardiac function
    B. An elderly client with dementia
    C. A middle-aged client suffering from a Stage II pressure ulcer
    D. A two-year-old that has had gastroenteritis for four days

18. An overweight client with gout is discussing his diet with the nurse. During their discussion, the client should demonstrate an understanding of which foods have a high purine content. Which of the following foods would be MOST appropriate for this client?

    A. Liver
    B. Broccoli
    C. Lentils
    D. Wheat bran

19. A client has been diagnosed with terminal cancer. Shortly after the diagnosis she turns to the nurse and asks: "What should I do?" The nurse responds: "What do you think would be best for you and your family?"
The nurse has used the therapeutic communication technique of

    A. Acknowledging
    B. Refraining
    C. Metacommunication
    D. Reflecting

20. Which of the following is NOT considered a task involved in the orientation phase of the nurse-client relationship?

    A. Exploring the client's thoughts and feelings
    B. Exploring one's own feelings and fears
    C. Clarifying the problem
    D. Structuring and developing the contract

21. One of the first clinical signs of hypovolemia associated with fluid volume deficit is

    A. tachycardia
    B. edema
    C. bradycardia
    D. shortness of breath

22. A nurse is asked to obtain an arterial blood gas from a client. Of the following, the _____ artery is the LEAST appropriate site for obtaining the blood sample.

    A. femoral
    B. brachial
    C. subclavian
    D. radial

23. Parasthesia is a condition that may in itself become the etiology for other nursing diagnoses, such as

    A. knowledge deficit
    B. fibromyalgia
    C. dehydration
    D. risk for injury

24. A client diagnosed with acute pain may exhibit the defining characteristic of

    A. weight change
    B. sympathetic nervous system responses
    C. depression
    D. sleep pattern changes

25. A food label contains the following information:
    2 grams of protein
    12 grams of fat
    15.5 grams of carbohydrate
    Using the 4-4-9 method, the nurse calculates the number of total calories to be

    A. 36
    B. 97
    C. 178
    D. 256

25.____

KEY (CORRECT ANSWERS)

1. A
2. C
3. A
4. D
5. C

6. C
7. B
8. A
9. D
10. C

11. B
12. B
13. D
14. A
15. C

16. B
17. C
18. B
19. D
20. B

21. A
22. C
23. D
24. B
25. C

TEST 2

DIRECTIONS: Each question or incomplete statement is followed by several suggested answers or completions. Select the one that BEST answers the question or completes the statement. *PRINT THE LETTER OF THE CORRECT ANSWER IN THE SPACE AT THE RIGHT.*

1. Which of the following is an example of palliative surgery? 1._____

    A. Vascular grafting
    B. Nephrectomy
    C. Laparatomy
    D. Nerve block

2. A client has a respiratory disease that causes a chronic lack of oxygen. The nurse would need to expect and be most watchful for 2._____

    A. peripheral edema
    B. wheezing upon exhaling
    C. flushed skin
    D. clubbing of the digits

3. In reviewing the file of a client who is scheduled for an IV pyelogram, which of the following should receive the nurse's special attention? 3._____

    A. Hypertension
    B. Iodine allergy
    C. Diabetes mellitus
    D. Latest bowel movement

4. Which of following is NOT an advantage associated with the use of closed questions in interviewing a client? 4._____

    A. Greater potential for revealing a client's emotional state
    B. Ease of documentation
    C. Less skill required of the interviewer
    D. More effective control of answers

5. Of the possible complications associated with blood transfusion, the most serious is 5._____

    A. allergic reaction
    B. fever
    C. hemolysis
    D. dizziness

6. Which of the following cranial nerves is NOT assessed by evaluating the eyes and vision? 6._____

    A. First
    B. Third
    C. Fifth
    D. Sixth

7. A 78-year-old client is brought to the emergency department after suffering vomiting and diarrhea for the last 48 hours. During the nursing assessment, the nurse observes that the client's skin is dry and can be tented, and that the client complains of an itching sensation. In developing a plan of care for the client, the most appropriate diagnosis would be

   A. risk for fall related to sensory deficit, as manifested by prolonged diarrhea and vomiting
   B. risk for fluid volume deficit related to prolonged diarrhea and vomiting
   C. risk for fluid volume excess related to prolonged diarrhea and vomiting
   D. nutrition imbalanced: less than body requirements, related to prolonged diarrhea and vomiting

8. A client who is several days post-surgery complains that none of his family has been to see him since the operation. The nurse responds: "That was your son who was here just this morning, wasn't it—The man who brought those flowers?"
   The type of therapeutic communication technique being used by the nurse is

   A. reflection
   B. focusing
   C. clarifying
   D. confrontation

9. Each of the following is a factor that commonly contributes to constipation, EXCEPT

   A. anxiety or stress
   B. decreased activity level
   C. low dietary fiber
   D. routine use of laxatives

10. The most significant contributing factor in cardiac disease is

    A. hypotension
    B. congenital heart defects
    C. alcohol abuse
    D. atherosclerosis

11. Clients are often encouraged to perform deep breathing exercises after surgery, in order to

    A. counteract respiratory acidosis
    B. increase cardiac output
    C. expand residual volume
    D. increase blood volume

12. Which of the following hormones acts to preserve sodium ions in the body's cells?

    A. Thyrocalcitonin
    B. Androstenone
    C. Cortisone
    D. Aldosterone

13. Which of the following is NOT an example of tertiary care?

    A. Neurosurgery
    B. Promoting workplace safety
    C. Hospice care
    D. Burn care

14. A client has died. Because proper handling of a client's body after death is an important intervention, the nurse should

    A. cover the client completely with a sheet before family members are allowed into the room
    B. apply makeup, jewelry, and any other accessories that the person wore in life before allowing the family into the room
    C. make sure the body looks as clean and natural as possible
    D. leave the body exactly as it was at the moment of death until a physician has arrived to formalize the death pronouncement

15. The nurse is meeting a new client. Which of the following would be MOST effective in initiating the nurse-client relationship?

    A. Asking the client why she was brought to the hospital.
    B. Explaining the purpose of and plan for the relationship
    C. Waiting until the client indicates a readiness to establish a relationship.
    D. Describing her family background, and then asking the client to do the same.

16. Together, a nurse and a client devise a nursing care plan with one goal being the maintenance of adequate fluid volume. The achievement of this goal can most accurately be measured by

    A. auscultation for heart and vascular sounds
    B. palpating for skin turgor, pulse, and heart rhythm
    C. monitoring bowel elimination patterns
    D. monitoring serum glucose

17. Nursing care and treatment of pressure sores is executed under each of the following general guidelines or recommended practices, EXCEPT the

    A. use of alcohol to clean and dress sores
    B. frequent repositioning of the client
    C. tissue sampling from infected sores
    D. application of cornstarch to the bedsheet

18. Clients should be screened for tuberculosis every

    A. six months
    B. year
    C. 2 years
    D. 5 years

19. Which of the following represents a primary source of data during the assessment phase of the nursing process?

    A. The client states that she has been suffering from intermittent dizzy spells.
    B. The client's spouse says the she has seemed severely fatigued lately.
    C. The client's chart documents a history of epilepsy.
    D. The client's temperature is 99° F.

20. A client with a broken left hand is awaiting an X-ray. Which of the following nonpharmacological interventions is most appropriate to help the client reduce pain prior to the procedure?

    A. Applying ice directly over the break
    B. Turning of the lights and eliminating other sensory stimuli
    C. Applying ice to the left elbow
    D. Applying warmth directly over the break

21. A nurse is planning an educational program on the detection of cancer, to be presented at a community clinic. Which of the following elements is LEAST likely to help address the various learning styles of the clients?

    A. A lecture
    B. Specific examples/case studies
    C. Audiovisuals
    D. Collaborative activities

22. Which of the following is an example of an outcome evaluation?

    A. A review of nursing documentation for compliance with institutional standards
    B. A survey to analyze staffing patterns
    C. Checking a client's temperature before administering a new medication
    D. An audit that records the number of postoperative infections

23. Which of the following tasks is part of the working phase of the nurse-client relationship?

    A. Identifying client problems
    B. Establishing trust
    C. Developing a plan for interaction
    D. Reviewing progress and attainment of goals

24. Which of the following is the body's mechanism for preventing pressure sores?

    A. third-space movement
    B. ischemia
    C. vasoconstriction
    D. vasodilation/hyperemia

25. If a client is hearing-impaired, the nurse should establish and maintain therapeutic communication by

    A. learning sign language
    B. using an inteipreter
    C. using simple sentences
    D. orienting the client to sounds in the environment

KEY (CORRECT ANSWERS)

1.	D	11.	A
2.	D	12.	D
3.	B	13.	B
4.	A	14.	C
5.	C	15.	A
6.	A	16.	B
7.	B	17.	A
8.	C	18.	C
9.	A	19.	A
10.	D	20.	C

21.	A
22.	D
23.	A
24.	D
25.	C

TEST 3

DIRECTIONS: Each question or incomplete statement is followed by several suggested answers or completions. Select the one that BEST answers the question or completes the statement. *PRINT THE LETTER OF THE CORRECT ANSWER IN THE SPACE AT THE RIGHT.*

1. A nurse asks a client: "What kind of abdominal pain are you feeling today?" What kind of assessment is being performed?   1.____

   A. Time-lapsed
   B. Problem-focused
   C. Initial
   D. Emergency

2. A client has been placed on a high-fiber diet. Which of the following foods would be LEAST likely to contribute to the diet?   2.____

   A. Green peppers
   B. Cheese
   C. Apples
   D. Wheat bread

3. A "chronic" illness is generally defined as one that lasts for more than   3.____

   A. six weeks
   B. 3 months
   C. 6 months
   D. 1 year

4. Which of the following is NOT a sign of cardiac arrest?   4.____

   A. Crepitations auscultated in lungs
   B. No carotid pulse
   C. Dilated pupils
   D. Apnea

5. For a client who is admitted with gastrointestinal bleeding, one of the earliest and most important blood tests will be the   5.____

   A. complete blood count
   B. Coombs test
   C. arterial blood gases
   D. lipid panel

6. A nursing care plan for a client with a diagnosis of chronic pain related to compression of the spinal nerves involves two goals: the client will achieve a sense of pain relief within 1 month, and the client will perform self-care measures with less discomfort on self-report within 14 days. Which of the following would be an appropriate evaluation of the effectiveness of the care plan?   6.____

   A. Observing whether client has returned to social activities within 14 days
   B. Observing the client's facial expression in response to the application of localized heat
   C. Observing client's freedom of movement and facial expressions for signs of discomfort
   D. Asking if client's pain has remained localized within initially described boundaries

7. In planning client teaching, the nurse's instruction should be most significantly guided by the knowledge that

   A. each client has unique learning needs
   B. a client's cultural background is the most important factor in determining his or her learning needs
   C. all clients share the same basic learning needs
   D. a client's learning needs are most strongly correlated with his or her life stage

8. One of the goals of a nursing care plan is for a client to return to within 10 percent of his ideal body weight. Each of the following would be an appropriate outcome to go along with this goal, EXCEPT

   A. the client loses 2 kg per week
   B. the client gains 2 kg per week
   C. the client verbalizes positive feelings about weight loss or gain
   D. the client selects appropriate foods to facilitate weight gain or loss

9. A client is recovering from a stroke and is aphasic. To establish and maintain therapeutic communication with this client, the nurse should

   A. ask brief questions that require "yes" or "no" answers
   B. be sure to provide some introductory language before each procedure or activity
   C. make as many decisions as feasible for the client, to avoid agitating her
   D. speak very slowly and enunciate clearly

10. A client is semiconscious and likely to obstruct her own airway with her tongue. If the client requires respiratory intubation and there are no contraindications, a(n) _____ tube should be used.

    A. oropharyngeal
    B. endotracheal
    C. tracheostomy
    D. nasopharyngeal

11. A nurse asks a client to close his eyes, and then places a spoon in his palm and asks the client to identify the object. Which evaluation is the nurse performing?

    A. Stereognosis
    B. Tactile spatial acuity
    C. Texture discrimination
    D. Proprioception

12. A 38-year-old woman has a diagnosis of nocturia, probably caused by pregnancy. The nurse should recommend that the client

    A. restrict fluid intake in evening and nighttime hours
    B. consult a urologist
    C. make use of a nighttime alarm to alert her when an episode is occurring
    D. avoid eating citrus fruits

13. A doctor has ordered that a client take 6 ml of a medication in solution. The nurse's equipment is marked for fluid ounces (oz). How many ounces should the nurse administer?

    A. 0.2
    B. 0.8
    C. 1.2
    D. 2.4

13.____

14. A nurse is assessing a new client for possible impairment of verbal communication. Each of the following should be a component of the assessment, EXCEPT

    A. vision
    B. level of education
    C. hearing
    D. cognitive function

14.____

15. While recovering from surgery, a client avoids eye contact with the attending nurse, both while being cared for and when speaking. This is most likely a sign that the client is feeling

    A. ashamed
    B. fearful
    C. angry
    D. weak and defenseless

15.____

16. In nurse-client communication, which of the following variables is an emotional/psychological barrier to effective reception of a message?

    A. Using one's personal experience or frame of reference in interpreting
    B. Lack of context
    C. Distorting the message to comply with one's own expectations
    D. Insufficient vocabulary

16.____

17. Total parenteral nutrition (TPN) is usually contraindicated in clients whose gastrointestinal tracts are functional within _____ following an illness, surgery, or trauma.

    A. 24 hours
    B. 3 to 5 days
    C. 7 to 10 days
    D. 1 month

17.____

18. A client is undergoing oxygen therapy. The nurse can most effectively evaluate the effectiveness of this therapy by observing changes in

    A. blood volume
    B. serum electrolyte values
    C. arterial blood gases
    D. respiration

18.____

19. Which of the following nursing skills is most likely to be required during the pre-interaction phase of the nurse-client relationship?

    A. Analyzing one's one strengths and limitations
    B. Exploring relevant stressors
    C. Overcoming resistance behaviors
    D. Establishing trust

20. A nurse is instructed to give an IM injection into the ventrogluteal muscle. Each of the following would be a landmark used for this procedure, EXCEPT the

    A. lateral femoral condyle
    B. iliac crest
    C. greater trochanter
    D. anterior superior iliac spine

21. A nurse observes that a client's stool is green, loose, and has a strong odor. Based on this assessment, the next step of the nursing process that should be implemented is

    A. evaluating
    B. assessing
    C. implementing
    D. diagnosing

22. The main consequence of repeated vomiting is

    A. fluid and electrolyte loss
    B. dental caries
    C. metabolic alkalosis
    D. sleep disorder

23. Of the following medical conditions, which is most appropriate for the use of a nursing critical pathway?

    A. Knee replacement surgery
    B. Polyuria associated with pregnancy
    C. Viral infection acquired during travel
    D. Ear blockage by impacted cerumen

24. Coping or defense mechanisms that are used by clients include each of the following EXCEPT

    A. projection   B. reinvention
    C. compensation   D. denial

25. A client who recently suffered a herniated spinal disc complains of pain in her foot. During the nursing assessment, the nurse discovers no problems with the foot. The client's pain is best described as

    A. referred   B. neuropathic
    C. phantom   D. somatic

KEY (CORRECT ANSWERS)

1. B	11. A
2. B	12. A
3. B	13. A
4. A	14. B
5. A	15. D
6. C	16. C
7. A	17. C
8. C	18. C
9. A	19. A
10. A	20. A

21. D
22. A
23. A
24. B
25. A

EXAMINATION SECTION
TEST 1

DIRECTIONS: Each question or incomplete statement is followed by several suggested answers or completions. Select the one that BEST answers the question or completes the statement. *PRINT THE LETTER OF THE CORRECT ANSWER IN THE SPACE AT THE RIGHT.*

1. Which of the following is NOT a characteristic of the nursing care plan?

    A. It focuses on the present, rather than the future.
    B. It is based on identifiable health and nursing problems.
    C. It is a product of a deliberate systematic process.
    D. Its focus is holistic, rather than localized.

2. What method of wound debridement is generally least damaging?

    A. Scissors
    B. Chemical
    C. Wet to dry dressings
    D. Mechanical

3. Which of the following types of medications is LEAST likely to increase a client's risk of falling?

    A. antidepressants
    B. laxatives
    C. antibiotics
    D. diuretics

4. For most adults, healthy elimination patterns usually require a fluid intake of at least _____ ml daily.

    A. 750-1250
    B. 1500-2200
    C. 2000-3000
    D. 3500-5000

5. Which of the following is NOT a clinical guideline for assessing possible decubitus sites on a partially immobilized client?

    A. Avoiding incandescent light
    B. Inspecting for abrasions/excoriations
    C. Palpating skin temperature over pressure areas
    D. Elevating room temperature during assessment

6. During the assessment phase, a nurse will need to validate data when
    I. the data lack objectivity
    II. there is a discrepancy between what the client is saying and what the nurse is observing
    III. the data are not relevant to the client's presenting problem

    A. I only   B. I and II   C. II only   D. I, II and III

7. Following a mastectomy, a client says to a nurse: "The scar isn't as bad as I thought it was going to be." The client's eyes tear up and she looks anxious when she says this. Her message is an example of

   A. the Hawthorne effect
   B. congruence
   C. understatement
   D. metacommunication

8. In the _____ stage of the nursing process, the nurse ensures that the client is receiving the prescribed therapy at the appropriate times.

   A. evaluating
   B. diagnosing
   C. assessing
   D. planning/implementing

9. Among the following, the example that best represents "passive immunity" is

   A. a newborn receiving breast milk from his mother
   B. an infected person taking antibiotic medication
   C. an infected person producing antibodies
   D. a person receiving an influenza vaccine

10. The most common form of dementia is

    A. dementia due to Parkinson's disease
    B. AIDS dementia complex
    C. vascular dementia
    D. Alzheimer's disease

11. Which of the following positions puts the client at greatest risk for aspirating secretions?

    A. Sim's
    B. Fowler's
    C. Lateral
    D. Supine

12. The main factor that differentiates chronic pain from acute pain is that a client who is experiencing chronic pain is more likely to have

    A. a tissue injury
    B. a rapid pulse
    C. warm, dry skin
    D. dilated pupils

13. A client is refusing a blood transfusion because she says the procedure goes against her religious beliefs. The most appropriate action for the nurse to take is to

    A. notify a close family member who might persuade the client to undergo the procedure
    B. seek a court order compelling the client to submit to the procedure
    C. provide all the information the client needs to make an informed decision
    D. ask questions that probe the client's rationale, such as: "Do you think God would want for you to bleed to death?"

14. Which of the following nursing notes is an example of subjective data?

    A. Pulse is erratic
    B. Client's gait is unsteady
    C. Client's left hand is cool to the touch
    D. Client complains of headache

15. Each of the following would be an appropriate nursing intervention for a client with a chest drainage system, EXCEPT

    A. Placing the client in the Sim's position
    B. Monitoring the integrity of the drainage system
    C. Maintaining the water seal area of the unit
    D. Using clamps when appropriate

16. Which of the following is characteristic of the chronic cellular response phase of the inflammatory response?

    A. erythema
    B. hyperemia
    C. granuloma
    D. margination

17. When a nurse is preparing to teach a client, it is most useful for the nurse to know the client's

    A. educational background
    B. personal preferences
    C. family status
    D. developmental stage

18. For a client with sensory deficit, a nurse can appropriately increase environmental stimuli by

    A. using the television to provide intermittent auditory and visual stimuli
    B. installing a nightlight near the client's bed
    C. freeing the room of unnecessary clutter
    D. establishing a mealtime routine

19. A nurse informs a client: "Your arterial blood gases will be evaluated at seven p.m. tonight." Later, the client seems surprised and upset by the arterial blood draw. In informing the client about the procedure, the nurse's words probably required a greater measure of

    A. clarity
    B. simplicity
    C. timing
    D. tact

20. Which of the following is a term that denotes an isotonic gain of water and electrolytes? 20.____

    A. Dehydration
    B. Superhydration
    C. Fluid volume deficit
    D. Fluid volume excess

21. Of following clients, the one most likely to suffer a vitamin B deficiency would be the one who 21.____

    A. is on a low-residue diet
    B. abuses alcohol
    C. is pregnant
    D. does not regularly exercise

22. A nurse is attempting to establish a therapeutic environment for a confused elderly client. Of the following, the nurse should place the highest priority on 22.____

    A. a fixed routine
    B. supportive group interactions
    C. a trusting relationship
    D. a variety of activities

23. A client with a respiratory disease is only able to breathe when he is in an upright or standing position. In charting the client's condition, the nurse would use the medical term_____ to describe this condition. 23.____

    A. orthopnea
    B. tachypnea
    C. bradypnea
    D. apnea

24. A client is to have oxygen delivered in concentrations between 60 and 70 percent, at an average flow of 6.5 liters per minute. What type of mask should be used? 24.____

    A. Simple face mask
    B. Nonrebreather
    C. Partial rebreather
    D. Venturi

25. An elderly client was admitted to the emergency room three hours ago and has been hydrated with half-normal saline. During a subsequent assessment, the nurse observes a rapid pulse and shortness of breath. The nurse suspects that the client is showing signs of 25.____

    A. hypovolemia
    B. hypernatremia
    C. hypokalemia
    D. hypervolemia

KEY (CORRECT ANSWERS)

1. A
2. B
3. C
4. C
5. D

6. B
7. D
8. D
9. A
10. D

11. D
12. C
13. C
14. D
15. A

16. D
17. D
18. D
19. B
20. D

21. B
22. C
23. A
24. C
25. D

TEST 2

DIRECTIONS: Each question or incomplete statement is followed by several suggested answers or completions. Select the one that BEST answers the question or completes the statement. *PRINT THE LETTER OF THE CORRECT ANSWER IN THE SPACE AT THE RIGHT.*

1. In order to keep nurse-client communications therapeutic, the nurse should 1.____

    A. continue pushing the client toward some insights into his or her health behaviors
    B. make sure the conversation lasts for as long as the client wants to remain engaged
    C. make sure conversations remain goal-centered
    D. include prescriptive and directive language in the conversation

2. Which of the following body fluids is NOT associated with bloodborne pathogens? 2.____

    A. Vaginal secretions
    B. Pleural fluid
    C. Cerebrospinal fluid
    D. Nasal secretions

3. During an assessment interview, the nurse should use _____ questions to validate or clarify information. 3.____

    A. rhetorical
    B. direct
    C. open-ended
    D. reflective

4. A typical nursing intervention aimed at promoting the transport of oxygen and carbon dioxide is to 4.____

    A. reduce stress, in order to optimize cardiac output
    B. perform percussion, vibration, and postural drainage
    C. encourage coughing or deep breathing
    D. increase the amount of dietary fiber

5. A nurse is trying to help an elderly client regain urinary continence. Which of the following interventions would NOT be helpful? 5.____

    A. Teaching Kegel exercises
    B. Prompted voiding
    C. Restricting fluid intake
    D. Habit training/toilet scheduling

6. Kegel exercises are designed to strengthen the pubococcygeal muscle. Benefits associated with this exercise include 6.____
    I. reduced menstrual pain
    II. preparation for normal vaginal childbirth
    III. increased sexual gratification
    IV. improved urinary continence

    A. I and II
    B. I, III and IV
    C. III and IV
    D. I, II, III and IV

7. Each of the following is a risk factor that contributes to the formation of pressure ulcers, EXCEPT

    A. incontinence
    B. low blood protein
    C. inactivity
    D. lowered body temperature

8. Which of the following nursing activities poses the greatest risk for stress or injury to the nurse's back?

    A. Turning a client in bed
    B. Transferring a client in or out of bed
    C. Helping a client stand from a sitting position
    D. Helping a client walk

9. A nurse learns that a client does not appear to completely understand the risks of the surgery for which he is scheduled tomorrow. The nurse should notify the

    A. client's family
    B. surgical unit
    C. institution's administrative office
    D. surgeon

10. Client _____ behaviors are often encountered during the introductory phase of the nurse-client relationship, and may be due to difficulty in acknowledging the need for help, fear of exposing and facing feelings, and anxiety about changing behavior patterns.

    A. affiliative
    B. hostile
    C. resistive
    D. dependent

11. A nurse is establishing a therapeutic relationship with a client whose cultural background is vastly different from his own. It is important for the nurse, in establishing this relationship, to

    A. not mention the difference to the client, but remain aware of it throughout interactions
    B. ignore or minimize the difference
    C. wait for the client to mention the difference
    D. acknowledge the difference forthrightly

12. Together, the nurse and client devise a nursing care plan that includes the goal of maintaining fluid and electrolyte balances within normal limits. Each of the following would be an evaluation that could help measure outcomes for this goal, EXCEPT

    A. monitoring bowel elimination patterns
    B. weighing the client
    C. palpation for edema and skin breakdown
    D. monitoring vital signs for tachycardia, dysrhythmias, hypertension, and dyspnea

13. Under the nurse's teaching, a client is learning how to use crutches after a knee operation. The nurse should instruct the client to do each of the following, EXCEPT to

    A. adjust the length of the crutches frequently and independently, until they are comfortable
    B. regularly inspect the crutch tips
    C. remain as erect as possible when using them
    D. use the arms, and not the armpit pads, to support weight

14. A nurse is teaching a 24-year-old client with insulin-dependent diabetes to manage his diet, sugars, and insulin regimen. The client will most likely be interested in learning this information from the nurse if the nurse

    A. makes the client sufficiently aware that the disease can be life-threatening
    B. reminds the client that he has several family members who rely on him to remain healthy and able-bodied
    C. is able to fully communicate the future implications of uncontrolled diabetes
    D. is able to relate the need for control of certain factors in the client's present-day life

15. A client reports to the emergency department complaining of angina and shortness of breath. Before performing a physical assessment of this client, the nurse obtains a history. Which of the following data will be relevant for this client?

    A. History of diabetes or smoking
    B. History of atrial fibrillation
    C. History of taking dietary supplements
    D. Allergy history

16. Dorothea Orem's nursing model is based on the principle that

    A. the best people to care for a client are his or her family, with help from medical professionals
    B. all clients wish to care for themselves
    C. the nurse acts as a gatekeeper, both for information and therapeutic care
    D. the client is an interrelated set of systems: biological, psychological, and social

17. A nurse who is preparing a client for a sigmoidoscopy would

    A. explain to the client that she will have to swallow a chalky substance before the examination
    B. explain the client that no fluids can be ingested within 24 hours prior to the examination
    C. administer an enema on the morning of the examination
    D. collect a stool specimen from the client

18. A nurse is preparing a client for a series of diagnostic tests. When explaining the tests to the client, the nurse should

    A. provide specific and detailed information about each test involved in the series
    B. provide minimal answers to client questions if the client appears anxious
    C. provide enough information to help the client understand the procedures, but not so much as to overwhelm her
    D. wait until just prior to each test, in order to postpone unnecessary anxiety

19. The leading cause of injury in older adults is

    A. medication dosage error
    B. automobile accidents
    C. exposure/hypothermia
    D. falling

20. A client has end stage renal disease. Upon reporting for his shift, the nurse learns that the client's vital signs have been dropping throughout the day. The nurse enters the client's room and sees that her dentures and bed linens are dirty, and her hair is unkempt. His plan for intervention should include

    A. recommending that the client remove her dentures
    B. asking the client what she needs to be more comfortable
    C. telling the client that her hair must be washed
    D. asking the client if she can get herself out of bed so that the linens can be changed

21. The nurse who wants to assess a client's temperature at its highest daily level should take temperature readings at

    A. 8 p.m. and midnight
    B. 3 p.m. and 9 p.m.
    C. noon and 5 p.m.
    D. 3 a.m. and 7 a.m.

22. A client has been placed on a soft diet. Which of the following foods would NOT be allowed?

    A. Tofu
    B. Oatmeal
    C. Raisins
    D. Yogurt

23. A client's medication order reads "Keflex 250 mg po." The drug is available as Keflex 125 mg/ml. The nurse should give _____ ml.

    A. 2
    B. 12
    C. 20
    D. 45

24. A nurse who, throughout every facet of his work, shows that he is answerable to himself and those in authority is demonstrating that he is

    A. accountable
    B. responsible
    C. ethical
    D. beneficent

25. A nurse finds a client's distraught mother in the client's room, long after visiting hours have been ended. The client is asleep. The nurse tells the mother in a calm, patient voice that she will have to go home for the night. The mother responds, but the nurse does not attend to her response because he is thinking that the institution's policy, in this case, is not helpful to the client or his family. This kind of distraction in communication is known as

    A. scapegoating
    B. intrapersonal communication
    C. derailing
    D. cross-talk

KEY (CORRECT ANSWERS)

1.	C	11.	D
2.	D	12.	A
3.	B	13.	A
4.	A	14.	D
5.	C	15.	A
6.	C	16.	B
7.	D	17.	C
8.	B	18.	C
9.	D	19.	D
10.	C	20.	B

21. A
22. C
23. A
24. A
25. B

TEST 3

DIRECTIONS: Each question or incomplete statement is followed by several suggested answers or completions. Select the one that BEST answers the question or completes the statement. *PRINT THE LETTER OF THE CORRECT ANSWER IN THE SPACE AT THE RIGHT.*

1. A therapeutic relationship
    I. involves an emotional commitment
    II. is goal-directed
    III. is planned
    IV. focuses on client needs

    A. I and II
    B. I, II and III
    C. II, III and IV
    D. I, II, III and IV

    1.____

2. A brachial pulse is taken typically to

    A. obtain the most accurate reading possible
    B. measure blood pressure
    C. to calculate resting heart rate
    D. determine cerebral circulation

    2.____

3. The most important difference between a nursing diagnosis and a medical diagnosis is that

    A. medical diagnoses are evidence-based, while nursing diagnoses are anecdotal
    B. nurses are not allowed to engage in medical diagnosis
    C. nursing diagnoses focus on human responses to stimuli, while medical diagnoses focus on the disease process.
    D. nursing diagnoses focus on health promotion, while medical diagnoses focus on treatment

    3.____

4. A client's wound is draining thick yellow material. Which of the following descriptions would be LEAST appropriate in describing the wound?

    A. Purulent
    B. Pyogenic
    C. Serous
    D. Suppurative

    4.____

5. A client has been admitted to the emergency room complaining of a headache and weakness. The nurse observes that she appears confused and has warm, flushed skin. Her vital signs are as follows: T 101.8; HR 124; R 22; and BP 128/90. A blood gas sample was taken on room air, with the following results: pH 7.35; pCO_2 58; pO_2 70; HCO_3 23. The client is at risk for

    A. metabolic acidosis
    B. metabolic alkalosis
    C. respiratory acidosis
    D. respiratory alkalosis

    5.____

6. A client is referred to a nurse by a local women's shelter, where she has fled a violent marriage. The client tells the nurse she is having trouble deciding whether to continue the relationship with her husband. The most appropriate nursing diagnosis for this client is

   A. risk for injury
   B. readiness for enhanced spiritual well-being
   C. decisional conflict
   D. energy field disturbance

7. Which of the following is LEAST likely to be a site for a skinfold test during a nursing assessment?

   A. Subiliac
   B. Triceps
   C. Subscapula
   D. Thigh

8. Weight loss, described as "severe" once it exceeds _____ percent, is one of the clinical signs of fluid volume deficit.

   A. 5
   B. 8
   C. 12
   D. 20

9. Which of the following is NOT a fluid/electrolyte condition that is typically caused by stress?

   A. Hypervolemia
   B. Reduced cellular metabolism
   C. Sodium retention
   D. Water retention

10. When evaluating a family's coping resources, a nurse should consider the

    A. structure of the family
    B. availability of support
    C. individual roles of family members
    D. family's preventive health practices

11. Which of the following is MOST likely to be a therapeutic communication technique when used by a nurse?

    A. Challenging
    B. Advising
    C. Disagreeing
    D. Restating

12. A client who has recently broken his arm complains of a dull, generalized pain along his forearm. This type of pain is best described as

    A. somatic
    B. cutaneous
    C. phantom
    D. visceral

13. A nurse is teaching a client about a low-cholesterol diet. Which of the following activities is MOST likely to facilitate retention?   13._____

    A. breaking down the lesson into individual units that are followed by quizzes
    B. under the nurse's supervision, having the client develop a weekly menu by selecting foods
    C. assigning reading and computer-aided activities
    D. using visual aids with bold line drawings

14. Which of the following nursing interventions is MOST appropriate for a client with a urinary tract infection?   14._____

    A. Facilitate access to toilet
    B. Encourage fluid intake
    C. Decrease calcium intake
    D. Teach Kegel exercises

15. With a completely or partially immobilized client, many nursing interventions for the respiratory system are aimed at promoting expansion of the chest and lungs. Of the following, the most effective intervention for this purpose is   15._____

    A. isometric exercises
    B. physiotherapy
    C. frequent position changes
    D. aerobic exercise

16. Together, a nurse and client are working on a plan to reduce the client's health risk factors. Which of the following interventions would be LEAST effective in assisting the client?   16._____

    A. Asking the client identify three goals for change
    B. Helping the client compose a plan for change
    C. Allowing the client to establish a reasonable time period for change
    D. Writing up a behavioral plan and then asking the client to adhere to it

17. The open systems model of nursing care is driven by the principle that communication should be used by the nurse to   17._____

    A. promote wellness
    B. heal the client
    C. widen the client's support network
    D. help the client adapt to his or her environment

18. The most appropriate demonstration of critical thinking by an inexperienced nurse would occur when he   18._____

    A. asks the client many focused questions
    B. relies on what he has witnessed other nurses do in similar situations
    C. admits uncertainty about how to perform a procedure, and asking for help
    D. studies the institutional policies and procedures manual

19. A client is to undergo a test for occult blood in the stool. For three days prior to the test, it is important for the client to take each of the following precautions, EXCEPT to

    A. avoid oral iron supplements
    B. avoid alcohol or caffeine
    C. undergo an assessment for hemorrhoids
    D. avoid the ingestion of red meat

20. Which of the following processes in nursing diagnosis occurs FIRST?

    A. Making a decision on the problem based on validation
    B. Observing/noting changes in physical status
    C. Taking necessary steps to rule out other hypotheses
    D. Determining the possible alternatives that could have caused changes in physical status

21. A client will most likely respond favorably to a nurse's verbal communication if the nurse

    A. remains professional and uses medical and technical terms for conditions and procedures
    B. opens up and reveals something about himself during communication
    C. maintains the same tone of voice throughout the conversation
    D. uses consistency in both verbal and nonverbal communication

22. Serum osmolality values are used during the assessment of a client's fluid and electrolyte balance, primarily to measure the extent of

    A. hypervolemia
    B. fluid volume excess
    C. dehydration
    D. fluid volume deficit

23. Before reminding a client of the importance of consistently taking his prescribed medication on schedule, a nurse decides what tone of voice to use and what gestures, if any, will be used to reinforce the message. The nurse is engaging in a process known as

    A. verbal cues
    B. inductive bias
    C. sending
    D. encoding

24. "To Err is Human: Building a Safer Health System," the influential report published by the Institute of Medicine in 2000, between 44,000 and 98,000 people die in the United States each year from _____ more than die from motor vehicle accidents, breast cancer, or Alzheimer's disease.

    A. heart disease
    B. illegal drug use
    C. AIDS
    D. medical errors

25. A nurse is administering oxygen to a client with emphysema. The nurse uses an oxygen analyzer to monitor levels of oxygen, knowing that high levels of oxygen over long periods of time are most likely to cause   25.____

    A. hyperventilation
    B. damage to the retina and cornea
    C. irreversible brain damage
    D. pulmonary edema

KEY (CORRECT ANSWERS)

1. C	11. D
2. B	12. A
3. C	13. B
4. C	14. B
5. C	15. C
6. C	16. D
7. A	17. D
8. B	18. C
9. B	19. B
10. B	20. B

21. D
22. C
23. D
24. D
25. B

EXAMINATION SECTION
TEST 1

DIRECTIONS: Each question or incomplete statement is followed by several suggested answers or completions. Select the one that BEST answers the question or completes the statement. *PRINT THE LETTER OF THE CORRECT ANSWER IN THE SPACE AT THE RIGHT.*

1. The nurse-client relationship is characterized by each of the following, EXCEPT 1.____

    A. positive regard
    B. therapeutic self-disclosure
    C. abstraction
    D. empathy

2. Which of the following is an example of an open-ended question? 2.____

    A. Did you leave the bed to urinate last night?
    B. When did you first begin to notice the pain?
    C. Is somebody coming to pick you up this morning?
    D. What happened to your shoulder?

3. Of the following, which is LEAST likely to cause REM sleep deprivation? 3.____

    A. A regularly scheduled 60-hour work week
    B. Sleep apnea
    C. Barbiturates
    D. Alcohol

4. When assessing a client's communication abilities, a nurse needs to evaluate both the client's communication style and 4.____

    A. impairments or barriers to communication
    B. education level
    C. medical history
    D. posture

5. The term "aphagia" refers to 5.____

    A. the inability to swallow
    B. the inability to speak
    C. difficult or painful swallowing
    D. an absence of white blood cells

6. During the assessment phase, a nurse acquires each of the following items of data. Which would require validation? 6.____

    A. The client says she feels feverish
    B. The client's pulse is 102
    C. The client's blood pressure is 112/65
    D. The client's chart indicates a history of asthma

7. During the assessment interview, a nurse attempts to use active listening skills. Which of the following is an element of this skill set?

   A. Responding quickly to the client and trying to summarize the client's statements
   B. Interrupting the client only when clarification is needed
   C. Asking for crucial items of information
   D. Listening for principal themes in the client's communication

8. Each of the following is a recognized stage in the body's inflammatory response to infection, EXCEPT

   A. exudate
   B. vascular response
   C. passive immunity
   D. reparation

9. Generally, a humidifying device will be required when oxygen is administered to a client at a flow rate of _____ liters/minute or more.

   A. 2
   B. 4
   C. 6
   D. 8

10. During an assessment interview, a nurse attempts to assess the client's personal identity. Which of the following questions is an appropriate means of assessing this?

    A. What kind of people do you most enjoy being around?
    B. Do you have any meaningful relationships with family members?
    C. Do you think this problem has anything to do with your choices or behaviors?
    D. If you could change anything about yourself, what would it be?

11. Possible causes of polyuria include each of the following, EXCEPT

    A. extremely low fluid intake
    B. congestive heart failure
    C. intestinal obstruction
    D. liver failure

12. In nursing, a process recording is primarily useful for

    A. insuring that all interventions and medications are having the desired effects
    B. ensuring that the nurse adheres to an established care plan
    C. analyzing the effectiveness of nurse-client communication in modifying client behaviors
    D. establishing a therapeutic relationship

13. When a client develops contracts the human immunodeficiency virus (HIV), he loses _____ immunity.

    A. passive
    B. adaptive
    C. cellular
    D. humoral

14. A client with non-Hodgkin's lymphoma is receiving leurocristine. The nurse should make sure the client's diet is

    A. low-fat
    B. high in fluids but low in residue
    C. low in protein, but with increased iron
    D. high in fluids and dietary fiber

15. A client's medication order reads "Chlorpropamide 250 mg qd. The medication is available as Diabinese, .25 gram tablets. How many tablets should the nurse give to the client in one dose?

    A. half
    B. 1
    C. one-and-half
    D. 2

16. A sleep history taken during a nursing assessment typically includes each of the following, EXCEPT

    A. content of dreams
    B. bedtime rituals
    C. use of sleep medications
    D. client satisfaction with sleep

17. A 38-year-old client is admitted to the hospital with a diagnosis of chronic renal insufficiency. He is weak, hypotensive, and has low sodium and high potassium levels. The focus of his nursing care plan should be

    A. restoring electrolyte balance
    B. increasing urinary output
    C. increasing carbohydrate intake
    D. postural drainage

18. A client visits a clinic with a twisted ankle that has swollen. Of the following chronic conditions, which would contraindicate the use of ice on the ankle?

    A. Chronic obstructive pulmonary disease
    B. Osteoporosis
    C. Glaucoma
    D. Diabetes mellitus

19. Prior to a surgical procedure, a client asks the nurse to stay and pray with him and his wife. The nurse is an agnostic who does not attend church services and has never prayed before. The most appropriate nursing action would for the nurse to

    A. stay with the client and either join in the prayer or remain silent
    B. explain that prayer is not a part of her personal belief system
    C. try to explain with humor that she is an agnostic and her prayers are unlikely to do any good
    D. offer to have the hospital chaplain perform a service

20. Which of the following nursing interventions is LEAST appropriate for a client with chronic renal failure?

    A. Hourly assessment for hyper- or hypovolemia
    B. Promote maintenance of skin integrity
    C. Hourly assessment for signs of uremia
    D. Monitor and prevent changes in fluid and electrolyte balance

21. During auscultation, the nurse notes a high-pitched musical sound during expiration. This would be documented as

    A. rhonchi
    B. rales
    C. crepitations
    D. wheeze

22. Each of the following is involved in a typical nutritional assessment, EXCEPT

    A. the dietary history
    B. a comparison of weight to body build
    C. mid-upper arm circumference measurement
    D. girth measurements

23. Which of the following nursing diagnoses is written in PES format?

    A. Potential for impaired skin integrity related to immobility
    B. Impaired communication related to laryngectomy, as manifested by an inability to talk,
    C. At risk for aspiration
    D. Decreased caloric intake related to altered nutrition: Less than body requirements

24. A nurse is administering oxygen to a client with emphysema. An oxygen analyzer is used to monitor levels of oxygen, and is calibrated using room air, which is about _____ percent oxygen

    A. 10
    B. 20
    C. 40
    D. 60

25. A father is frustrated because his five-year-old son cannot stay dry at night. The most appropriate suggestion by the nurse would be that

    A. bedwetting is often a sign of an underlying psychological problem
    B. the father should ask the doctor about the possibility of prescribing Desmopressin
    C. while frustrating, bedwetting is a condition that is not normally appropriate for treatment until a child reaches the age of six or seven
    D. the child should be awakened at the same time every night to void his bladder

KEY (CORRECT ANSWERS)

1. C
2. D
3. A
4. A
5. A

6. A
7. D
8. C
9. A
10. D

11. A
12. C
13. C
14. D
15. B

16. A
17. A
18. D
19. A
20. A

21. D
22. D
23. B
24. B
25. C

TEST 2

DIRECTIONS: Each question or incomplete statement is followed by several suggested answers or completions. Select the one that BEST answers the question or completes the statement. *PRINT THE LETTER OF THE CORRECT ANSWER IN THE SPACE AT THE RIGHT.*

1. In planning a menu for a vegetarian client, the nurse will need to take special care that the client's food contains adequate amounts of

   A. protein
   B. carbohydrate
   C. fiber
   D. vitamin A

   1._____

2. The word "macule" refers to a

   A. flat area of discoloration on the skin
   B. raised or elevated area
   C. blister-like raised area filled with fluid
   D. raised area containing pus

   2._____

3. Which of the following is MOST likely to be the causative factor in ischemia?

   A. aneurysm
   B. respiratory distress
   C. atherosclerosis
   D. anemia

   3._____

4. During the assessment phase of the nursing process, the nurse applies critical thinking when she

   A. thinks ahead to the therapeutic goals that are likely to be established
   B. asks closed-ended questions
   C. expresses doubt about the data provided by the client
   D. asks questions that are culturally sensitive

   4._____

5. The most common infecting organism associated with nosocomial infections is

   A. Enterococcus
   B. Staphylococcus aureus
   C. Lactobacillus
   D. E. coli

   5._____

6. In the following nursing diagnosis-Ineffective airway clearance related to decreased energy as manifested by an ineffective cough-the etiology of the diagnosis is represented by

   A. decreased energy
   B. an ineffective cough
   C. as manifested by
   D. ineffective airway clearance

   6._____

7. A client with gastroenteritis and severe diarrhea is MOST at risk for losing excessive amounts of

   A. chloride
   B. potassium
   C. sodium
   D. phosphate

8. Which of the following behaviors-on the part of the nurse-is known to inhibit effective nurse-client communication?

   A. Maintaining silence
   B. Stating observations
   C. Paraphrasing
   D. Showing approval or disapproval

9. Typically, a nurse may facilitate pulmonary ventilation through each of the following means, EXCEPT

   A. suctioning
   B. stress reduction
   C. percussion
   D. hydration

10. Of the following, which as at greatest risk for developing an upper respiratory infection?

    A. 30-year-old with Stage I HIV infection
    B. 45-year-old pregnant client
    C. 60-year-old nonsmoker
    D. 4-year-old preschooler

11. While bathing a client, the nurse assesses the client's skin. Which of the following would necessitate a referral to another health professional?

    A. Pitted edema at the ankles
    B. Rough, flaking skin in exposed areas
    C. Keratosis pilaris
    D. Angular stomatitis

12. A client with hyperpnea

    A. is hyperventilating
    B. will need to exercise or otherwise raise his heart rate to improve blood oxygenation
    C. is experiencing an excessively high rate of alveolar ventilation
    D. presents a prolonged gasping inspiration followed by a very short, usually inefficient, expiration

13. A client with obesity is at greater risk of suffering _____ postoperatively than a client who is not obese.

    A. infection
    B. respiratory distress
    C. anaphylaxis
    D. delayed healing

14. A client has not adhered to a diet designed to manage her diabetes. Of the following, which statement or question by the nurse would be MOST likely to motivate the client to comply with dietary restrictions?

    A. I understand the diet is hard for you to stick to. Can you tell me why you find it so difficult?
    B. I'm having trouble understanding why you won't stick to the diet when we agreed upon it together.
    C. The diet has been designed to lengthen your life expectancy. Do you understand the consequences if you don't adhere to it?
    D. Is there somebody at home who can make sure you adhere to the diet?

15. Which of the following is an interdependent nursing action?

    A. Developing a nursing care plan
    B. Preparing a client for diagnostic tests
    C. Changing sterile dressings
    D. Teaching a client about hygiene

16. Which of the following communication tasks is typically part of the planning phase of the nursing process?

    A. Seeking the involvement of additional health resources
    B. Discussing methods of implementation with client
    C. Meeting the client
    D. Examining the need for adjustments and changes

17. For a client with mild hypothermia, the most appropriate intervention is

    A. administering warm IV fluids
    B. applying blankets
    C. applying an electric blanket
    D. turning up the room thermostat

18. Which of the following is NOT a therapeutic communication technique?

    A. Stating observations
    B. Clarifying
    C. Summarizing
    D. Offering opinions

19. During the psychosocial assessment of an 8-year-old client, it would be most helpful for the nurse to

    A. read the client a story or play a video prior to the interview
    B. provide some toys for the client to play with during the interview
    C. provide a nutritious snack
    D. establish a quiet and private setting

20. A nurse who wants a client to obtain maximum benefits after postural drainage should encourage the client to

    A. use bronchodilators
    B. remain lying down

C. elevate the feet
D. cough deeply

21. A nurse is developing a nutrition program for 6- and 7-year-old children. Given known health problems for children in this age group, the program should include

    A. distinguishing between HDL and LDL cholesterol
    B. identifying foods that contain water-soluble vitamins
    C. recognizing the importance of taking daily vitamin supplements
    D. identifying foods that may contribute to obesity

22. The most likely reaction of a client who has been recently transferred to the intensive care unit would be

    A. defiance
    B. confusion
    C. fear
    D. relief

23. When assessing a client's pain, the most important factor to consider is the

    A. likelihood that the pain will interfere with normal functioning
    B. client's own perception of the pain
    C. client's vital signs
    D. underlying cause of the pain

24. During the orientation stage of an initial interview with the client, the nurse should

    A. establish his authority and background in interviewing clients
    B. indicate what client health behaviors will be most desirable
    C. stick to closed questioning
    D. explain the purpose of the interview

25. A doctor has prescribed 5 tablespoons of an anti-diarrhea medication. The nurse's equipment is only marked for metric measurements. How many ml will the nurse administer?

    A. 12
    B. 32.5
    C. 75
    D. 130

KEY (CORRECT ANSWERS)

1. A
2. A
3. C
4. D
5. D
6. A
7. B
8. D
9. B
10. D

11. A
12. C
13. D
14. A
15. A
16. B
17. B
18. D
19. D
20. D

21. D
22. C
23. B
24. D
25. C

TEST 3

DIRECTIONS: Each question or incomplete statement is followed by several suggested answers or completions. Select the one that BEST answers the question or completes the statement. *PRINT THE LETTER OF THE CORRECT ANSWER IN THE SPACE AT THE RIGHT.*

1. Nontherapeutic responses to client concerns include 1.____

    A. Reflecting
    B. Focusing
    C. Summarizing
    D. Probing

2. A nurse is working with a client who needs to learn how to perform her own colostomy care. It is most important that the nurse assess and facilitate 2.____

    A. readiness
    B. comfort
    C. motivation
    D. knowledge

3. The early treatment of diabetic acidosis would involve 3.____

    A. NPH insulin
    B. Respiratory intubation
    C. IV fluids
    D. Restricted sodium intake

4. Which of the following nursing skills is MOST likely to be required during the termination phase of the nurse-client relationship? 4.____

    A. Summarizing
    B. Clarifying
    C. Goal-setting
    D. Risk-taking

5. For a client who has a significant body odor, the most appropriate solution is 5.____

    A. a lesson in personal hygiene
    B. a bath or shower
    C. an alcohol-based deodorant
    D. antiperspirant

6. Symptoms of alveolar hyperventilation include 6.____

    A. numbness
    B. warm, dry skin
    C. pallor
    D. convulsions

7. The nurse is preparing to communicate discharge information to an elderly client of Chinese descent who speaks English well, but it is his second language. The best way to communicate with this client is to

    A. provide brief, simple explanations, and speak slowly
    B. provide some literature that he can read on his own later
    C. find an interpreter or family member to help
    D. provide comprehensive explanations of all information

8. Which phase of the nursing process involves the systematic and continuous collection, organization, validation, and documentation of data?

    A. Evaluating
    B. Assessing
    C. Planning
    D. Diagnosing

9. During the nursing assessment of a client with heart disease, the nurse becomes concerned that the client might be suffering from hypoxia. Each of the following is a clinical sign of hypoxia, EXCEPT

    A. intercostal retraction
    B. deep, rapid breaths
    C. cyanosis
    D. flaring nostrils

10. Digitalis preparations often involve the depletion of _____ as a side effect.

    A. phosphate
    B. potassium
    C. iron
    D. calcium

11. The label on a bottle of atropine states that the strength of each tablet is "gr 1/120." The client's medication order says that she should receive 0.5 g of atropine. The nurse should give the client _____ tablet.

    A. half
    B. 1
    C. one-and-half
    D. 2

12. A client complains of polyuria, pain on urination, and an unpleasant smell. The nurse calls for a urine sample. Which of the following is the most likely problem?

    A. Renal calculi
    B. Urinary tract infection
    C. Glomerulonephritis
    D. Acute renal failure

13. _____ infections are defined as those due to any aspect of medical therapy.

    A. Occult
    B. Nosocomial

C. Iatrogenic
D. Exanthematic

14. When ending an interview, the most appropriate communication technique for the nurse to use is usually

    A. a firm handshake
    B. reflecting
    C. summarizing
    D. self-disclosure

15. A 13-year-old client is experiencing painful abdominal cramps during menstruation. The most appropriate intervention for this would be to instruct the client to

    A. perform mild stretching exercises of the lower back and abdominal muscles
    B. rest and apply an ice pack to the abdomen
    C. decrease fluid intake
    D. rest and apply warmth to the abdomen

16. A nurse is developing an initial plan of care for a client. The plan should include

    A. a request for possible psychological consultation
    B. the client's vital signs on admission
    C. a nursing diagnosis
    D. a list of medications currently taken by the client

17. A client is about to undergo an adrenalectomy. It is MOST important for the nurse to insure _____ during the preoperative period.

    A. adequate nutrition
    B. increased fluid intake
    C. complete rest
    D. electrolyte balance

18. Which of the following clients might be legally allowed to give informed consent to a medical procedure?

    A. A client who is under sedation
    B. A client who experiences intermittent episodes of dementia who appears lucid at the time of consent
    C. An unconscious client
    D. A client whose injury or disability does not enable her to sign the consent form

19. A client who has recently suffered a laceration to her forehead complains of a throbbing localized pain on the surface of her head. This type of pain is best described as

    A. somatic
    B. neuropathic
    C. cutaneous
    D. visceral

20. A nursing care plan includes the goal of appropriate client response to stimuli. Which of the following outcomes would MOST clearly show that this goal has been met?

    A. Client is able to formulate sounds within 24 hours of admission
    B. Client and family openly discuss plans for discharge with a social worker by the fifth day of hospitalization
    C. Client is able to transmit a clear message to a nurse or family member by the second day of hospitalization
    D. Client is able to nonverbally acknowledge the receipt of a verbal message within 24 hours of admission

21. To examine the size of a client's liver, the nurse moves her hands over the surface of the client's abdomen. This examination technique is known as

    A. auscultation
    B. percussion
    C. palpation
    D. inspection

22. In communicating with toddlers or preschoolers, a nurse should be sure to

    A. prevent the child from handling equipment
    B. avoid nonverbal cues
    C. deflect difficult questions by offering a toy or snack
    D. focus the conversation on the child's personal needs and concerns

23. Which of the following is an example of ablative surgery?

    A. Mitral valve replacement
    B. Colostomy
    C. Tonsillectomy
    D. Arthroplasty

24. Likely causes of fluid volume deficit include each of the following, EXCEPT

    A. excess steroid intake
    B. bleeding
    C. third-space movement
    D. decreased fluid intake

25. A client has been placed on a low-residue diet. Which of the following foods would NOT be allowed?

    A. Oatmeal
    B. Butter
    C. Cottage Cheese
    D. Canned, peeled vegetables

KEY (CORRECT ANSWERS)

1.	D	11.	B
2.	A	12.	B
3.	C	13.	C
4.	A	14.	C
5.	B	15.	D
6.	A	16.	C
7.	A	17.	C
8.	B	18.	D
9.	B	19.	C
10.	B	20.	D

21. C
22. D
23. C
24. A
25. A

EXAMINATION SECTION
TEST 1

DIRECTIONS: Each question or incomplete statement is followed by several suggested answers or completions. Select the one that BEST answers the question or completes the statement. *PRINT THE LETTER OF THE CORRECT ANSWER IN THE SPACE AT THE RIGHT.*

Questions 1-15.

DIRECTIONS: In the following questions numbered 1 through 15, the word in capitals is the name of an anatomical part which is a segment of a larger structure or system For each question, select the letter preceding the structure or system of which the word in capitals is a part.

1. ESOPHAGUS
   - A. circulatory system
   - B. bronchi
   - C. submaxillary
   - D. respiratory system

2. ALVEOLI
   - A. nervous system
   - B. lungs
   - C. endocrine system
   - D. muscle

3. DELTOID
   - A. upper arm
   - B. rib cage
   - C. circulatory system
   - D. superior vena cava

4. FEMORAL ARTERY
   - A. right ventricle
   - B. left auricle
   - C. circulatory system
   - D. lymphatic system

5. BRACKIAL PLEXUS
   - A. circulatory system
   - B. nervous system
   - C. respiratory system
   - D. bronchi

6. ERYTHROCYTE
   - A. lymph glands
   - B. skeletal system
   - C. blood
   - D. large intestine

7. STERNUM
   - A. spinal column
   - B. muscular system
   - C. nervous system
   - D. skeletal system

8. THYMUS
   - A. endocrine system
   - B. pituitary gland
   - C. parathyroids
   - D. adrenals

9. MANDIBLE
   - A. pelvis
   - B. head
   - C. liver
   - D. stomach

10. PECTORAL

    A. skeletal system B. patella
    C. chest   D. digestive tract

11. CORNEA

    A. arm   B. eye   C. blood   D. lymph

12. CRANIUM

    A. circulatory system B. left auricle
    C. skeletal system   D. abdomen

13. TRAPEZIUS

    A. breastbone   B. muscular system
    C. endocrine system D. spinal column

14. MEGALOBLAST

    A. blood   B. pelvis   C. spleen   D. head

15. ADRENAL

    A. mouth   B. respiratory system
    C. liver   D. endocrine system

Questions 16-25.

DIRECTIONS: The following questions numbered 16 through 25 are concerned with various categories of diseases. For each question, select the letter preceding the disease or condition which MOST properly belongs to the category listed.

16. BONE DISEASE

    A. arrhythmia   B. arthritis
    C. edema   D. gastritis

17. DISEASE OF THE DIGESTIVE SYSTEM

    A. diabetes   B. osteomyelitis
    C. ileitis   D. conjunctivitis

18. DISEASE OF THE RESPIRATORY SYSTEM

    A. cyanosis   B. poliomyelitis
    C. jaundice   D. bronchiectasis

19. DISEASE OF THE HEART

    A. hepatitis   B. influenza
    C. encephalitis   D. myocarditis

20. DISEASE OF THE BLOOD

    A. leukemia   B. diphtheria
    C. pneumonia   D. colitis

21. NUTRITIONAL DISEASE 21.____

    A. hyperemia   B. mononucleosis
    C. trichinosis   D. scurvy

22. DISEASE OF THE NERVOUS SYSTEM 22.____

    A. amebiasis   B. parkinsonism
    C. ascariasis   D. tapeworm

23. PARASITIC DISEASE 23.____

    A. salmonella   B. neuralgia
    C. hemophilia   D. bursitis

24. SKIN DISEASE 24.____

    A. hydrocephalus   B. leprosy
    C. adenitis   D. angina

25. DISEASE OF THE URINARY TRACT 25.____

    A. myasthenia gravis   B. colitis
    C. hydronephrosis   D. dermatitis

KEY (CORRECT ANSWERS)

1. D	11. B
2. B	12. C
3. A	13. B
4. C	14. A
5. B	15. D
6. C	16. B
7. D	17. C
8. A	18. D
9. B	19. D
10. C	20. A

21. D
22. B
23. A
24. B
25. C

TEST 2

DIRECTIONS: Each question or incomplete statement is followed by several suggested answers or completions. Select the one that BEST answers the question or completes the statement. *PRINT THE LETTER OF THE CORRECT ANSWER IN THE SPACE AT THE RIGHT.*

Questions 1-10.

DIRECTIONS: Questions 1 through 10 are concerned with various categories of diseases. For each question, select the letter preceding the disease or condition which MOST properly belongs to the category listed.

1. DISEASE OF THE HEART
   A. diabetes
   B. tachycardia
   C. osteoporosis
   D. adenitis

2. SKIN DISEASE
   A. cholelithiasis
   B. colitis
   C. psoriasis
   D. encephalitis

3. DISEASE OF THE BLOOD
   A. polycythemia
   B. ileitis
   C. psoitis
   D. dermatitis

4. DISEASE OF THE RESPIRATORY SYSTEM
   A. dysentery
   B. angina
   C. hemophilia
   D. pneumonia

5. DISEASE OF THE DIGESTIVE SYSTEM
   A. periastitis
   B. bronchiectasis
   C. enteritis
   D. pertussis

6. PARASITIC DISEASE
   A. ascariasis
   B. nephritis
   C. hyperemia
   D. neuralgia

7. NUTRITIONAL DISEASE
   A. entasis
   B. pellagra
   C. amebiasis
   D. diphtheria

8. BONE DISEASE
   A. gangrene
   B. epilepsy
   C. osteochondritis
   D. bronchitis

9. DISEASE OF THE NERVOUS SYSTEM
   A. mononucleosis
   B. gallstones
   C. jaundice
   D. multiple sclerosis

10. DISEASE OF THE URINARY TRACT   10._____

    A. hydrocephalus   B. glomerulonephritis
    C. cyanosis   D. bursitis

Questions 11-25.

DIRECTIONS: For the following questions 11 through 25, select the letter preceding the part or system of the body which is CHIEFLY affected by the disease in capitals.

11. CONJUNCTIVITIS   11._____

    A. ear   B. intestines
    C. eye   D. liver

12. EMPHYSEMA   12._____

    A. heart   B. bronchial tubes
    C. pancreas   D. lymph nodes

13. CHOLELITHIASIS   13._____

    A. muscles   B. liver
    C. bones   D. common bile duct

14. PYELONEPHRITIS   14._____

    A. intestinal tract   B. arterial walls
    C. ligaments   D. urinary tract

15. EPILEPSY   15._____

    A. nervous system   B. pancreas
    C. thyroid   D. stomach

16. DYSENTERY   16._____

    A. tendons   B. kidneys
    C. intestines   D. brain

17. ERYTHROBLASTOSIS   17._____

    A. kidneys   B. blood
    C. endocrine system   D. large intestine

18. GLAUCOMA   18._____

    A. blood vessels   B. cortex
    C. cerebellum   D. eye

19. OSTEOPOROSIS   19._____

    A. bones   B. central nervous system
    C. adrenals   D. lymph nodes

20. MENINGITIS   20._____

    A. nasal passages   B. intestinal tract
    C. spinal cord   D. urinary tract

21. BURSITIS   21._____
    A. urinary tract   B. bones
    C. nasal passages   D. heart

22. ENDOCARDITIS   22._____
    A. cortex   B. kidneys   C. pancreas   D. heart

23. DIVERTICULOSIS   23._____
    A. thyroid   B. endocrine system
    C. intestinal tract   D. kidneys

24. ENCEPHALITIS   24._____
    A. brain   B. vessels   C. kidneys   D. eye

25. ILEITIS   25._____
    A. nervous system   B. blood
    C. liver   D. intestinal tract

KEY (CORRECT ANSWERS)

1. B	11. C
2. C	12. B
3. A	13. D
4. D	14. D
5. C	15. A
6. A	16. C
7. B	17. B
8. C	18. D
9. D	19. A
10. B	20. C

21. B
22. D
23. C
24. A
25. D

EXAMINATION SECTION
TEST 1

DIRECTIONS: Each question or incomplete statement is followed by several suggested answers or completions. Select the one that BEST answers the question or completes the statement. *PRINT THE LETTER OF THE CORRECT ANSWER IN THE SPACE AT THE RIGHT.*

1. Normally, upon exposure to air, blood clots form within _____ minutes. 1._____

   A. 30 seconds to two
   B. three to ten
   C. ten to fifteen
   D. fifteen to thirty

2. The red blood cells of the body are produced in the 2._____

   A. spongy area of the long bones, in the ribs, and in the vertebrae
   B. ends of the long bones and the spleen
   C. liver and the flat bones
   D. pancreas and the liver

3. All of the following statements are correct EXCEPT: 3._____

   A. The figures used for the recording of blood pressure represent in millimeters the height of a column of mercury in the sphygmomanometer.
   B. In high blood pressure cases, progressive damage to the blood vessels takes place, whereas hypertension is limited to harder than normal work by the heart to pump the same amount of blood around to the tissues.
   C. In the recording of blood pressure, the larger figure represents the maximum pressure in the arteries with each heart beat.
   D. The smaller figure in the recording of an individual's blood pressure registers the minimum pressure between heart beats.

4. The physician can actually see the arteries and veins at work when he 4._____

   A. measures the pressure of the walls of the blood vessels
   B. uses the ophthalmoscope in examining the eyes
   C. applies a fluoroscope in examining a patient
   D. uses the electrocardiograph

5. The blood-clotting process in the body is started by the breaking up of 5._____

   A. plasma
   B. platelets
   C. white blood cells
   D. red blood cells

6. The condition that impairs the elasticity and function of the blood vessel walls and reduces the volume of blood that may pass through the afflicted arteries is 6._____

   A. hypertension
   B. vascular occlusion
   C. high blood pressure
   D. hardening of the arteries

7. All of the following statements are correct EXCEPT: 7._____

   A. There is more limited mobility of the big toe of the foot compared to that of the thumb on the hand.

B. The foot bones are held together in such a way as to form springy lengthwise and crosswise arches.
C. The much greater solidity of the big toe as compared to the fingers on the hand help the foot to support body weight.
D. The phalanges of the foot are relatively more important than those of the hand and have a greater role in the functioning of the foot than those in the hand.

8. The inside of the shaft of a long bone is filled with

   A. yellow marrow
   B. compact bony cells
   C. red blood cells
   D. gelatinous tissue

9. Children's bones do not break so easily as those of older persons because their bones

   A. are less flexible
   B. do not carry so heavy a weight
   C. contain more cartilage
   D. receive better nutritional foods

10. All of the following associations are correct EXCEPT:

    A. Intracutaneous - within the layers of the skin
    B. Hypodermic - beneath the skin
    C. Subcutaneous - sweat glands over the entire skin surface
    D. Diaphoresis - perceptible perspiration

11. The PRIMARY purpose of melanin is to

    A. provide variation in the toughness of the skin
    B. prevent the more dangerous rays of the sun from damaging tissues
    C. convert surface skin on certain parts of the body into horny material
    D. dilate the blood vessels in the skin

12. Of the following, the SAFEST treatment for corns on toes is to

    A. apply a medicated moleskin plaster to the area
    B. wear well-fitted shoes
    C. cut off the mass of dead skin cells on the surface of the corn
    D. apply a corn remover

13. Of the following statements, the CORRECT one is:

    A. Suntan preparations enable an individual to stay in the sun longer with less risk of burning than without their use.
    B. Suntan lotions increase the speed of one's natural tanning mechanism.
    C. Suntan preparations shut out burning ultraviolet rays.
    D. The application of suntan preparations is more effective when used during exposure to direct mid-day hours of sun rather than used on hazy, lightly overcast days.

14. To soften water,

    A. calcium in a fluid state is added to the water supply
    B. fluorides in small amounts are added to the water supply
    C. sodium is substituted for the calcium and magnesium in the water
    D. sodium is taken from the water supply by the addition of chlorine

15. All of the following are important in tooth development EXCEPT vitamin

   A. A   B. C   C. B   D. D

16. Of the following, the gland MOST closely related to muscular efficiency is the

   A. adrenal   B. gonads   C. pituitary   D. thyroid

17. The INCORRECT association of gland and location is:

   A. Pineal - brain cavity
   B. Parotid - below and in front of the ear
   C. Submaxillary - below each lower jaw
   D. Thymus - at the larynx

18. A urine analysis does NOT test for the

   A. possibility of diabetes
   B. presence of albumin
   C. evidence of bladder or kidney inflammation
   D. growth of polyps in the urinary tract

19. All of the following are basic taste sensations EXCEPT _____ sensations.

   A. hot and cold   B. sweet
   C. bitter   D. sour

20. The accumulation of an oxygen debt by a normally healthy individual engaged in sport activity is related MOST directly to

   A. lack of endurance
   B. limited residual air
   C. strenuous exercise
   D. failure of the hemoglobin to combine with oxygen

21. The CHIEF cause of heart disease in persons under 40 years of age is

   A. heredity   B. rheumatic fever
   C. obesity   D. elevated blood pressure

22. Binocular vision is MOST important in

   A. forming impressions of depth
   B. providing a clear image of item on which eyes are focused
   C. reducing strain in each of the eyes
   D. intensifying receipt of light rays on the retina

23. The INCORRECT association is:

   A. Cornea - transparent part of the outer layer of the eye
   B. Lens - part of the eye where light first enters to be focused on the retina
   C. Iris - muscle which controls the size of the pupil
   D. Sclera - hard protective outer layer of the eye

24. Of the following, the CORRECT statement is:

   A. Wearing eyeglasses will always make a person's eyes stronger.

B. If a person is able to see clearly, he can be sure he doesn't need glasses.
C. Glancing occasionally at some distant object when doing close work with the eyes helps prevent eye strain.
D. Wearing sunglasses gives the eyes complete protection from the sun.

25. All of the following are correct reasons as to why it is necessary to maintain good posture when reading a book EXCEPT:

    A. Reading with the head bent forward strains the neck muscles
    B. Viewing print at a sharp angle strains the eye muscles in their effort to focus
    C. Studying a page in a book while lying down distorts the image on the page
    D. Interpreting the printed page while sitting in a slouched position results in eye inflammation

26. In order to avoid eye fatigue during the viewing of a television program, the lighting arrangement in the room should provide light that

    A. is reflected on the screen
    B. brings about subdued general illumination of the room
    C. provides sharp contrast between the television screen and the surrounding area
    D. is located in the line of vision toward the screen

27. The SAFEST method of acquiring a suntan is the one in which

    A. a preparation is applied to provide a protective covering during the exposure time
    B. gradual exposure allows the skin to build natural resistance by increased pigmentation and thickening for an even tanning
    C. exposure of the skin is started with reflected rays from water rather than from morning rays of direct sunlight
    D. skin is exposed to noon-day rays

28. No amount of vitamin D will serve to promote normal bone development unless the diet includes, in adequate quantities,

    A. calcium and phosphorus B. sodium and sulfur
    C. iron and magnesium D. potassium and carbon

29. All of the following associations concerning milk are correct EXCEPT:

    A. Pasteurization - destruction of the common pathogens found in milk
    B. Homogenization - process of emulsifying milk
    C. Irradiation - sterilization of raw milk
    D. Centrifugalization - separation of cream from the milk

30. It is INCORRECT to state that cholesterol

    A. metabolism is related to atherosclerosis
    B. is a normal and essential constituent of human tissue
    C. levels in the blood are related to intake of animal fats
    D. levels in the blood are lowered by intake of saturated fats

31. Of the following, the one that is NOT an after-effect of rickets is

    A. bow-legs B. chicken breast
    C. knock-knees D. clubfoot

32. All of the following concerning amino acids are correct EXCEPT:

    A. All amino acids contain carbon, hydrogen, oxygen, and nitrogen
    B. Excess amino acids are stored in the involuntary musculature of the body
    C. Proteins are made up of amino acids
    D. Amino acids play an important role in maintaining both natural and acquired resistance to infection

33. Of the following, the CORRECT statement is:

    A. All people with rosy complexions are healthy
    B. Any food that does not smell or taste spoiled is safe to eat
    C. All children with heart murmurs will surely have heart trouble later on in life
    D. Most persons who look thin and underweight are not necessarily in poor health

34. In your health guidance period, you have a pupil with a long, thin trunk. Classifying by somatotypes, you would list this pupil as a(n)

    A. mesomorph   B. endomorph   C. holomorph   D. ectomorph

35. All of the following associations are correct EXCEPT:

    A. Muscle cramp - sustained involuntary contractions
    B. Muscle twitch - minor irregular spasm
    C. Muscle spasticity - sustained tension
    D. Muscle hypertrophy - decreased size due to loss of elasticity

36. All of the following statements are correct EXCEPT: The

    A. mitral valve is between the left auricle and the left ventricle
    B. tricuspid valve is between the right auricle and the right ventricle
    C. aortic-semilunar valve is between the aorta and the right auricle
    D. pulmonary semilunar valve is between the right ventricle and the pulmonary artery

37. Urea is made in the

    A. kidneys   B. liver
    C. ureter   D. urinary bladder

38. Definite sensory centers in the brain have been found for all of the following EXCEPT

    A. hearing   B. pain   C. vision   D. equilibrium

39. Saliva is associated with all of the following glands EXCEPT the

    A. submaxillary   B. parotid
    C. fundic   D. sublingual

40. Plasma is more advantageous than whole blood in an emergency because it

    A. contains more white corpuscles
    B. does not have to be typed
    C. contains more red corpuscles
    D. contains more platelets

6 (#1)

41. The last year was characterized by a decrease in all of the following EXCEPT

   A. poliomyelitis cases
   B. tuberculosis deaths
   C. infant and maternal deaths from childbirth
   D. heart disease and blood vessel disturbances

41.___

42. All of the following associations are correct EXCEPT:

   A. Paul Burkholder - chloromycetin
   B. Philip Hench - cortisone
   C. Selman Waksman - streptomycin
   D. Benjamin Duggar - insulin

42.___

43. Tobacco has the effect of temporarily decreasing the appetite because it causes an increased concentration of blood

   A. sugar   B. protein   C. salts   D. starches

43.___

44. The present state of research in the relationship between the incidence of lung cancer and smoking indicates the presence of a definite relationship between lung cancer and

   A. cigarette smoking   B. pipe smoking
   C. cigar smoking   D. all of the above

44.___

45. If a pupil is overweight only because of food intake, the teacher can help guide him by all of the following admonitions EXCEPT:

   A. *Gradually change your eating habits*
   B. *Eliminate your breakfast*
   C. *Be content to reduce slowly*
   D. *Practice self-control*

45.___

46. All of the following are enzymes of pancreatic juice EXCEPT

   A. amylopsin   B. ptyalin   C. steapsin   D. trypsin

46.___

47. A sprain in any part of the body PRIMARILY involves the _____ tissue.

   A. ligament   B. nerve   C. skin   D. muscle

47.___

48. A victim with a fractured neck should ALWAYS be transported lying on

   A. the stomach, face downward
   B. a stretcher
   C. his back, face upward
   D. a blanket

48.___

49. All of the following statements are correct EXCEPT

   A. In a fracture, crepitus is usually present, but in a dislocation there is no crepitus.
   B. In a fracture, deformity may vary in extent while in a dislocation, the deformity is usually marked.

49.___

C. In a dislocation, deformity recurs after the part is placed in its normal position, while in a fracture there is no deformity after the bone is placed in normal position.
D. In a dislocation, the head of the bone rotates with the rest of the bone, whereas in a fracture the bone moves as two bones or as a bone with a loose end.

50. All of the following are complete fractures EXCEPT a(n) _____ fracture.   50.____
    A. impacted   B. greenstick   C. Colles'   D. Pott's

KEY (CORRECT ANSWERS)

1. B	11. B	21. B	31. D	41. D
2. A	12. B	22. A	32. B	42. D
3. B	13. A	23. B	33. D	43. A
4. B	14. C	24. C	34. D	44. A
5. B	15. C	25. D	35. D	45. B
6. D	16. A	26. B	36. C	46. B
7. D	17. D	27. B	37. B	47. A
8. A	18. D	28. A	38. B	48. C
9. C	19. A	29. C	39. C	49. C
10. C	20. C	30. D	40. B	50. B

TEST 2

DIRECTIONS: Each question or incomplete statement is followed by several suggested answers or completions. Select the one that BEST answers the question or completes the statement. *PRINT THE LETTER OF THE CORRECT ANSWER IN THE SPACE AT THE RIGHT.*

1. The stimulant theobromine is found in all of the following EXCEPT   1.____

   A. cocoa   B. chocolate   C. tea   D. coffee

2. Recent research indicates that the appetite center or food intake control is located in the   2.____

   A. pancreatic gland
   B. hypothalamus located at the base of the brain
   C. nerve centers that are directly controlled by the big muscles
   D. duodenum

3. In general, all of the following act to reduce the vitamin content in any food EXCEPT   3.____

   A. storage at room temperature for long periods
   B. freezing
   C. excessive heat
   D. prolonged cooking

4. All of the following are vitamins EXCEPT   4.____

   A. thiamine   B. niacin   C. heparin   D. biotin

5. All of the following associations are correct EXCEPT: 5.____

   A. Antidermatitis - vitamin B_6
   B. Antihemorrhagic - vitamin K
   C. Antineuritic - vitamin B_1
   D. Antisterility - vitamin G

6. All of the following associations are correct EXCEPT: 6.____

   A. Sodium and potassium - normal beating of heart
   B. Iron and copper - making of hemoglobin
   C. Calcium and phosphorus - formation of bone
   D. Chlorine and sulphur - oxidative processes

7. Dry skim milk   7.____

   A. has the same butterfat content as homogenized milk
   B. contains considerably more fat and vitamin A than whole milk
   C. has butterfat removed
   D. loses a good deal of its nutritional value when stored for several months

8. A pupil should be referred for the pitch tone test if the FINAL score in the first audiometer test screening shows a hearing loss of

   A. 1 to 5 decibels in both ears
   B. 6 to 9 decibels in one ear
   C. 12 or more decibels in one or both ears
   D. 9 decibels in both ears

9. MOST cases of deafness are caused by troubles in the

   A. outer ear   B. inner ear
   C. eustachian tube   D. middle ear

10. After a group of pupils has had the audiometer test and before another group of pupils uses the ear phones, it is advisable for the teacher to

    A. cleanse the ear phones with alcohol and cotton
    B. dip the ear phones in a solution of peroxide and water
    C. continue the testing without touching the ear phones
    D. tell the next group of pupils to rub the ear phones with a handkerchief or piece of tissue

11. In MOST large cities, sewage is purified by

    A. aeration   B. chemical action
    C. exposure to sunlight D. isolation

12. The use of hard water for bathing is less satisfactory than the use of soft water because of all of the following reasons EXCEPT:

    A. Hard water contains more calcium and magnesium than soft water
    B. Hydrolysis is slower in hard water than in soft water
    C. The use of detergents made necessary by bathing in hard water produces a drying effect on the skin
    D. The additional use of soap and the more vigorous rubbing required by the use of hard water may irritate the skin

13. Research on the fluoridation of public water supplies at the recommended concentration indicates that

    A. there is a significant difference in the general death rate between areas where fluoride is present and those where it is absent
    B. the amount of fluoride useful for the prevention of tooth decay is well below the toxic level
    C. the continued consumption of water treated with fluoride is harmful to adults suffering from chronic illnesses
    D. the fluoridation of water has caused a comparatively high incidence of disfiguring mottled tooth enamel

14. The poisonous character of carbon monoxide is due to its tendency to unite chemically with

    A. synovial fluid   B. cerebro-spinal fluid
    C. hemoglobin   D. gastric juice

15. With regard to a tourniquet, the one CORRECT first aid procedure, according to the American Red Cross, is

   A. loosening it after 20 minutes
   B. having it released only by a physician
   C. placing it on the wound
   D. having it applied only by a physician or nurse

16. Of the following procedures for the periodic check-up of pupils' height and weight by the health guidance teacher, the MOST desirable is the one in which the teacher

   A. judges the pupil's height and weight and records his (her) judgment as satisfactory or unsatisfactory on the pupil's health envelope
   B. asks the pupil whether he has increased in height and lost or gained any weight and records the answers on the pupil's health envelope
   C. measures but does not record the pupil's height and weight on the pupil's record since variations in these items indicate that height-weight charts are obsolete
   D. measures the pupil's height and weight and records the findings as a means of evaluating the cumulative record of growth of the pupil

17. In cases of lordosis, there is a marked tendency to assume a position of round shoulders because in such cases,

   A. the body compensates for the backward shifting of the body weight
   B. too much weight is thrown on the forward edges of the lumbar vertebrae
   C. the erector spinal muscles in the thoracic region are shortened
   D. the pelvis tilts backward

18. All of the following associations of conditions and causes are correct EXCEPT:

   A. Carbuncle - infection of a sebaceous gland
   B. Wart - excessive growth of papillae of the skin
   C. Mole - overdevelopment of pigment cells under the epidermis
   D. Boil - infection, usually at the site of a hair follicle

19. All of the following associations are correct EXCEPT:

   A. Macula - point of clearest vision at the center of the retina
   B. Organ of corti - sense of hearing
   C. Tympanic membrane - sound vibrations
   D. Mastoid cells - body balance

20. All of the following associations are correct EXCEPT:

   A. Peristalsis - wavelike contractions that pass along a tube
   B. Catalysis - breaking down of body cells
   C. Catharsis - purgation
   D. Metastasis - transfer of disease from a primary focus to a distant one

21. A lesion in the cerebellum may cause

   A. aphasia   B. ataxia   C. atavism   D. asthenia

22. All of the following associations concerning inflammation are correct EXCEPT:

    A. Heat - calor
    B. Redness - rubor
    C. Pain - dolor
    D. Swelling - aden

23. When the term *febrile* is associated with a physical condition, it means that the condition is characterized by

    A. fibroids
    B. weakness of an organ
    C. fever
    D. decreased respiration

24. All of the following associations are correct EXCEPT:

    A. Hepatic - pertaining to the liver
    B. Herpetic - pertaining to hair
    C. Hemiplegic - pertaining to paralysis of one side of the body
    D. Hematic - pertaining to the blood

25. All of the following are important components of the visual act proper EXCEPT

    A. accommodation
    B. interpretation
    C. convergence
    D. fusion

26. Of the following, the LEAST desirable practice in viewing television is to

    A. have the room dark
    B. view the screen from directly in front
    C. have moderate indirect lighting of the room
    D. frequently shift the eyes away from the screen

27. Of the following, the INCORRECT association is:

    A. Sclera - white of the eye
    B. Cornea - window of the eye
    C. Lens - pupil of the eye
    D. Iris - shutter of the eye

28. If the length of the anteroposterior diameter of the eye is too great, the resulting condition is

    A. farsightedness
    B. nearsightedness
    C. astigmatism
    D. trachoma

29. When the health guidance teacher tests pupils' vision by means of the Snellen chart, he(she) is testing the pupils'

    A. near acuity
    B. distance acuity
    C. depth perception
    D. peripheral vision

30. All of the following statements concerning body temperature in normal, healthy persons are correct EXCEPT:

    A. During the 24-hour day, the highest temperature is registered in the late afternoon or early evening
    B. During the 24-hour day, the lowest temperature is registered between 2 and 4 A.M., provided the person is not working on a night job

C. The more or less rhythmic rise and fall of body temperature is not established until adolescence
D. In most normal people, the variations of temperature are so small that it is difficult to detect them without the use of a special thermometer

31. It has been found that, for most people, the BEST room temperature is about _____ °F with relative humidity of about _____.

   A. 70; 50%   B. 65; 40%   C. 68; 68%   D. 75; 75%

32. The MOST accurate of the following tuberculin tests is the

   A. Moro Test, using a tuberculin ointment
   B. Von Pirquet Test, applying tuberculin to the scratched skin
   C. Mantoux Test, injecting tuberculin preparation between the layers of the skin
   D. Patch Test, applying tuberculin ointment to the skin by gauze and adhesive plaster

33. All of the following statements concerning tetanus are true EXCEPT:

   A. Tetanus infection is likely only with puncture-type wounds
   B. Barnyard soil probably has the highest incidence of tetanus infestation
   C. Insignificant wounds often cause tetanus infection
   D. Immediate cleansing of a wound is a prime step in avoiding tetanus

34. All of the following are symptoms of a simple fracture of a bone EXCEPT

   A. deformity
   B. swelling
   C. a wound through the skin
   D. tenderness of the area to touch

35. A student who appears in the playground with an infected wound should be barred from physical activities PRIMARILY because

   A. other children may be infected
   B. a scab may be ruptured
   C. the spread of infection is likely
   D. pain may result

36. Traumatic shock following injury is directly attributable to

   A. pain
   B. loss of blood through external or internal bleeding
   C. psychological reactions
   D. failure of enough blood to circulate

37. Of the following, the substance that is NOT commonly used as an emetic is

   A. salt water   B. soap suds
   C. baking soda   D. ammonia water

38. All of the following statements concerning heat exhaustion are correct EXCEPT:

   A. In heat exhaustion, perspiration is usually profuse.
   B. Unconsciousness resulting from heat exhaustion is rare.

C. Salt tablets help to prevent heat exhaustion.
D. Body temperature rises rapidly.

39. Of the following, the gland MOST closely related to muscular efficiency is the

    A. adrenal   B. thyroid   C. gonads   D. pituitary

40. A deficiency of vitamin A in the diet may result in a condition known as

    A. beri-beri   B. scoliosis
    C. night blindness   D. scurvy

41. The condition in which a student is unable to focus both eyes on an object at the same time is termed

    A. strabismus   B. hyperopia
    C. emmetropia   D. scotoma

42. The *pressure point* MOST effective in controlling arterial bleeding of the forearm is located

    A. near the wrist
    B. near the elbow
    C. on the outer surface of the upper arm halfway between the shoulder and the elbow
    D. behind the inner end of the collarbone

43. The time interval between the entrance of infectious germs into the body and the appearance of the first symptoms is known as the _____ period.

    A. active   B. incubation   C. sequelae   D. prodromal

44. A condition which may result from a deficiency of vitamin C is known as

    A. beri-beri   B. rickets   C. scurvy   D. impetigo

45. Of the following, the contagious disease of the skin that the playground teacher should recognize in order to protect others is

    A. conjunctivitis   B. lordosis
    C. Osgood Schlatter's disease D. impetigo

46. Of the following, the symptom of heatstroke MOST frequently noted is

    A. an absence of perspiration
    B. mental confusion
    C. headache
    D. dilated pupils

47. A puncture wound is considered serious from the point of view that

    A. bleeding may be hard to stop
    B. injury to tissue may be extensive
    C. infection is likely to result
    D. multiple injury may result

48. Astigmatism is due PRIMARILY to

    A. a loss of elasticity in the lens
    B. the eyeballs' being too long
    C. an irregularity in the curvature of the eyeball
    D. an imbalance of eye muscles

49. With regard to respiration, it is CORRECT to state that

    A. in forced expiration, all of the air in the chest can be expelled
    B. the presence of carbon dioxide in the blood causes the brain area that controls breathing to act
    C. contraction of the muscles of the chest causes expiration
    D. every time one swallows, the windpipe is covered by the uvula

50. With regard to strains, all of the following are correct EXCEPT

    A. application of heat relieves the pain
    B. rubbing downward on the injured part aids the return flow of blood in the veins
    C. gentle massage helps loosen up the muscles
    D. rest is necessary

KEY (CORRECT ANSWERS)

1. D	11. B	21. B	31. A	41. A
2. B	12. B	22. D	32. C	42. D
3. B	13. B	23. C	33. A	43. B
4. C	14. C	24. B	34. C	44. C
5. D	15. B	25. B	35. C	45. D
6. D	16. D	26. A	36. D	46. A
7. C	17. A	27. C	37. D	47. C
8. C	18. A	28. B	38. D	48. C
9. D	19. D	29. B	39. A	49. B
10. A	20. B	30. C	40. C	50. B

TEST 3

DIRECTIONS: Each question or incomplete statement is followed by several suggested answers or completions. Select the one that BEST answers the question or completes the statement. *PRINT THE LETTER OF THE CORRECT ANSWER IN THE SPACE AT THE RIGHT.*

1. A short lapse of consciousness and a sudden momentary pause in conversation or movement is MOST suggestive of   1.____

    A. nephrosis
    B. autism
    C. Friedreich's ataxia
    D. petit mal seizure

2. Which one of the following diseases usually has a very poor prognosis?   2.____

    A. Hodgkin's disease
    B. Slipped epiphysis
    C. Cerebral palsy
    D. Eczema

3. Mononucleosis is an abnormal condition of the   3.____

    A. blood   B. liver   C. nerves   D. colon

4. Increased thirst, increased urination, loss of weight, and general fatigue are common symptoms of   4.____

    A. arthrogryposis
    B. diabetes
    C. hepatitis
    D. arthritis

5. Which one of the following is a disease of the ear?   5.____

    A. Ostitis
    B. Otitis
    C. Omphalitis
    D. Ophthalmia

6. Glomerulonephritis is a disease of the   6.____

    A. heart   B. stomach   C. kidney   D. larynx

7. Which one of the following is the disease that would MOST likely impair the ability to ambulate?   7.____

    A. Diabetes
    B. Colitis
    C. Bronchiectasis
    D. Spina bifida

8. The lay term *hunchback* is synonymous with   8.____

    A. kyphosis
    B. scoliosis
    C. torticollis
    D. spondylolisthesis

9. Which one of the following diseases involves a malformation of the heart?   9.____

    A. Hydrocele
    B. Tetralogy of Fallot
    C. Myasthenia gravis
    D. Lordosis

10. Of the following, the disease which would be included under the general classification *orthopedic* is   10.____

    A. lupus erythematosus
    B. lymphedema
    C. Osgood-Schlatter's
    D. opthalmospasm

105

11. Of the following cardiac classifications, the one the teacher would be LEAST likely to encounter is   11.____

    A. 4A   B. 3C   C. 4E   D. 2C

12. A fusion operation upon the spine is often undertaken to correct   12.____

    A. pelvimetry   B. paroxysm
    C. epiphysistis   D. scoliosis

13. The treatment program for slipped epiphysis is MOST similar to the program for   13.____

    A. torticollis   B. Perthe's disease
    C. polydactylism   D. nephrosis

14. Which one of the following is MOST likely to be associated with production of large quantities of mucous?   14.____

    A. Kyphosis   B. Bronchiectasis
    C. Lymphodenoma   D. Thyroid deficiency

15. Poor bladder control is MOST frequently associated with   15.____

    A. rheumatic fever   B. hemophilia
    C. club foot   D. torticollis

16. Which one of the following conditions is caused by the inflammation of the lower part of the intestine?   16.____

    A. Pyelitis   B. Transverse myelitis
    C. Regional ileitis   D. Hepatitis

17. In contrast with former treatment methods that called for intramuscular injections, oral medication is now frequently provided for treating   17.____

    A. diabetes   B. colitis   C. thyroiditis   D. myelitis

18. A cardiac child classified as 4E would be MOST apt to   18.____

    A. be placed in a health conservation class
    B. receive home instruction
    C. be placed in a regular class with limited physical activity
    D. be placed in a regular class following a short stay in a special class

19. An underweight child with a cardiac condition should be encouraged to   19.____

    A. add candy to his diet
    B. add carbohydrates such as bread and milk desserts to his diet
    C. maintain weight below normal since this insures a margin of safety should illness occur
    D. increase his intake of fluids and salt

20. When correctly used, the term *allergen* refers to   20.____

    A. a person who is allergic
    B. an antihistamine medication
    C. a substance which produces allergy
    D. the tendency to inherit an allergy

21. Which of the following is congenital?

    A. Meningitis
    B. Gastroenteritis
    C. Chronic bronchitis
    D. Osteogenesis imperfecta

22. Spasm is a common characteristic of

    A. slipped epiphysis
    B. otitis
    C. muscular dystrophy
    D. asthma

23. A disease usually characterized by frequent vomiting and cramps is

    A. colitis
    B. bronchitis
    C. myocarditis
    D. empyemia

24. A lateral curvature of the spine is characteristic of

    A. scoliosis   B. lordosis   C. hypnosis   D. stenosis

25. Which of the following is one of the GREAT dangers of many forms of anemia?

    A. Brain deterioration
    B. Secondary infection
    C. Mental deficiency
    D. Bleeding

26. Arteriosclerosis is a disturbance of the _____ system.

    A. skeletal
    B. endocrine
    C. nervous
    D. circulatory

27. Of the following disorders, which one is NOT a form of cerebral palsy?

    A. Little's disease
    B. Athetosis
    C. Mitral's stenosis
    D. Spastic paralysis

28. The chin is rotated away from the side of the short, prominent muscle; the head is tilted toward the affected side.
    These symptoms are characteristic of

    A. talipes
    B. torticollis
    C. ligamentitis
    D. bursitis

29. A patient designated by a physician as *Class IID* is suffering from

    A. diabetes
    B. polio
    C. tuberculosis
    D. heart disease

30. A dorsal curvature is generally referred to as

    A. lordosis   B. kyphosis   C. scoliosis   D. curatosis

31. A disease that usually occurs in overweight boys and girls between the ages of ten and thirteen years and is characterized by upper tibial epiphysitis is known as _____ disease.

    A. Pott's
    B. Charcot-Tooth's
    C. Little's
    D. Osgood-Schlatter's

32. A child whose walk is characterized by a scissors gait, with inward rotation and adduction of the legs, is probably suffering from

    A. Erb's palsy
    B. spasticity
    C. osteogenesis imperfecta
    D. spina bifida

33. Which of the following children will *generally* be placed in a regular class rather than in a health conservation class?

    A. Cardiopathic children
    B. Epileptic children
    C. Children with orthopedic handicaps
    D. Tuberculosis children

34. Which one of the following groups encompasses the LARGEST number of children? _____ children.

    A. Malnourished
    B. Crippled
    C. Cardiac
    D. Tuberculous

35. Rickets, a disease of nutrition manifested by disturbances in the general health and in the bones and joints, is caused by a lack of vitamin

    A. A
    B. B
    C. C
    D. D

36. Rheumatic fever

    A. most often strikes children between the ages of nine and ten
    B. is generally thought to be a streptococcal infection
    C. is generally accompanied by pain in the region of the heart
    D. is contagious

37. A young girl in your health conservation class has to have a blood transfusion every two weeks.
    She probably is suffering from

    A. gastritis
    B. hepatitis
    C. nephritis
    D. Cooley's disease

38. Differential diagnosis is MOST difficult in distinguishing between cases of

    A. poliomyelitis and meningitis
    B. aphasia and brain damage
    C. spasticity and athetosis
    D. leukemia and anemia

39. The MOST common complaint made by psychiatric patients is concerned with

    A. depression
    B. panic
    C. insomnia
    D. fatigue

40. The one of the following which is MOST likely to cause the reappearance in old age of a previously compensated neurosis is

    A. decrease in social status, loss of persons and possessions or presence of injuries and illnesses
    B. decrease in sensory and cognitive capacities resulting in poor reality testing

C. cerebro-arteriosclerosis or other cerebrovascular disturbance
D. decrease in financial resources, resulting in heightened anxiety

41. Infectious mononucleosis is also known as   41._____

   A. Hodgkin's disease   B. glandular fever
   C. chorea   D. bronchiectasis

42. Which one of the following is non-inflammatory?   42._____

   A. Cystitis   B. Nephritis   C. Nephrosis   D. Pyelitis

43. Idiopathic epilepsy may be BEST characterized as a condition which   43._____

   A. is of unknown origin
   B. is a result of some trauma
   C. is not amenable to treatment
   D. may be safely ignored

44. Which one of the following conditions is characterized by loss of weight, sleeplessness, irritability, and bulging eyes?   44._____

   A. Tuberculosis   B. Overactive thyroid
   C. Myasthenia gravis   D. Frederick's ataxia

45. Cardiac involvement may result from a previous acute, infectious disease. The disease referred to is   45._____

   A. streptococcus sore throat
   B. measles
   C. uremia
   D. enteric fever

46. A type of facial paralysis due to a neuritis of the facial nerve in the Fallopian canal is called   46._____

   A. Paget's disease   B. Bell's palsy
   C. endocarditis   D. encephalitis

47. A slipped epiphysis occurs MOST frequently in   47._____

   A. early adolescence   B. late adolescence
   C. pre-adolescence   D. early childhood

48. An electroencephalogram would NOT ordinarily be used in connection with   48._____

   A. epilepsy   B. ataxia   C. pyelitis   D. meningitis

49. Which of the following is characterized by lifeless muscle?   49._____

   A. Pott's disease   B. Flaccid paralysis
   C. Scoliosis   D. Colitis

50. Of the following diseases, the one that is NOT directly attributable to a specific vitamin deficiency is   50._____

   A. scurvy   B. beri-beri   C. tularemia   D. pellagra

KEY (CORRECT ANSWERS)

1. D	11. A	21. D	31. D	41. B
2. A	12. D	22. D	32. B	42. C
3. A	13. B	23. A	33. B	43. A
4. B	14. C	24. A	34. A	44. B
5. B	15. A	25. B	35. D	45. A
6. C	16. C	26. D	36. B	46. B
7. D	17. C	27. C	37. D	47. A
8. A	18. B	28. B	38. B	48. C
9. B	19. B	29. D	39. A	49. B
10. C	20. C	30. B	40. A	50. C

EXAMINATION SECTION
TEST 1

DIRECTIONS: Each question or incomplete statement is followed by several suggested answers or completions. Select the one that BEST answers the question or completes the statement. *PRINT THE LETTER OF THE CORRECT ANSWER IN THE SPACE AT THE RIGHT.*

1. In the sick room, a *newspaper bag* is used for 1.____

    A. filing sickroom data
    B. physiotherapy
    C. catching drippings while eating
    D. disposal of waste material

2. The SAFEST way to dust the sick room is with a(n) 2.____

    A. oiled sponge
    B. feather duster
    C. damp cloth
    D. dry cloth

3. Small rugs should be removed from the sick room because they 3.____

    A. collect dust
    B. cause extra work
    C. may spread infection
    D. are a hazard

4. Disinfection may be effected by boiling dishes for _____ minutes. 4.____

    A. 5   B. 10   C. 15   D. 20

5. The safe care of the thermometer after use includes 5.____

    A. two soapings and two rinsings
    B. storing in alcohol
    C. soaking in an antiseptic solution
    D. washing under running cold water

6. A sheet stained by body discharges should FIRST be 6.____

    A. boiled
    B. rinsed in cold water
    C. soaked in warm water and soap
    D. bleached

7. Food left on the communicable patient's tray should be 7.____

    A. wrapped in newspaper and disposed
    B. boiled 5 minutes before disposing
    C. boiled 15 minutes before disposing
    D. boiled 10 minutes before disposing

8. It is recommended that the clothing of a person who has a contagious disease should be 8.____

    A. *boiled* for 10 minutes in thick heavy suds
    B. *heated* for 5 minutes in green soap solution
    C. *boiled* for 5 minutes in bleach solution
    D. *boiled* for 10 minutes in ammonia solution

9. Disease is MOST commonly spread through

   A. clothing B. dishes C. food D. contact

10. The PREFERRED treatment for a case of frostbite is to rewarm the area by

    A. rubbing it to stimulate circulation
    B. exposing it to open air room temperature
    C. immersing it in water as warm as the patient can stand
    D. immersing it in water at body temperature

11. In giving first aid treatment to a child who complains of feeling faint, one should

    A. carry him out of the room
    B. give him a drink of cool water
    C. gently massage his head and neck
    D. have him lower his head between his knees and breathe deeply

12. When one of the ligaments that support a joint is stretched or torn, the resulting condition is described as a(n)

    A. fracture   B. dislocation
    C. sprain   D. infection

13. To reduce swelling, one should apply

    A. hot applications   B. cold applications
    C. a bandage   D. an electric heating pad

14. First aid for a person who has fainted is

    A. administer a hot beverage
    B. hold the head back and open the mouth
    C. administer aromatic spirits of ammonia
    D. lower the head below heart level

15. For first aid for poisons swallowed in capsule or tablet form, administer a

    A. laxative   B. dilutant
    C. regurgitive   D. stimulant

16. Of the following types of wound, the one MOST likely to occasion infection is a(n)

    A. incision puncture B. laceration
    C. abrasion   D. incision

17. The MOST frequent cause of home accidents is

    A. burns   B. sharp instruments
    C. falls   D. poisons

18. *Do not move the patient* is a first-aid precept which is applicable particularly in cases of

    A. bleeding and fainting   B. fracture and shock
    C. sunstroke and asphyxia   D. burns and heat exhaustion

19. Among the following, the INCORRECT first aid treatment for nose bleed is   19._____

    A. press nostrils together lightly
    B. apply cold wet towels to the face
    C. apply cold applications to the base of the neck
    D. assume sitting position with the head dropped back

20. First aid for poisoning by mouth: The FIRST step is to   20._____

    A. telephone the doctor
    B. save the label on the box of poison
    C. dilute the poison
    D. administer antidote of strong tea, milk of magnesia, and crumbled burned toast

21. Treat a chemical burn with   21._____

    A. mild iodine and a sterile dressing
    B. quantities of clear water
    C. light bandage
    D. soap dressing

22. For wounds in which bleeding is NOT severe,   22._____

    A. cleanse thoroughly, using plain soap and running water
    B. wash the wound with peroxide
    C. clean the area with iodine 3.5% in alcohol 70%
    D. bandage, after applying lysol

23. While waiting for a doctor, the approved first aid treatment for frostbite is to   23._____

    A. thaw the frozen limb rapidly in a warm water bath not over 104° F
    B. thaw the frozen limb very slowly in cold water
    C. rub the frostbite with snow
    D. apply ice packs

24. The *universal antidote* for victims of poisoning is made up of   24._____

    A. charcoal, aspirin, and tannic acid
    B. burnt toast, tea, and aspirin
    C. ipecac and tannic acid
    D. activated charcoal, tannic acid, and magnesium oxide

25. The recommended first aid procedure for a burn is   25._____

    A. submersion in comfortably cold water or cloths soaked in ice water
    B. cover the skin with ointment
    C. cover the burn with a paste of baking soda
    D. cover the burn with boric acid solution

26. First aid care of a third degree burn requires   26._____

    A. oil and chalk mixture   B. sterile dressing
    C. antiseptic solution   D. healing ointment

27. A *water blister* should be

    A. opened and drained
    B. left unbroken
    C. painted with iodine and bandaged
    D. soaked in hot epsom salt solution

28. In MOST cases, to get a doctor in an emergency, call the

    A. nearest doctor
    B. nearest hospital
    C. Red Cross
    D. police emergency 911

29. Intravenous injections may be legally administered by the

    A. registered nurse
    B. practical nurse
    C. nursing aide
    D. home nurse

30. The MAXIMUM degrees Fahrenheit of a hot water bottle should be

    A. 100   B. 200   C. 130   D. 180

31. The three bones known as the *hammer, anvil, and stirrup* are all found in the human

    A. nose   B. eye   C. knee   D. ear

32. The vascular system of the body is MOST directly responsible for

    A. circulation of blood and lymph
    B. respiration
    C. metabolism
    D. balance and coordination

33. The heart muscles receive nourishing blood from the

    A. aorta
    B. coronary artery
    C. pulmonary vein
    D. pulmonary artery

34. Bones are joined to one another with

    A. sinews   B. tendons   C. ligaments   D. membranes

35. A magenta-colored tongue is evidence of deficiency of

    A. vitamin A   B. thiamin   C. niacin   D. riboflavin

KEY (CORRECT ANSWERS)

1. D
2. C
3. D
4. A
5. D

6. B
7. D
8. A
9. D
10. D

11. D
12. C
13. B
14. D
15. C

16. A
17. C
18. A
19. C
20. C

21. B
22. A
23. A
24. D
25. A

26. B
27. B
28. D
29. A
30. C

31. D
32. A
33. B
34. C
35. B

TEST 2

DIRECTIONS: Each question or incomplete statement is followed by several suggested answers or completions. Select the one that BEST answers the question or completes the statement. *PRINT THE LETTER OF THE CORRECT ANSWER IN THE SPACE AT THE RIGHT.*

1. A bed roll is a support for the patient's　　　　　　　　　　　　　　　　　　　1._____

   A. head　　　　B. knees　　　　C. back　　　　D. feet

2. The MAIN purpose of a good nursing chart is to　　　　　　　　　　　　　　　2._____

   A. aid the nurse's memory
   B. help the doctor in diagnosis and treatment
   C. prevent lawsuits
   D. protect the hospital

3. When an ice bag is applied, it should be　　　　　　　　　　　　　　　　　　3._____

   A. kept filled with ice
   B. strapped in place
   C. removed every 15 or 20 minutes
   D. removed every hour

4. Average adult temperature by rectum is _____ °F.　　　　　　　　　　　　　　4._____

   A. 98.6　　　　B. 97.6　　　　C. 99.6　　　　D. 100.6

5. Average adult pulse rate for a man is　　　　　　　　　　　　　　　　　　　　5._____

   A. 64　　　　B. 72　　　　C. 80　　　　D. 96

6. The accepted treatment in severe and extensive radiation burns is to　　　　　6._____

   A. apply tannic acid generously
   B. apply wet sodium bicarbonate dressing
   C. bandage the burned area firmly
   D. put the patient to bed

7. A bed cradle is a device for supporting the　　　　　　　　　　　　　　　　　7._____

   A. back　　　　　　　　　　B. knees
   C. bed covering　　　　　　D. food tray

8. Pediculosis capitus refers to　　　　　　　　　　　　　　　　　　　　　　　　8._____

   A. baldness　　　　　　　　B. athlete's foot
   C. lice　　　　　　　　　　D. tics

9. A subjective symptom is one that the patient　　　　　　　　　　　　　　　　9._____

   A. feels　　　　B. hears　　　　C. sees　　　　D. smells

10. A bed cradle　　　　　　　　　　　　　　　　　　　　　　　　　　　　　　10._____

    A. keeps the patient's weight off the bed
    B. keeps the knees up

116

C. elevates the feet
D. keeps the weight of the covers off the patient

11. The MOST reliable temperature is that found in the

    A. rectum   B. axilla
    C. mouth   D. none Of the above

12. An antiseptic solution recommended in first aid for slight skin scratches (abrasions) is

    A. concentrated boric acid
    B. tincture of merthiolate 1:1000
    C. iodine 2%
    D. tincture of green soap

13. Persons who are likely to come in contact with communicable diseases are immunized by

    A. heredity   B. environment
    C. asepsis   D. biotics

14. The temperature of water for a hot water bottle should NOT exceed _____ ° F.

    A. 100   B. 150   C. 125   D. 175

15. The recently developed treatment for arthritis is

    A. x-ray   B. cortisone
    C. aureomycin   D. gold injections

16. A MOST important need of the aged person is

    A. adequate food
    B. sunshine
    C. companionship with old, familiar friends
    D. exercise

17. Re-educating the aged person to become self-sufficient is referred to as

    A. rejuvenation   B. stabilization
    C. rehabilitation   D. regeneration

18. The aged citizen is BEST cared for in

    A. communities developed for older people
    B. the home environment
    C. nursing homes
    D. hospitals for the aged

19. The octogenarian in a home where there are children should be

    A. expected to train the children
    B. isolated from the rest of the family
    C. catered to
    D. protected from noise and children's activities.

20. The aged person should be treated 20.____

    A. to correct his helplessness
    B. by ignoring his helplessness as much as possible
    C. by solicitous care
    D. with understanding as an individual

21. In growing old, the BEST way to achieve happiness is to 21.____

    A. supervise others for security
    B. advise young folks from experience
    C. adopt positive attitudes of acceptance
    D. undertake babysitting

22. The BEST guide to a safe and efficient dentrifice is 22.____

    A. flavor   B. price
    C. A.D.A. seal   D. manufacturer's label

23. One cause of tooth decay is 23.____

    A. malnutrition   B. too little meat to chew
    C. lack of iron   D. lack of carbohydrates

24. When sugar is lodged in the teeth, cavities enlarge rapidly because bacteria use it to 24.____

    A. form acids which dissolve calcium salts
    B. form enzymes which dissolve calcium salts
    C. form toxins which soften teeth
    D. assimilate calcium salts

25. One of the CHIEF causes of tooth decay is 25.____

    A. malnutrition
    B. too little chewing exercise
    C. bland foods
    D. too much roughage in the diet

26. Concerning teeth, 26.____

    A. dental caries appear most frequently between ages 12 and 20
    B. dental tartar should not be removed
    C. orthodontia is unimportant
    D. fluorides prevent all decay

27. Enariel forming cells of the teeth are sensitive to a deficiency of vitamin 27.____

    A. A   B. B   C. C   D. D

28. To prevent falling, an aged person should wear shoes that have 28.____

    A. open toes   B. crepe rubber soles
    C. foam rubber inner soles   D. rubber heels

29. The study of old age and its diseases is known as 29.____

    A. phrenetics   B. psychosomatics
    C. pediatrics   D. geriatrics

30. Senility is marked by loss of

   A. sight
   B. coordination
   C. hearing
   D. memory

31. Geriatric means

   A. pertaining to gymnastics
   B. the hygienic care of children
   C. care of the eyes
   D. characteristic of old age

32. A person who feels inferior to others may adopt a superior *bossy* attitude toward them. This behavior is an example of

   A. compensation
   B. rationalization
   C. regression
   D. identification

33. When an individual provides excuses for his behavior rather than facing reality, he is said to be

   A. regressing
   B. rationalizing
   C. ventilating
   D. projecting

34. The substitution of an activity in which a person can succeed for one in which he may fail is called

   A. compensation
   B. projection
   C. sublimation
   D. rationalization

35. Daily flossing and regular teeth cleaning by a dental hygienist prevents

   A. cavities
   B. plaque formation
   C. malocclusion
   D. all of the above

KEY (CORRECT ANSWERS)

1. B
2. B
3. C
4. A
5. B

6. C
7. C
8. C
9. A
10. D

11. A
12. C
13. D
14. C
15. B

16. C
17. C
18. B
19. D
20. D

21. C
22. C
23. A
24. A
25. A

26. A
27. A
28. D
29. D
30. D

31. D
32. A
33. B
34. A
35. B

READING COMPREHENSION
UNDERSTANDING AND INTERPRETING WRITTEN MATERIAL
EXAMINATION SECTION
TEST 1

Questions 1-8.

DIRECTIONS: Each question or incomplete statement is followed by several suggested answers or completions. Select the one that BEST answers the question or completes the statement. *PRINT THE LETTER OF THE CORRECT ANSWER IN THE SPACE AT THE RIGHT.*

Questions 1 and 2.

DIRECTIONS: Your answers to Questions 1 and 2 must be based ONLY on the information given in the following paragraph.

Hospitals maintained wholly by public taxation may treat only those compensation cases which are emergencies and may not treat such emergency cases longer than the emergency exists; provided, however, that these restrictions shall not be applicable where there is not available a hospital other than a hospital maintained wholly by taxation.

1. According to the above paragraph, compensation cases

    A. are regarded as emergency cases by hospitals maintained wholly by public taxation
    B. are seldom treated by hospitals maintained wholly by public taxation
    C. are treated mainly by privately endowed hospitals
    D. may be treated by hospitals maintained wholly by public taxation if they are emergencies

2. According to the above paragraph, it is MOST reasonable to conclude that where a privately endowed hospital is available,

    A. a hospital supported wholly by public taxation may treat emergency compensation cases only so long as the emergency exists
    B. a hospital supported wholly by public taxation may treat any compensation cases
    C. a hospital supported wholly by public taxation must refer emergency compensation cases to such a hospital
    D. the restrictions regarding the treatment of compensation cases by a tax-supported hospital are not wholly applicable

Questions 3-7.

DIRECTIONS: Answer Questions 3 through 7 ONLY according to the information given in the following passage.

THE MANUFACTURE OF LAUNDRY SOAP

The manufacture of soap is not a complicated process. Soap is a fat or an oil, plus an alkali, water and salt. The alkali used in making commercial laundry soap is caustic soda. The salt used is the same as common table salt. A fat is generally an animal product that is not a liquid at room temperature. If heated, it becomes a liquid. An oil is generally liquid at room temperature. If the temperature is lowered, the oil becomes a solid just like ordinary fat.

At the soap plant, a huge tank five stories high, called a *kettle,* is first filled part way with fats and then the alkali and water are added. These ingredients are then heated and boiled together. Salt is then poured into the top of the boiling solution; and as the salt slowly sinks down through the mixture, it takes with it the glycerine which comes from the melted fats. The product which finally comes from the kettle is a clear soap which has a moisture content of about 34%. This clear soap is then chilled so that more moisture is driven out. As a result, the manufacturer finally ends up with a commercial laundry soap consisting of 88% clear soap and only 12% moisture.

3. An ingredient used in making laundry soap is

   A. table sugar B. potash
   C. glycerine   D. caustic soda

4. According to the above passage, a difference between fats and oils is that fats

   A. cost more than oils
   B. are solid at room temperature
   C. have less water than oils
   D. are a liquid animal product

5. According to the above passage, the MAIN reason for using salt in the manufacture of soap is to

   A. make the ingredients boil together
   B. keep the fats in the kettle melted
   C. remove the glycerine
   D. prevent the loss of water from the soap

6. According to the passage, the purpose of chilling the clear soap is to

   A. stop the glycerine from melting
   B. separate the alkali from the fats
   C. make the oil become solid
   D. get rid of more moisture

7. According to the passage, the percentage of moisture in commercial laundry soap is

   A. 12%   B. 34%   C. 66%   D. 88%

8. The x-ray has gone into business. Developed primarily to aid in diagnosing human ills, the machine now works in packing plants, in foundries, in service stations, and in a dozen ways to contribute to precision and accuracy in industry.
The above statement means *most nearly* that the x-ray

   A. was first developed to aid business
   B. is of more help to business than it is to medicine
   C. is being used to improve the functioning of business
   D. is more accurate for packing plants than it is for foundries

8._____

Questions 9-25.

DIRECTIONS: Each question consists of a statement. You are to indicate whether the statement is TRUE (T) or FALSE (F). *PRINT THE LETTER OF THE CORRECT ANSWER IN THE SPACE AT THE RIGHT.*

Questions 9-12.

DIRECTIONS: Read the paragraph below about *shock* and then answer Questions 9 through 12 according to the information given in the paragraph.

SHOCK

While not found in all injuries, shock is present in all serious injuries caused by accidents. During shock, the normal activities of the body slow down. This partly explains why one of the signs of shock is a pale, cold skin, since insufficient blood goes to the body parts during shock.

9. If the injury caused by an accident is serious, shock is sure to be present.   9._____

10. In shock, the heart beats faster than normal.   10._____

11. The face of a person suffering from shock is usually red and flushed.   11._____

12. Not enough blood goes to different parts of the body during shock.   12._____

Questions 13-18.

DIRECTIONS: Questions 13 through 18, inclusive, are to be answered SOLELY on the basis of the information contained in the following statement and NOT upon any other information you may have.

Blood transfusions are given to patients at the hospital upon recommendation of the physicians attending such cases. The physician fills out a *Request for Blood Transfusion* form in duplicate and sends both copies to the Medical Director's office, where a list is maintained of persons called *donors* who desire to sell their blood for transfusions. A suitable donor is selected, and the transfusion is given. Donors are, in many instances, medical students and employees of the hospital. Donors receive twenty-five dollars for each transfusion.

13. According to the above paragraph, a blood donor is paid twenty-five dollars for each transfusion.   13._____

14. According to the above paragraph, only medical students and employees of the hospital are selected as blood donors. 14.___

15. According to the above paragraph, the *Request for Blood Transfusion* form is filled out by the patient and sent to the Medical Director's office. 15.___

16. According to the above paragraph, a list of blood donors is maintained in the Medical Director's office. 16.___

17. According to the above paragraph, cases for which the attending physicians recommend blood transfusions are usually emergency cases. 17.___

18. According to the above paragraph, one copy of the *Request for Blood Transfusion* form is kept by the patient and one copy is sent to the Medical Director's office. 18.___

Questions 19-25.

DIRECTIONS: Questions 19 through 25, inclusive, are to be answered SOLELY on the basis of the information contained in the following passage and NOT upon any other information you may have.

Before being admitted to a hospital ward, a patient is first interviewed by the Admitting Clerk, who records the patient's name, age, sex, race, birthplace, and mother's maiden name. This clerk takes all of the money and valuables that the patient has on his person. A list of the valuables is written on the back of the envelope in which the valuables are afterwards placed. Cash is counted and placed in a separate envelope, and the amount of money and the name of the patient are written on the outside of the envelope. Both envelopes are sealed, fastened together, and placed in a compartment of a safe.

An orderly then escorts the patient to a dressing room where the patient's clothes are removed and placed in a bundle. A tag bearing the patient's name is fastened to the bundle. A list of the contents of the bundle is written on property slips, which are made out in triplicate. The information contained on the outside of the envelopes containing the cash and valuables belonging to the patient is also copied on the property slips.

According to the above passage,

19. patients are escorted to the dressing room by the Admitting Clerk. 19.___

20. the patient's cash and valuables are placed together in one envelope. 20.___

21. the number of identical property slips that are made out when a patient is being admitted to a hospital ward is three. 21.___

22. the full names of both parents of a patient are recorded by the Admitting Clerk before a patient is admitted to a hospital ward. 22.___

23. the amount of money that a patient has on his person when admitted to the hospital is entered on the patient's property slips. 23.___

24. an orderly takes all the money and valuables that a patient has on his person. 24.___

25. the patient's name is placed on the tag that is attached to the bundle containing the patient's clothing. 25.___

KEY (CORRECT ANSWERS)

1. D
2. A
3. D
4. B
5. C

6. D
7. A
8. C
9. T
10. F

11. F
12. T
13. T
14. F
15. F

16. T
17. T
18. F
19. F
20. F

21. T
22. F
23. T
24. F
25. T

TEST 2

DIRECTIONS: Each question or incomplete statement is followed by several suggested answers or completions. Select the one that BEST answers the question or completes the statement. *PRINT THE LETTER OF THE CORRECT ANSWER IN THE SPACE AT THE RIGHT.*

Questions 1-4.

DIRECTIONS: Questions 1 through 4 are to be answered in accordance with the following paragraphs.

One fundamental difference between the United States health care system and the health care systems of some European countries is the way that hospital charges for long-term illnesses affect their citizens.

In European countries such as England, Sweden, and Germany, citizens can face, without fear, hospital charges due to prolonged illness, no matter how substantial they may be. Citizens of these nations are required to pay nothing when they are hospitalized, for they have prepaid their treatment as taxpayers when they were well and were earning incomes.

On the other hand, the United States citizen, in spite of the growth of payments by third parties which include private insurance carriers as well as public resources, has still to shoulder 40 percent of hospital care costs, while his private insurance contributes only 25 percent and public resources the remaining 35 percent.

Despite expansion of private health insurance and social legislation in the United States, out-of-pocket payments for hospital care by individuals have steadily increased. Such payments, currently totalling $23 billion, are nearly twice as high as ten years ago.

Reform is inevitable and, when it comes, will have to reconcile sharply conflicting interests. Hospital staffs are demanding higher and higher wages. Hospitals are under pressure by citizens, who as patients demand more and better services but who as taxpayers or as subscribers to hospital insurance plans, are reluctant to pay the higher cost of improved care. An acceptable reconciliation of these interests has so far eluded legislators and health administrators in the United States.

1. According to the above passage, the one of the following which is an ADVANTAGE that citizens of England, Sweden, and Germany have over United States citizens is that, when faced with long-term illness,

    A. the amount of out-of-pocket payments made by these European citizens is small when compared to out-of-pocket payments made by United States citizens
    B. European citizens have no fear of hospital costs no matter how great they may be
    C. more efficient and reliable hospitals are available to the European citizen than is available to the United States citizens
    D. a greater range of specialized hospital care is available to the European citizens than is available to the United States citizens

1.___

2. According to the above passage, reform of the United States system of health care must reconcile all of the following EXCEPT
    A. attempts by health administrators to provide improved hospital care
    B. taxpayers' reluctance to pay for the cost of more and better hospital services
    C. demands by hospital personnel for higher wages
    D. insurance subscribers' reluctance to pay the higher costs of improved hospital care

3. According to the above passage, the out-of-pocket payments for hospital care that individuals made ten years ago was APPROXIMATELY _____ billion.
    A. $32   B. $23   C. $12   D. $3

4. According to the above passage, the GREATEST share of the costs of hospital care in the United States is paid by
    A. United States citizens
    B. private insurance carriers
    C. public resources
    D. third parties

Questions 5-8.

DIRECTIONS: Questions 5 through 8 are to be answered SOLELY on the basis of the information contained in the following passage.

Effective cost controls have been difficult to establish in most hospitals in the United States. Ways must be found to operate hospitals with reasonable efficiency without sacrificing quality and in a manner that will reduce the amount of personal income now being spent on health care and the enormous drain on national resources. We must adopt a new public objective of providing higher quality health care at significantly lower cost. One step that can be taken to achieve this goal is to carefully control capital expenditures for hospital construction and expansion. Perhaps the way to start is to declare a moratorium on all hospital construction and to determine the factors that should be considered in deciding whether a hospital should be built. Such factors might include population growth, distance to the nearest hospital, availability of medical personnel, and hospital bed shortage.

A second step to achieve the new objective is to increase the ratio of out-of-hospital patient to in-hospital patient care. This can be done by using separate health care facilities other than hospitals to attract patients who have increasingly been going to hospital clinics and overcrowding them. Patients should instead identify with a separate health care facility to keep them out of hospitals.

A third step is to require better hospital operating rules and controls. This step might include the review of a doctor's performance by other doctors, outside professional evaluations of medical practice, and required refresher courses and re-examinations for doctors. Other measures might include obtaining mandatory second opinions on the need for surgery in order to avoid unnecessary surgery, and outside review of work rules and procedures to eliminate unnecessary testing of patients.

A fourth step is to halt the construction and public subsidizing of new medical schools and to fill whatever needs exist in professional coverage by emphasizing the medical training of physicians with specialities that are in short supply and by providing a better geographic distribution of physicians and surgeons.

5. According to the above passage, providing higher quality health care at lower cost can be achieved by the

   A. greater use of out-of-hospital facilities
   B. application of more effective cost controls on doctors' fees
   C. expansion of improved in-hospital patient care services at hospital clinics
   D. development of more effective training programs in hospital administration

6. According to the above passage, the one of the following which should be taken into account in determining if a hospital should be constructed is the

   A. number of out-of-hospital health care facilities
   B. availability of public funds to subsidize construction
   C. number of hospitals under construction
   D. availability of medical personnel

7. According to the above passage, it is IMPORTANT to operate hospitals efficiently because

   A. they are currently in serious financial difficulties
   B. of the need to reduce the amount of personal income going to health care
   C. the quality of health care services has deteriorated
   D. of the need to increase productivity goals to take care of the growing population in the United States

8. According to the above passage, which one of the following approaches is MOST LIKELY to result in better operating rules and controls in hospitals?

   A. Allocating doctors to health care facilities on the basis of patient population
   B. Equalizing the workloads of doctors
   C. Establishing a physician review board to evaluate the performance of other physicians
   D. Eliminating unnecessary outside review of patient testing

Questions 9-14.

DIRECTIONS: Questions 9 through 14 are to be answered SOLELY on the basis of the information contained in the following passage.

The United States today is the only major industrial nation in the world without a system of national health insurance or a national health service. Instead, we have placed our prime reliance on private enterprise and private health insurance to meet the need. Yet, in a recent year, of the 180 million Americans under 65 years of age, 34 million had no hospital insurance, 38 million had no surgical insurance, 63 million had no out-patient x-ray and laboratory insurance, 94 million had no insurance for prescription drugs, and 103 million had no insurance for physician office visits or home visits. Some 35 million Americans under the age of 65 had no health insurance whatsoever. Some 64 million additional Americans under age 65 had health insurance coverage that was less than that provided to the aged under Medicare.

Despite more than three decades of enormous growth, the private health insurance industry today pays benefits equal to only one-third of the total cost of private health care, leaving the rest to be borne by the patient—essentially the same ratio which held true a decade ago. Moreover, nearly all private health insurance is limited; it provides partial benefits, not comprehensive benefits; acute care, not preventive care; it siphons off the young and healthy, and ignores the poor and medically indigent. The typical private carrier usually pays only the cost of hospital care, forcing physicians and patients alike to resort to wasteful and inefficient use of hospital facilities, thereby giving further impetus to the already soaring costs of hospital care. Valuable hospital beds are used for routine tests and examinations. Unnecessary hospitalization, unnecessary surgery, and unnecessarily extended hospital stays are encouraged. These problems are exacerbated by the fact that administrative costs of commercial carriers are substantially higher than they are for Blue Shield, Blue Cross, or Medicare.

9. According to the above passage, the PROPORTION of total private health care costs paid by private health insurance companies today as compared to ten years ago has

   A. *increased* by approximately one-third
   B. *remained* practically the same
   C. *increased* by approximately two-thirds
   D. *decreased* by approximately one-third

10. According to the above passage, the one of the following which has contributed MOST to wasteful use of hospital facilities is the

    A. increased emphasis on preventive health care
    B. practice of private carriers of providing comprehensive health care benefits
    C. increased hospitalization of the elderly and the poor
    D. practice of a number of private carriers of paying only for hospital care costs

11. Based on the information in the above passage, which one of the following patients would be LEAST likely to receive benefits from a typical private health insurance plan?
    A

    A. young patient who must undergo an emergency appendectomy
    B. middle-aged patient who needs a costly series of x-ray and laboratory tests for diagnosis of gastrointestinal complaints
    C. young patient who must visit his physician weekly for treatment of a chronic skin disease
    D. middle-aged patient who requires extensive cancer surgery

12. Which one of the following is the MOST accurate inference that can be drawn from the above passage?

    A. Private health insurance has failed to fully meet the health care needs of Americans.
    B. Most Americans under age 65 have health insurance coverage better than that provided to the elderly under Medicare.
    C. Countries with a national health service are likely to provide poorer health care for their citizens than do countries that rely primarily on private health insurance.
    D. Hospital facilities in the United States are inadequate to meet the nation's health care needs.

13. Of the total number of Americans under age 65, what percentage belonged in the combined category of persons with NO health insurance or health insurance less than that provided to the aged under Medicare?

    A. 19%   B. 36%   C. 55%   D. 65%

14. According to the above passage, the one of the following types of health insurance which covered the SMALLEST number of Americans under age 65 was

    A. hospital insurance
    B. surgical insurance
    C. insurance for prescription drugs
    D. insurance for physician office or home visits

Questions 15-17.

DIRECTIONS: Questions 15 through 17 are to be answered SOLELY on the basis of the information contained in the following passage.

Statistical studies have demonstrated that disease and mortality rates are higher among the poor than among the more affluent members of our society. Periodic surveys conducted by the United States Public Health Service continue to document a higher prevalence of infectious and chronic diseases within low income families. While the basic life style and living conditions of the poor are to a considerable extent responsible for this less favorable health status, there are indications that the kind of health care received by the poor also plays a significant role. The poor are less likely to be aware of the concepts and practices of scientific medicine and less likely to seek health care when they need it. Moreover, they are discouraged from seeking adequate health care by the depersonalization, disorganization, and inadequate emphasis on preventive care which characterize the health care most often provided for them.

To achieve the objective of better health care for the poor, the following approaches have been suggested: encouraging the poor to seek preventive care as well as care for acute illness and to establish a lasting one-to-one relationship with a single physician who can treat the poor patient as a whole individual; sufficient financial subsidy to put the poor on an equal footing with *paying patients*, thereby giving them the opportunity to choose from among available health services providers; inducements to health services providers to establish public clinics in poverty areas; and legislation to provide for health education, earlier detection of disease, and coordinated health care.

15. According to the above passage, the one of the following which is a function of the United States Public Health Service is

    A. gathering data on the incidence of infectious diseases
    B. operating public health clinics in poverty areas lacking private physicians
    C. recommending legislation for the improvement of health care in the United States
    D. encouraging the poor to participate in programs aimed at the prevention of illness

16. According to the above passage, the one of the following which is MOST characteristic of the health care currently provided for the poor is that it   16.____

    A. aims at establishing clinics in poverty areas
    B. enables the poor to select the health care they want through the use of financial subsidies
    C. places insufficient stress on preventive health care
    D. over-emphasizes the establishment of a one-to-one relationship between physician and patient

17. The above passage IMPLIES that the poor lack the financial resources to   17.____

    A. obtain adequate health insurance coverage
    B. select from among existing health services
    C. participate in health education programs
    D. lobby for legislation aimed at improving their health care

Questions 18-20.

DIRECTIONS: Questions 18 through 20 are to be answered SOLELY on the basis of the information contained in the following passage.

The concept of *affiliation,* developed more than ten years ago, grew out of a series of studies which found evidence of faulty care, surgery of *questionable* value and other undesirable conditions in the city's municipal hospitals. The affiliation agreements signed shortly thereafter were designed to correct these deficiencies by assuring high quality medical care. In general, the agreements provided the staff and expertise of a voluntary hospital—sometimes connected with a medical school—to operate various services or, in some cases, all of the professional divisions of a specific municipal hospital. The municipal hospitals have paid for these services, which last year cost the city $200 million, the largest single expenditure of the Health and Hospitals Corporation. In addition, the municipal hospitals have provided to the voluntary hospitals such facilities as free space for laboratories and research. While some experts agree that affiliation has resulted in improvements in some hospital care, they contend that many conditions that affiliation was meant to correct still exist. In addition, accountability procedures between the Corporation and voluntary hospitals are said to be so inadequate that audits of affiliation contracts of the past five years revealed that there may be more than $200 million in charges for services by the voluntary hospitals which have not been fully substantiated. Consequently, the Corporation has proposed that future agreements provide accountability in terms of funds, services supplied, and use of facilities by the voluntary hospitals.

18. According to the above passage, *affiliation* may BEST be defined as an agreement whereby   18.____

    A. voluntary hospitals pay for the use of municipal hospital facilities
    B. voluntary and municipal hospitals work to eliminate duplication of services
    C. municipal hospitals pay voluntary hospitals for services performed
    D. voluntary and municipal hospitals transfer patients to take advantage of specialized services

19. According to the above passage, the MAIN purpose for setting up the *affiliation* agreement was to

    A. supplement the revenues of municipal hospitals
    B. improve the quality of medical care in municipal hospitals
    C. reduce operating costs in municipal hospitals
    D. increase the amount of space available to municipal hospitals

20. According to the above passage, inadequate accountability procedures have resulted in

    A. unsubstantiated charges for services by the voluntary hospitals
    B. emphasis on research rather than on patient care in municipal hospitals
    C. unsubstantiated charges for services by the municipal hospitals
    D. economic losses to voluntary hospitals

Questions 21-25.

DIRECTIONS: Questions 21 through 25 are to be answered SOLELY on the basis of the information contained in the following passage.

The payment for medical services covered under the Outpatient Medical Insurance Plan (OMI) may be made, by OMI, directly to a physician or to the OMI patient. If the physician and the patient agree that the physician is to receive payment directly from OMI, the payment will be officially assigned to the physician; this is the assignment method. If payment is not assigned, the patient receives payment directly from OMI based on an itemized bill he submits, regardless of whether or not he has already paid his physician.

When a physician accepts assignment of the payment for medical services, he agrees that total charges will not be more than the allowed charge determined by the OMI carrier administering the program. In such cases, the OMI patient pays any unmet part of the $85 annual deductible, plus 10 percent of the remaining charges to the physician. In unassigned claims, the patient is responsible for the total amount charged by the physician. The patient will then be reimbursed by the program 90 percent of the allowed charges in excess of the annual deductible.

The rates of acceptance of assignments provide a measure of how many OMI patients are spared *administrative participation* in the program. Because physicians are free to accept or reject assignments, the rate in which assignments are made provide a general indication of the medical community's satisfaction with the OMI program, especially with the level of amounts paid by the program for specific services and the promptness of payment.

21. According to the above passage, in order for a physician to receive payment directly from OMI for medical services to an OMI patient, the physician would have to accept the assignment of payment, to have the consent of the patient, AND to

    A. submit to OMI a paid itemized bill
    B. collect from the patient 90% of the total bill
    C. collect from the patient the total amount of the charges for his services, a portion of which he will later reimburse the patient
    D. agree that his charges for services to the patient will not exceed the amount allowed by the program

22. According to the above passage, if a physician accepts assignment of payment, the patient pays 22.____

   A. the total amount charged by the physician and is reimbursed by the program for 90 percent of the allowed charges in excess of the applicable deductible
   B. any unmet part of the $85 annual deductible, plus 90 percent of the remaining charges
   C. the total amount charged by the physician and is reimbursed by the program for 10 percent of the allowed charges in excess of the $85 annual deductible
   D. any unmet part of the $85 annual deductible, plus 10 percent of the remaining charges

23. A physician has accepted the assignment of payment for charges to an OMI patient. The physician's charges, all of which are allowed under OMI, amount to $115. This is the first time the patient has been eligible for OMI benefits and the first time the patient has received services from this physician. 23.____
   According to the above passage, the patient must pay the physician

   A. $27   B. $76.50   C. $88   D. $103.50

24. In an unassigned claim, a physician's charges, all of which are allowed under OMI, amount to $165. The patient paid the physician the full amount of the bill. 24.____
   If this is the FIRST time the patient has been eligible for OMI benefits, he will receive from OMI a reimbursement of

   A. $72   B. $80   C. $85   D. $93

25. According to the above passage, if the rate of acceptance of assignments by physicians is high, it is LEAST appropriate to conclude that the medical community is generally satisfied with the 25.____

   A. supplementary medical insurance program
   B. levels of amounts paid to physicians by the program
   C. number of OMI patients being spared administrative participation in the program
   D. promptness of the program in making payment for services

KEY (CORRECT ANSWERS)

1.	B	11.	C	21.	D
2.	A	12.	A	22.	D
3.	C	13.	C	23.	C
4.	D	14.	D	24.	A
5.	A	15.	A	25.	C
6.	D	16.	C		
7.	B	17.	B		
8.	C	18.	C		
9.	B	19.	B		
10.	D	20.	A		

BASIC FUNDAMENTALS OF CLEANING OF PATIENT AND NON-PATIENT AREAS

CONTENTS

		Page
I.	Patient and Non-Patient Units	1
II.	Bed Washing	4
III.	Cleaning Lavatories, Urinals, Toilet Bowls, etc.	6
IV.	Cleaning of Shower Rooms	10
V.	Isolation (Regular and Reverse)	12
VI.	Miscellany	19
VII.	Chalkboard Maintenance	23
VIII.	Microbiology of the Hospital Environment	26
IX.	Chemistry of Detergent	31

BASIC FUNDAMENTALS OF CLEANING OF PATIENT AND NON-PATIENT AREAS

I. PATIENT AND NON-PATIENT UNITS

PURPOSE: To improve sanitation of the environment, to control cross-contamination and to maintain an acceptable appearance.

EQUIPMENT:

- Utility cart
- Vacuum or sweeping tool
- Treated cloths
- Germicidal detergent
- Gloves
- Buckets (two)
- Wringer on dolly (two)
- Mopheads and handles (two)
- Clean dyed cloths or sponges
- Plastic bags and ties
- Container for cigarette butts

SAFETY PRECAUTIONS:

1. Knock on door before entering.

2. Be as quiet as possible.

3. Do not transfer one patient's belongings to another patient's area (cross-contamination).

4. Change water frequently (every three to four rooms—depending on size and soilage factors).

PROCEDURE

Daily

1. Assemble equipment. Prepare solutions (for damp dusting operation, as well as the mopping operation). Take all necessary equipment to assigned area. Take inside unit.

2. Open windows if possible for ventilation. Take a good look at the unit and report any damage to furniture, equipment, walls, ceiling, or lights. Check furniture and walls for spots.

3. Put on gloves.

4. Collect trash (follow trash removal procedure).

CLEANING OF PATIENT AND NON-PATIENT AREAS

PROCEDURE

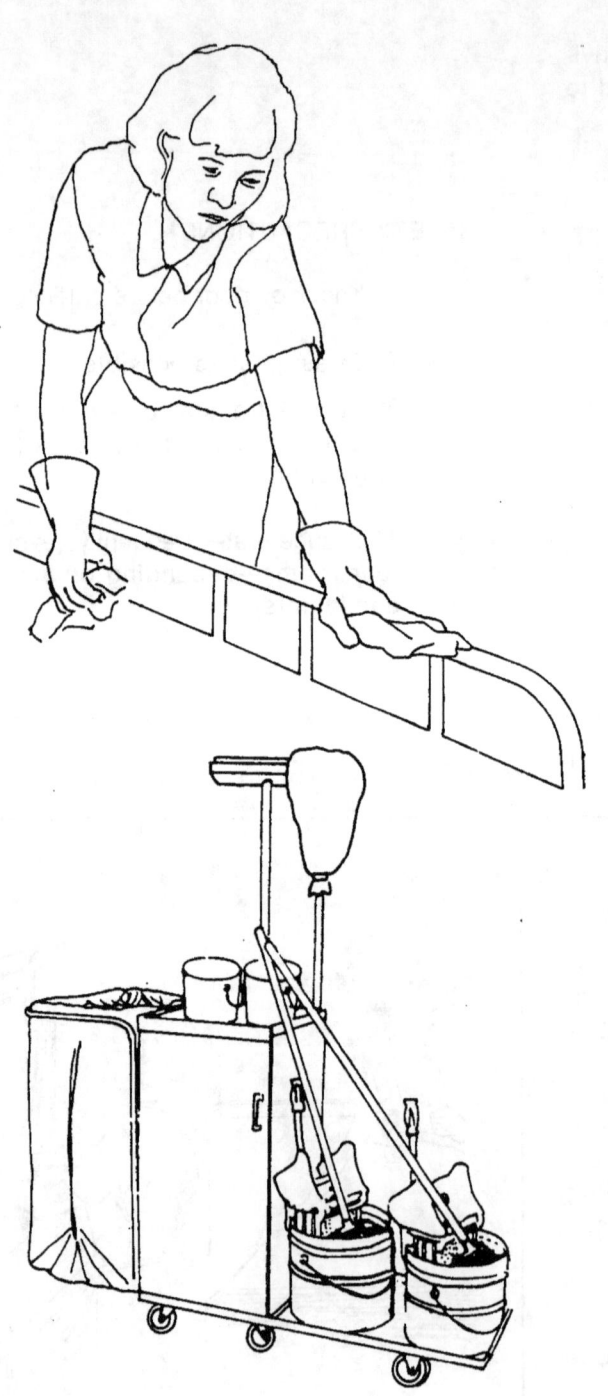

5. Empty ash trays into special container.

6. Dip clean cloth in germicide solution, wring out. Take second cloth in other hand. Wipe off bedside stands, bedrails, window sills, chairs, cabinets, and other furniture with the damp germicide cloth. Dry with dry cloth. Wash ash trays. Remove spots on wall and around light switches. Wipe off door knobs. Return cloth to germicide solution frequently for refreshing. (Wash beds on airing day.)

7. Vacuum floor (covered broom or the sweeping tool with treated cloth may be used to remove surface dust).

8. Wet mop floor area (follow wet mopping procedure).

9. Continue this procedure until all units are completed. Change water frequently.

10. Clean equipment and return to designated storage area. Restock utility cart.

Terminal

The same procedure is used as for daily maintenance with the following exceptions:

1. All furniture is pulled away from wall areas and the unit is given a thorough cleaning. In patient areas, bedside stands are washed inside and outside; beds and bedding accessories are washed.

2. In non-patient, as well as patient areas, walls—if soiled—are washed (as far as one can reach).

CLEANING OF PATIENT AND NON-PATIENT AREAS

PROCEDURE

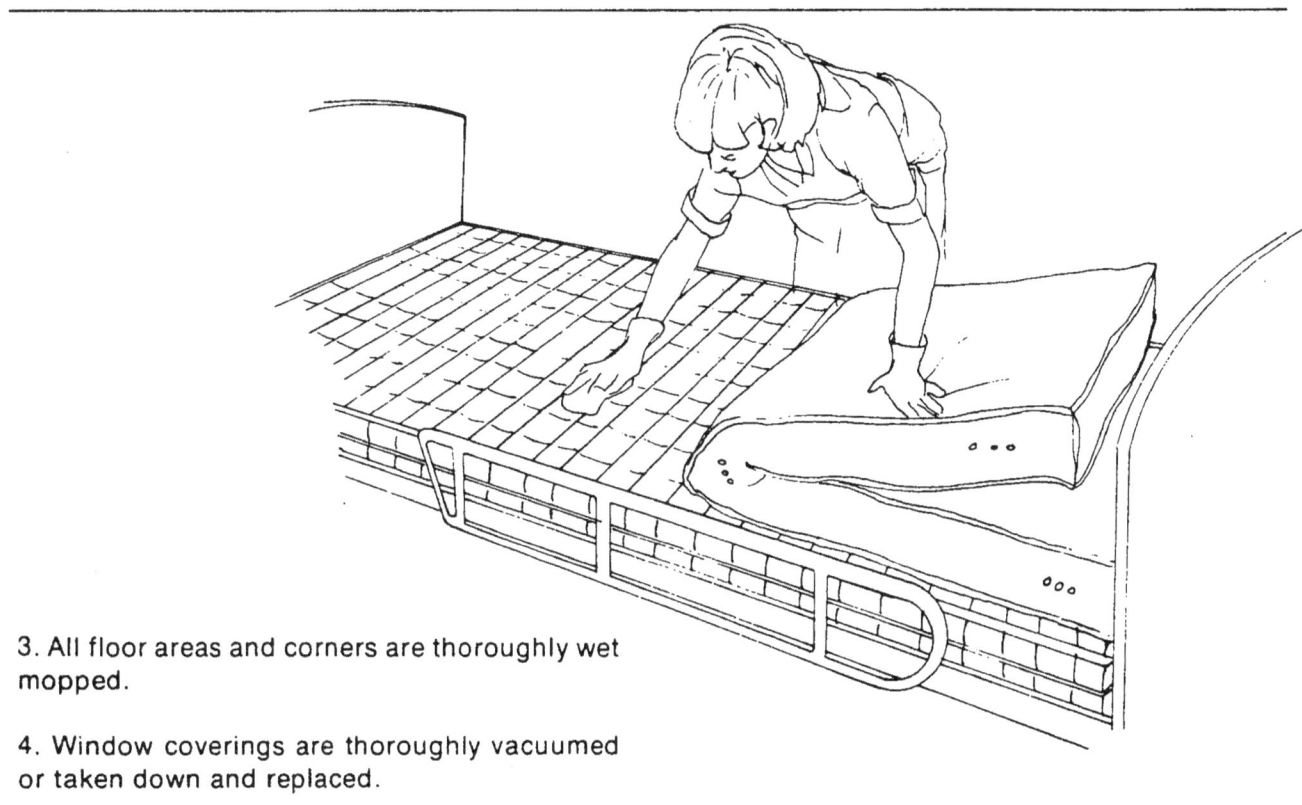

3. All floor areas and corners are thoroughly wet mopped.

4. Window coverings are thoroughly vacuumed or taken down and replaced.

5. Windows and light fixtures are cleaned.

6. All furniture is replaced in proper location.

Cleaning Treatment Rooms, Laboratories, and Research Areas

These areas are set up for treatment, diagnosis and other experiments, and must be kept free of dust and any other foreign matter that will interfere with the highest level of sanitation that can be obtained.

The same procedure is used as for the daily maintenance with the following precautions:

1. Do not clean tops of counters. However, Housekeeping is responsible for maintenance of walls, floors, windows, toilet facilities, outside of cabinets, trash containers, and trash removal.

2. Do not clean, touch, strike or drip water on equipment. However, if equipment is accidentally damaged, report immediately.

CLEANING OF PATIENT AND NON-PATIENT AREAS

II. BED WASHING

PURPOSE: To control odor and to prevent cross-contamination. Bed washing is performed once a week on airing days, as well as, when the unit is vacated.

EQUIPMENT:

    Utility cart
    Bucket (two)
    Cloths
    Vacuum cleaner (wet and dry)
    Germicidal detergent

SAFETY PRECAUTIONS:

1. Do not place bedding against body.

2. Do not use abrasives (cleansers, toilet brushes and other harsh materials) on metal. This harsh type treatment will scratch metal and cause it to bleed—rust.

3. Keep solution close to work site for frequent refreshing of the cloths.

4. Always put clean on cleaned.

5. Report all damaged furnishings.

6. If bedding is not plasticized or covered with plastic, check with supervisor for cleaning procedure.

PROCEDURE

1. Assemble equipment. Prepare solution. Take to assigned area.

2. Prepare a surface for placing small cleaned items (for example, wash and dry top of night stand).

3. Check bedding for foreign matter, tears, etc. (If plastic covering is torn, replace. If mattress is plasterized and is torn, ask that the mattress be replaced. If spring or frame is damaged, report to supervisor.)

4. Vacuum bedding, frame and springs.

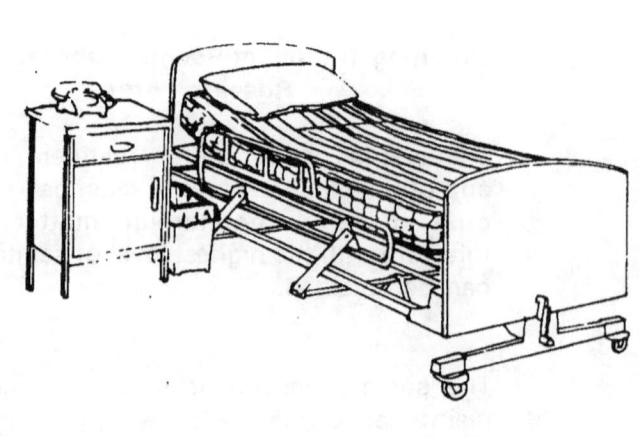

CLEANING OF PATIENT AND NON-PATIENT AREAS

PROCEDURE

5. Wash both sides of the pillow. Rinse and dry. Place on the cleaned surface (night stand).

6. Continue with the washing of the mattress. Start at the top and wash top side and edges of mattress. Rinse and dry.

> *NOTE: Some authorities state that the mattress should not be rinsed or dried because the longer the germicide solution is in contact with the surface, the lesser the chance for cross-contamination. However, if this method is used, all frames, springs, rails must be rinsed and dried.*

7. Turn top half of mattress over on bottom half (clean on cleaned) and wash the upper half of mattress and springs. Rinse and dry.

8. Wash the head frame and side rail (if any), washing from head to foot. Rinse and dry.

9. Continue to opposite side of bed. Turn top half of mattress on cleaned spring.

10. Turn bottom half of mattress over on top half. Wash mattress and spring. Rinse and dry.

11. Wash side rail (if any) and the foot frame of the bed. Rinse and dry. Do not overlook casters.

12. Rinse springs, head, and foot; and leave mattress to air (mattress may also be placed over head frame if gatch type bed is not in use).

13. Continue the above procedures until all beds are completed. Remember to change water frequently.

14. Clean equipment and return to designated storage area.

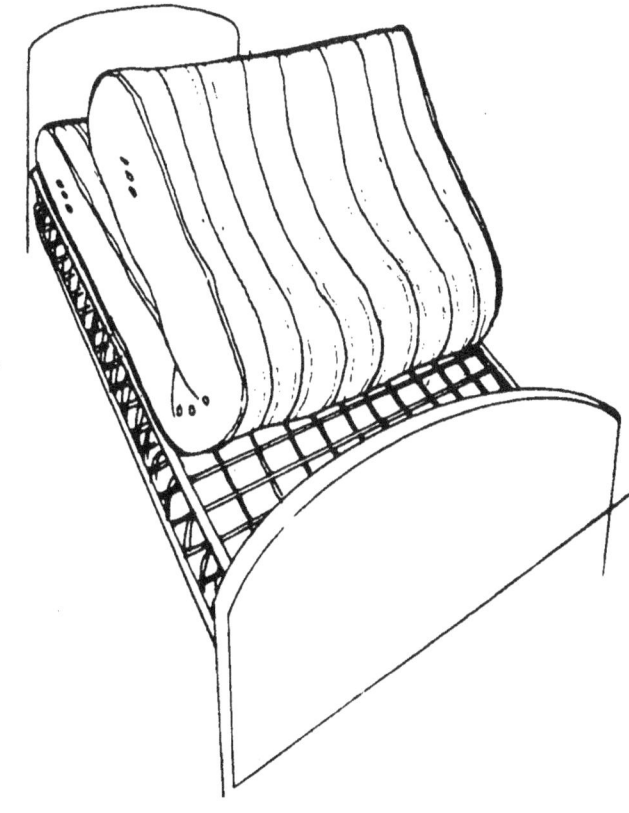

CLEANING OF PATIENT AND NON-PATIENT AREAS

III. CLEANING LAVATORIES, URINALS, TOILET BOWLS OR COMMODES, SINKS, PARTITIONS, MIRRORS

PURPOSE: To maintain cleanliness, control bacteria and odor, and for appearance. Toilet facilities are divided into two categories—private and public. Both must be cleaned at least once daily. However, a public facility may require several cleanings and policings per day.

EQUIPMENT:

Utility cart
Gloves
Small buckets (two)
Buckets on dolly (two)
Wringers (two)
Mopheads and handles (two)
Germicidal detergent
Cleanser
Toilet brush and carrier
Plunger
Out of order sign
Plastic liners
Nylon pad
Measuring cups
Counter brush
Dustpan
Mirror
Putty knife (short and long handle)
Spray bottle
Vacuum cleaner (wet and dry), or
Floor squeegee
Sweeping tool—treated cloths, or
Broom—Broom bags
Replacement supplies (paper towels, toilet tissue, soap—solid/liquid)

SAFETY PRECAUTIONS:

1. Always put room out of order. (Lock door or place "Out of Order" sign in front of door.

2. Always wear gloves.

3. Use recommended amount of detergent.

4. Turn lights off and make sure globe has cooled before washing.

5. Report any necessary repairs—lights, plumbing or fixtures.

6. Do not leave toilet brush in toilet area nor sitting in germicide solution.

7. It is a must to change all solutions (wash and rinse), mopheads and cleaning cloths or sponges before going to the next assignment.

CLEANING OF PATIENT AND NON-PATIENT AREAS

PROCEDURE

Daily

1. Assemble all equipment. Prepare solution. Take to designated area.

2. Place "Out of Order" sign in front of door.

3. Replace supplies (paper towels, soap, toilet tissue). As toilet tissue is being checked and replaced, in order to save steps, take sheets of toilet tissue and flush commodes.

4. Put on gloves.

5. Pour recommended amount of germicide into each commode and urinal.

6. Pick up large pieces of trash. Remove gum, tar, and other foreign matter from floor areas—use putty knife. Empty trash containers.

7. Dip cloths into germicide solution. Wring out. Wipe inside and outside of trash container. Rinse and dry. Replace liner.

8. Dust floor with covered broom, sweeping tool or vacuum.

9. Wash mirrors (spray glass cleaner or plain water on mirror). Rinse and dry.

10. Dip cloth or sponge into cleaning solution, wring out excess water. Wash all ledges, towel boxes, and window sills. Spot wash around all light switches. Wipe off globes, door knobs, and push and kick plates.

11. Dip cloth or sponge into germicidal solution, wring out, and wash faucets, soap dishes or dispensers (nylon pad can be used to remove difficult spots), wall areas around sink, outer

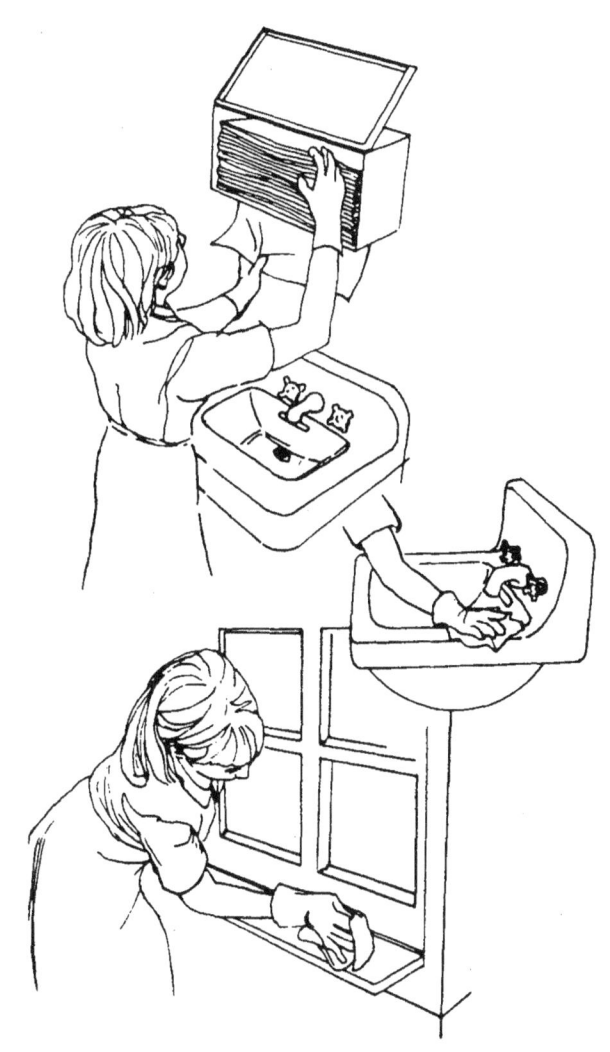

CLEANING OF PATIENT AND NON-PATIENT AREAS

PROCEDURE

surface of sink, and all exposed pipes, valves, and fixtures. Rinse and dry.

12. Dip cloth into germicidal solution. Wring out. Pour small amount of abrasive cleanser on cloth. Wash interior of sink. Rinse sink with water from faucets. Dry with clean cloth.

13. Clean commode and surrounding area:
   a. Dip cloth into germicidal solution, wring out. Wipe off all pipes, valves and fixtures. Spot wash wall areas and partitions. Rinse and dry.

   b. Continue with the procedure. Wash, rinse, and dry outer surface of the commode.

   c. Wash top and outer portion of seat. Rinse and dry.

   d. Wash underneath bottom of seat and outer rim of commode. Rinse and dry.

   e. Pour remaining water in bucket into commode. Take toilet brush and scrub interior of commode (inside rim as well as under the rim). Flush, wipe up splashes. Return brush to carrier.

14. Inspect commode. Check under rim of commode to see if all soil is removed. (A mirror may be used for this purpose.)

15. Wet mop floor. Follow the four-step wet mopping procedure. Start at back of room, and apply and pick up germicidal solution. Make sure to get into corners, around commode, and baseboards. Rinse and dry.

NOTE: Flooding system can be used instead of the wet mopping procedure.

CLEANING OF PATIENT AND NON-PATIENT AREAS

PROCEDURE

    a. Pour or spray excessive amount of germicidal solution on floor.

    b. Agitate with brush on side of wet pick-up tool, and pick up solution with wet and dry vacuum; or squeegee solution into floor drain with floor squeegee.

16. Remove all equipment. Inspect work.

17. Empty water and rinse buckets, change mopheads and cleaning cloths or sponges. Make fresh solution before going to next assignment.

18. Proceed to next assignment. If assignments are completed, wash and dry all equipment. Return to designated storage area. (Place mopheads and cleaning cloths in plastic bags for laundering.)

CLEANING OF PATIENT AND NON-PATIENT AREAS

IV. CLEANING OF SHOWER ROOMS

PURPOSE: To maintain cleanliness, control bacteria and odor, and for appearance.

EQUIPMENT:

- Utility cart
- Gloves
- Buckets (small, two)
- Buckets on dolly (two)
- Wringers (two)
- Mopheads and handles (two)
- Germicidal detergent
- Cleanser
- Toilet brush and carrier
- Plunger
- Out of Order signs
- Plastic liners
- Replacement supplies (paper towels, toilet tissue, soap solid/liquid)
- Nylon pad
- Measuring cups
- Counter brush
- Dustpan
- Mirror
- Putty knife (short and long handle)
- Spray bottle
- Vacuum cleaner (wet and dry)
- Floor Squeegee
- Clean dyed cloth or sponge
- Sweeping tool—treated cloths, or
- Broom—broom bags

SAFETY PRECAUTIONS:

1. Always put room out of order. (Lock door or place out of order sign in front of door.)

2. Always wear gloves.

3. Use recommended amount of detergent.

4. Turn lights off and make sure globe is cooled before washing.

5. Report any necessary repairs—lights, plumbing, or fixtures.

6. Do not leave toilet brush in toilet area nor sitting in germicide solution.

7. It is a must to change all solutions (wash and rinse), mopheads and cleaning cloths or sponges before going to the next assignment.

PROCEDURE

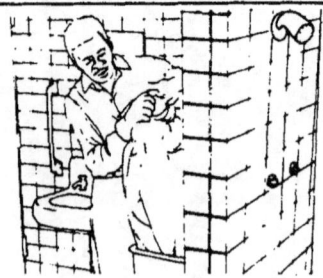

1. Assemble equipment. Prepare solutions. Take to designated area.

2. Place out of order sign in front of door or on door.

3. Put on gloves.

CLEANING OF PATIENT AND NON-PATIENT AREAS

PROCEDURE

4. Pick up all large pieces of trash, clothing, and soap chips. Place in proper containers.

5. Collect trash. Wipe trash container inside and outside. Replace liner.

6. Dip cloth into germicidal solution and wring out. Spot wash wall areas, window sills, and ledges. Return cloth to germicidal solution and refresh. Continue with procedure. Wipe around light switches, door knobs, kick and push plates, and water regulator control panels. Rinse and dry.

7. Clean bath tub—take germicidal cloth and wipe off all exposed pipes, faucets and fixtures, and exterior of tub. Rinse and dry.

8. Dip cloth or sponge in germicidal solution, wring out. Pour small amount of abrasive cleanser on cloth. Wash interior of tub. Rinse with water from faucets. Dry with clean cloth.

9. Change water (wash and rinse).

10. Spot wash all shower stall areas, partitions, and wall area. Rinse and dry. At least once a week, thoroughly wash, rinse and dry these areas.

11. Wet mop floor. Follow the four-step mopping procedure or the flooding system.

12. Inspect area. Take equipment to utility room. Clean and return to designated area. Restock utility cart.

CLEANING OF PATIENT AND NON-PATIENT AREAS

V. ISOLATION
(Regular and Reverse)

PURPOSE: To protect self and other persons outside of the Isolation unit from contracting a contagious disease, and to prevent the direct and indirect spread of the infectious organism. In Reverse Isolation, the purpose is to prevent infectious organisms from entering the Isolation unit.

EQUIPMENT:

    Utility cart
    Automatic mop assembly, or
    Buckets and Wringers on dolly (two)
    Mopheads and Handles (two)
    Buckets (two)
    Gloves (disposable)
    Gowns (disposable)
    Masks (disposable)
    20-gallon Galvanized can on dolly
    Large plastic liner
    Vacuum cleaner (wet and dry)
    Newspaper
    Toilet tissue
    Paper towels
    Soap (solid or liquid)
    Sponges or dyed cloths
    Germicidal detergent
    Plastic bags and ties (large and small)
    Orange laundry bag and hamper

SAFETY PRECAUTIONS:

1. At Saint Elizabeths Hospital, orange bags are used for any contaminated, launderable item.

2. Have as few pieces of furniture in room as possible—make sure it is washable.

3. Observe posted protective measures. Wear mask if specified. Wear gown and gloves when cleaning all Isolation units.

4. No one is allowed in the Isolation unit except persons caring for patient and area. Visitors must be referred to the charge nurse.

5. In Strict and Respiratory Isolation, if room does not have an adequate artificial ventilation system or functioning exhaust fan; a one-half hour airing period with windows open and doors closed may be indicated before cleaning.

6. Airing a room from which a patient is discharged, *is not* an effective terminal disinfection procedure.

7. Never use a broom or dust mop in this area.

8. Disinfectant fogging *should not be used*.

9. Leave equipment outside of door in Regular Isolation. Leave equipment in unit in Reverse Isolation.

10. Take off all jewelry (rings, watches, earrings) before putting on protective garments.

11. Make sure mask covers nose and mouth. Do not talk while wearing mask.

CLEANING OF PATIENT AND NON-PATIENT AREAS

Mask is only effective when dry. If for some reason, mask or gown becomes wet, change immediately.

12. Observe rules for trash removal.

13. Use paper towel to turn on faucets.

14. Make sure hands and equipment are thoroughly washed, rinsed, and dried.

15. The automatic mop assembly should always be used in the Isolation unit unless inoperative. The automatic mop assembly is a double compartment piece of equipment made of fiber glass that puts down clean germicidal solution and picks it up (in the compartment for soiled solution) in one operation. An automatic mop assembly is stored in each of the designated Isolation wings, as well as, the Operating Room (OR) and Bacteriology.

16. See also SEH Instruction 3530.3 in Policy and Procedures Manual.

PROCEDURE

Regular Daily Maintenance

1. Assemble equipment. Prepare solutions (for damp dusting, as well as for the mopping operation). Take to assigned area. Place outside of door entrance.

> NOTE: The Medical and Surgical Branch has designated certain units as Isolation units. These areas are set up to facilitate easier care of patient and area. Clean supplies are stored outside of units in metal cabinets. Sinks with foot or knee operated soap dispensers and faucets are intalled in most of the units or outside of units to facilitate easier hand washing technique in order to provide greater protection to patients.

2. Plug in vacuum cleaner and automatic mop assembly. Place near door entrance.

3. Put on protective garments (gowns, gloves, mask) outside of unit.

4. Dip two cloths into germicidal solution. Wring out. Pour a small amount of abrasive cleanser on one cloth. Take cloths, paper towels, plastic liners, and other necessary supplies into unit.

CLEANING OF PATIENT AND NON-PATIENT AREAS

PROCEDURE

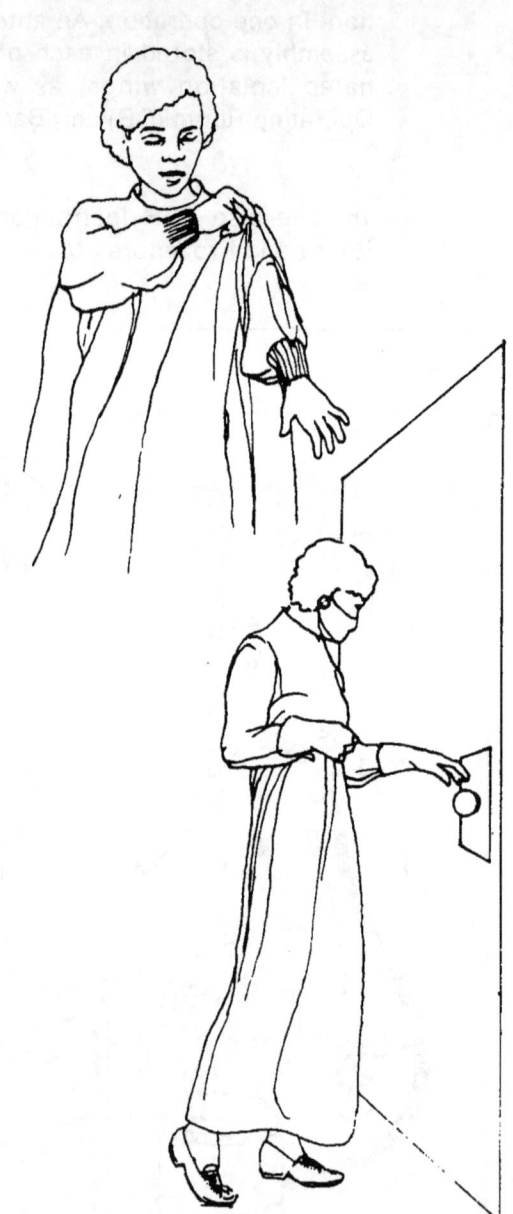

Place cloths on paper towel on night stand. Place paper towels into cabinet.

5. Pick up large pieces of trash. Tie trash liner and remove. Place in clean liner on carrier (20-gallon galvanized can) outside of door, or have a second person receive it in a clean liner (folded over hands). Dispose with regular trash. Wipe container inside and outside. Replace liner.

6. Refold germicidal cloth. Damp dust night stand, window sills, and bed frame. Refold cloth (remembering that cloth has eight sides or surfaces), and damp dust other furnishings. Rinse cloth out in sink.

7. Wash sink with second cloth. Wipe off all splashes on wall surfaces and paper towel box, soap dispenser, faucet, and foot pedal. Rinse and dry.

8. Vacuum area—*only wand and hose should be inside of unit/room.*

9. Turn on automatic mop assembly—*only hose and wand should be inside of unit/room*—start at back of room. Put down solution (squeeze solution release lever), agitate with sponge head, and pick up. If area is very soiled, repeat this procedure. Continue until area is completed. *If automatic mop assembly is inoperative, use the four-step wet mopping procedure.*

10. Remove disposable gloves. Place these and any other trash into step-on trash container.

11. Wash hands.

12. Remove mask (folding inward) and place in step-on trash container.

CLEANING OF PATIENT AND NON-PATIENT AREAS

PROCEDURE

13. Loosen gown and remove while inside room, fold contaminated area inward and roll into bundle. (If cloth, place into orange laundry bag; if paper, place in step-on container.)

14. Wash, rinse, and dry hands *outside of unit.*

15. If other Isolation units are to be cleaned, put on fresh protective garments for each unit/room and continue with the described cleaning procedures until completed. Then wash, rinse, and dry hands; put on clean gloves.

16. Move all equipment to utility room. Empty automatic mop assembly and vacuum cleaner. Prepare fresh germicidal solution. (Use paper towel to turn on faucet.) Dip clean cloth into germicidal solution. Wash inside and outside of all equipment. Rinse, and dry. Wash, rinse, and dry wands, hose, and any other equipment.

17. Place sponge heads into freshly prepared germicidal solution in moat or ten-gallon container. Soak for one-half hour. Remove and lay or hang in well ventilated area to dry.

18. Wash buckets and moats or other containers. Rinse and dry. Wipe off utility cart. Clean up area.

19. Remove gloves. (Remember when touching faucet, a paper towel is used.) Wash hands and arms thoroughly. Rinse and dry. Apply lotion. (It is also recommended that the face should be washed.)

20. Return equipment to designated storage area and continue with other assignments.

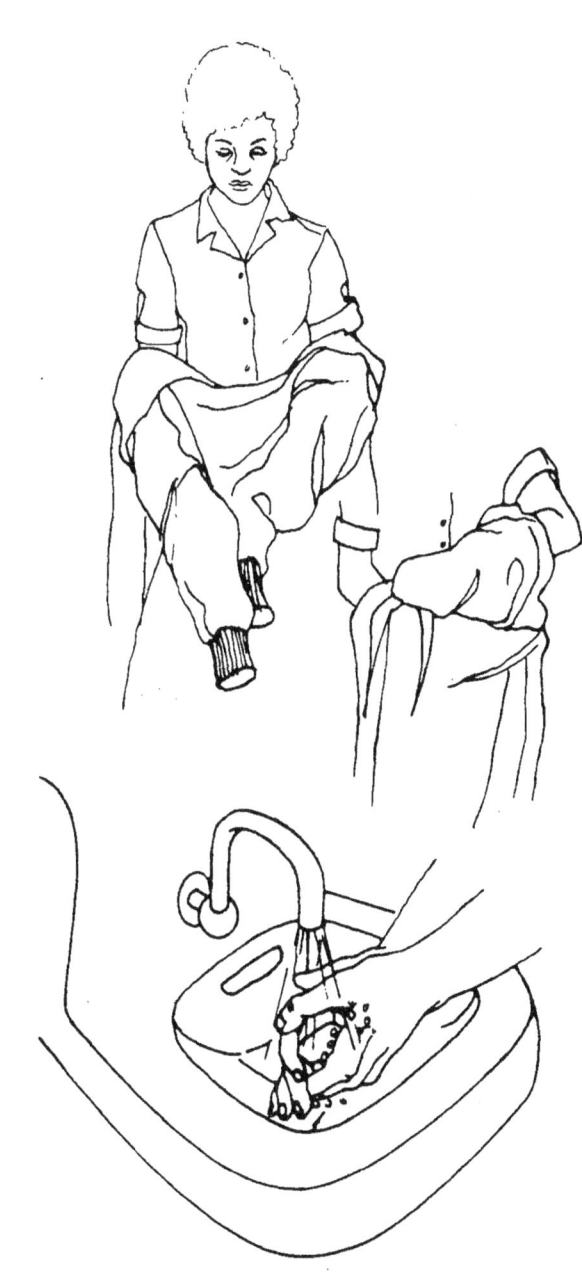

CLEANING OF PATIENT AND NON-PATIENT AREAS

PROCEDURE

Reverse

The main points to remember in this procedure which are common with burn cases are:

1. Care must be taken to keep contamination from entering unit/room and causing secondary infection.

2. Protective garments are worn to protect patient instead of being worn to protect employee.

3. All equipment and supplies must be sanitized or sterilized before taken to unit.

4. Once equipment has been taken into area, it *must* remain. *It cannot be taken back and forth.*

5. The unit is maintained daily with the objective of preventing infectious organisms from entering the unit.

Terminal Cleaning of Isolation Unit

1. Assemble equipment. Prepare germicidal solution. Take to designated area. Place as close to unit entrance as possible.

2. Plug in wet and dry vacuum and automatic mop assembly.

3. Put on protective garments (gown, gloves, mask).

4. Enter unit, take buckets (germicidal solution and rinse water), newspaper, plastic liners, abrasive cleanser, and cloths. Spread newspaper on chair. Place buckets, cloths, and plastic liners on newspaper.

CLEANING OF PATIENT AND NON-PATIENT AREAS

PROCEDURE

---

5. Collect and remove trash. Tie and place into clean plastic liner/bag, and discard with regular trash. Wash, rinse, and dry containers. Replace liners.

6. Remove drapery, curtains and shades from windows. Place in plastic liner and place in orange laundry bag, or prepare for autoclaving.

7. Dip cloth into germicidal solution, squeeze out excess water, and wash night stand inside and outside. Rinse and dry. Wash overbed table. Rinse and dry. Wash bedding, frame, and springs as described in bed washing procedure. Wash walls as far as one can reach. Wash window sills, windows, chairs, and other furnishings. Make sure that every object in the room is washed with germicidal solution. Wash, rinse, and dry paper towel cabinet. If any solution is left in buckets, empty into sink. Wash soap dispenser, faucet, foot pedals, and sink. Rinse and dry.

8. Vacuum floor. Remove newspaper and other equipment from area.

9. Turn on automatic mop assembly. Start at back of room. Put down germicidal solution (squeeze solution release lever). Agitate with sponge head, pick up. If area is very soiled, repeat procedure. (If automatic mop assembly is inoperative/not working, use the four-step wet mopping procedure.)

10. Remove protective garments as described in previous procedure—making sure not to contaminate self and uniform.

11. Wash hands. Put on clean gloves.

12. Take all equipment to utility room. Empty automatic mop assembly and wet and dry vac-

CLEANING OF PATIENT AND NON-PATIENT AREAS

PROCEDURE

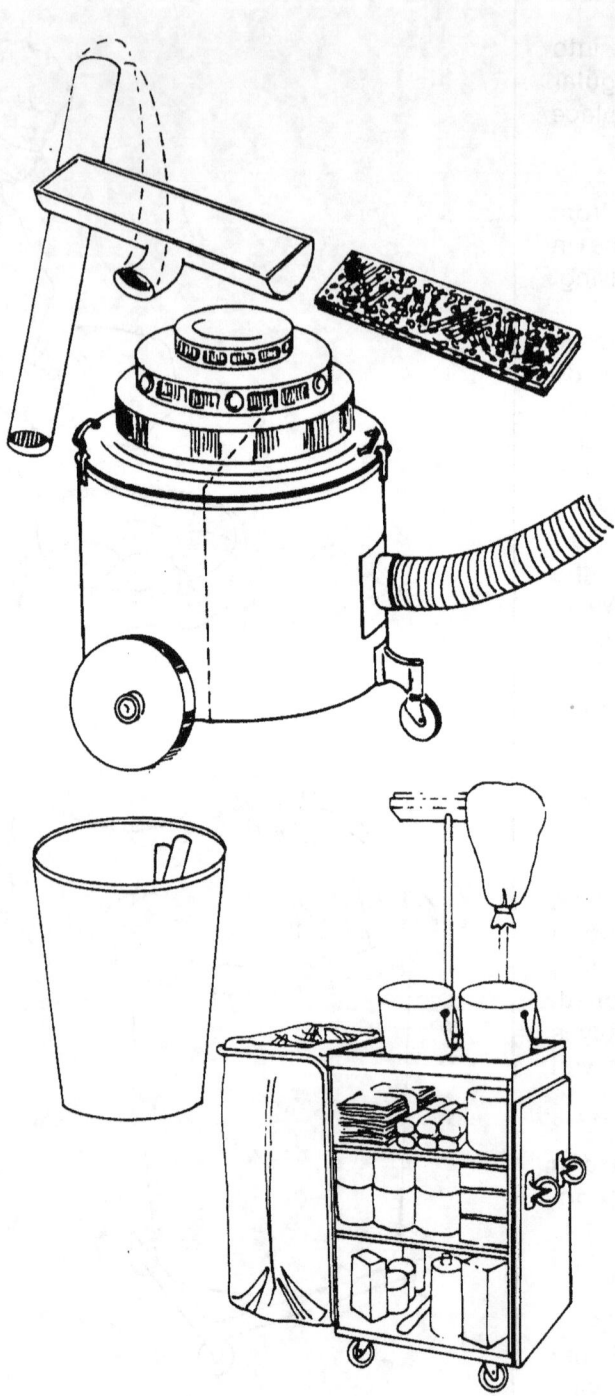

uum cleaner. Prepare fresh germicidal solution. (Be sure to use paper towel to turn faucet handles.) Wash, rinse, and dry all equipment (inside and outside, handles, wheels). Cleaning cloths and mopheads—if used—are placed in plastic liner/bag and placed in orange laundry bag.

13. Remove gloves. Wash hands, arms, and face thoroughly. Apply lotion.

14. Resupply unit/room with soap (solid or liquid), paper towels, and toilet tissue.

15. Return equipment to designated storage area. Restock utility cart.

16. Notify supervisor that the unit/room is ready. (Nursing personnel will make beds.)

17. Continue with other assignments.

MISCELLANEOUS

VI. MISCELLANY

PURPOSE: To remove soil deposits, prevent or control bacterial development and for appearance.

EQUIPMENT:

    Utility cart
    Buckets (two)
    Germicidal detergent
    Cloths
    Stainless steel polish
    Vacuum cleaner (Back-Pack or Wet and Dry)
    Cleanser
    Gloves
    Long-handle radiator brush
    Sponges
    High-pressure spray unit
    Double bucket mopping outfit
    Brush

SAFETY PRECAUTIONS:

1. Never use abrasive or harsh cleansers on metal surfaces.

2. Never allow your mouth to touch telephone surface.

1. Aluminum Cleaning:
a. Any aluminum surface is protected by a thin, tough film of oxide which forms on exposure to air. This film seals out dampness and other atmospheric conditions.

b. To Maintain Aluminum:

(1) Wash with mild germicidal solution.

(2) Rinse with clear water.

(3) Dry with soft cloth.

(4) Paste wax may be applied to surface but must be rubbed thoroughly.

2. Stainless Steel:
a. Stainless steel is a very hard durable metal but is easily scratched. Therefore, no harsh or abrasive materials can be used for its maintenance.

b. To Maintain Stainless Steel:

(1) Wash with a mild germicidal solution.

(2) Rinse with clear water.

(3) Wipe dry and polish.

(4) Lemon oil may be applied but must be rubbed in thoroughly.

(5) Saint Elizabeths Hospital uses a mixture of 1 part mineral oil and 3 parts alcohol to maintain stainless steel after it has been washed.

3. Radiators, Ventilation Grills, Air-Conditioners:
a. Hot water and steam are the most common heating systems in a hospital and the radiators are the most common device to deliver this type of heat. Radiators are usually made of cast iron, painted the same color as the wall or silver or a dark bronze color. They are recessed into wall and covered, or projected from wall and are covered or non-covered and are usually stationed/installed under windows. The circulation around the radiator carries dust to win-

dow glass, shades, curtains, drapery and other window parts and trim. Therefore, keeping the radiator clean will assist with keeping the window area clean.

b. To Maintain Radiators:

(1) Damp dust entire surface daily.

(2) Vacuum and wash every two weeks:
 (a) Place newspaper under radiator to catch dust and excess water.

 (b) Place crevice tool on vacuum cleaner and vacuum all inner portions of the columns, all hidden areas, wall areas and floor underneath.

 (c) Wash, rinse and dry (cover radiator brush with cloth to wash inner portion of columns).

 (d) Remove newspaper and discard. Wipe up any spills.

 (e) Clean equipment and return to designated storage area.

c. To Maintain Ventilation Grills:

(1) Vacuum.

(2) Wash with germicidal or wall washing agent. Include area around vents.

(3) Rinse and dry.

(4) Periodically, vents are scheduled for removal and thorough cleaning.

d. To Maintain Air-Conditioners:

(1) Most institutions are replacing radiators with air-conditioning equipment. Cleaning of the inside of the units and cleaning of filters are performed by the Electrical Engineering Department. However, the exterior surfaces and surrounding areas are maintained by the Housekeeping Aides.

(2) Damp dust daily:
 (a) Dip cloth in germicidal solution and wipe off all exterior surfaces and areas around air-conditioner.

 (b) Rinse and dry.

(3) Notify supervisor if air-conditioner is not working properly or grill and filters are soiled or clogged.

4. Telephones:
 a. Telephones are used by everyone and must be cleaned daily to remove soil, dust and other contamination to control the spread of bacteria and for appearance.

 b. To Maintain Telephones:

(1) Wash entire surface with germicidal solution (pay special attention to receiver).

(2) Rinse with clear water.

(3) Dry and polish with soft cloths.

5. Ice Machines, Ice Carts, Refrigerators:
 a. Housekeeping Aids maintain outside surfaces only.

 b. To Maintain Ice Machines, Ice Carts, Refrigerators:

(1) Wash outside surfaces daily with germicidal solution.

(2) Rinse and dry.

MISCELLANEOUS

6. Service/Utility Sinks, and Rooms:

a. Service sinks are installed in utility rooms to aid in the care of the equipment. They may be high or low and made of ceramic, fiber glass or stainless steel, and must be cleaned to prevent excess soil from accumulating.

b. To Maintain Service/Utility Sinks and Room:

(1) Clean each type daily with the recommended type of cleanser. Damp wipe outside surfaces and areas around sink.

(2) Rinse and dry.

(3) Sweep and mop floor areas. Place all equipment and supplies in their proper location. Leave room orderly.

(4) Inspect room.

7. Wheel Chairs:

a. Wheel chairs must be cleaned to insure good service for patient transportation. This procedure is usually performed by the nursing staff.

b. To Maintain Wheel Chairs:

(1) Wash surface with germicidal solution.

(2) Rinse and dry.

(3) Or, use high pressure machine and spray clean chairs.

(4) Rinse and dry.

(5) Return chairs to proper location.

(6) Wash equipment and return to designated storage area.

8. Linen, Linen Closet:

a. At many hospitals, the Housekeeping Aid's responsibility for linen is limited. However, since housekeeping in most areas of the Hospital is responsible for the delivery and removal of linen, they must be aware that soiled linen is separated into categories of flat work and body clothes—bagged in white bags and contaminated linen bagged in orange bags; that soiled and clean linens should not be delivered and removed in or on the same carrier.

b. Housekeeping is also responsible for shelving and floor care of the linen closet. Distribution and removal of clean and soiled linen is a daily assignment.

9. Uniforms:

a. The Hospital uniform is prescribed and furnished for use by designated employees while engaged in official duties.

b. Supervisors' Responsibility:

(1) Advising employees of pickup and delivery points and schedules.

(2) Making appropriate internal pickup and delivery arrangements with employees.

c. Employees' Responsibility:

(1) Inspect all soiled clothing before delivery to the pickup area to assure that damaged clothing is not sent to the Laundry.

(2) Prepare Form , a dry cleaning and laundry ticket. Both parts of the ticket must show the employee's last name, his initials, and division, service, section or building.

(3) Detach the claim stub from the dry clean-

ing and laundry ticket. Keep this stub for presentation when clean clothing is returned.

(4) Place soiled clothing in the individual container provided by the contractor and deliver the container and the ticket to the pickup point.

5. Pick up clean clothing as soon as possible after delivery.

(6) Report any instance of lost clothing to the employee in charge of the pickup point. The employee in charge will report the loss to the Property Section.

MISCELLANEOUS

VII. CHALKBOARD MAINTENANCE

GENERAL POINTS TO OBSERVE:

1. Chalkboards are the oldest visual aid to education. They are as indispensable to the faculty member as any piece of custodial equipment is to Housekeeping. Good chalkboard maintenance practices make friends, while poor practice creates complaints.

2. It is the employee's responsibility to see that each chalkboard has:
    a. Clean erasers
    b. Adequate supply of chalk
    c. Clean chalk tray
    d. Clean writing surface

3. ERASERS:
    a. Start with a good quality five-ply felt eraser.

    b. Have a supply large enough so that clean and dirty erasers can be rotated daily. An ideal situation would be to have enough to require eraser cleaning only once a week rather than daily.

    c. The technique for cleaning erasers is varied. In days gone by, the most efficient means was clapping them against the side of the building by a recalcitrant student. There are now cleaner sanitary methods. These include:

    (1) Vacuuming.

    (2) The commercial eraser cleaner—featuring a rotating brush with vacuum beneath.

    (3) The commercial cleaner with vibrating bars and vacuum beneath.

4. CHALK:
    a. Start with good quality *soft* chalk. The harder the chalk the more clay binders they contain. While the harder chalk gives off less dust and breaks less easily, it is also much harder to remove from the board. The clay binders imbed in the writing surface causing "ghost marks" or shadows which can be removed only with hard scrubbing.

    b. A special warning should be made about colored chalk. If at al possible, discourage its use. Most colored chalk contains wax of some kind. This wax imbeds deeply in the board and is very difficult to remove.

5. CHALK TRAYS:
    a. Chalk trays are designed to hold chalk and catch dust.

    b. After each day's use they should be cleaned with either a damp cloth or sponge.

6. WRITING SURFACE:
    a. Many of the new chalkboards are made of glass and require little, if any, "breaking in". However, be it slate, composition, metal or glass, follow the manufacturer's directions for the "break-in" period.

    b. A chalkboard used moderately may only require erasing with a clean eraser.

    c. Chalkboards may be cleaned with aerosol compounds. However, most of these compounds contain oil which can interfere with the writing process.

MISCELLANEOUS

d. Wet washing is the best technique for chalkboard maintenance.

e. Do not wash chalkboard if word "Save" or "Do Not Erase" is written.

EQUIPMENT:

    Utility cart
    Buckets (two)
    Sponges (two or more)
    Neutral detergent
    Vacuum clearner/attachments
    Cloths
    Gloves

SAFETY PRECAUTIONS:

PURPOSE: To remove chalk dust and maintain an attractive appearance.

1. Follow manufacturer's directions for "break-in" period.

PROCEDURE

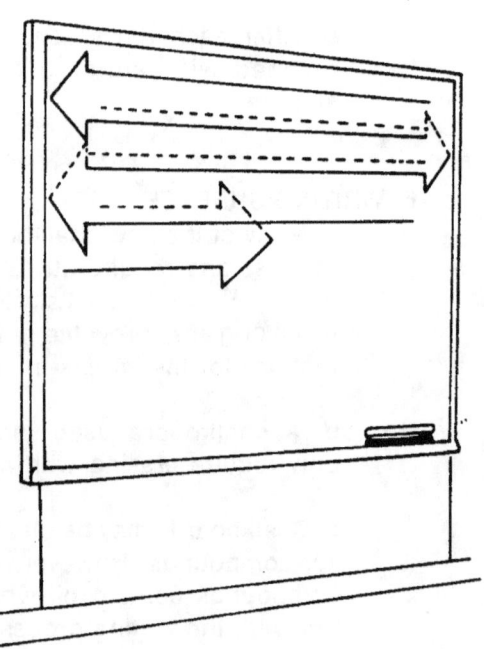

1. Assemble equipment. Prepare solution. Put on gloves.

2. Vacuum erasers and chalk tray. Wash chalkboard.

3. Dip sponge into cleaning solution. Squeeze out excess water.

4. Apply to surface in a continuous horizontal motion. Overlap each stroke. Continue this process until board is completed. (To expedite time, take a sponge in each hand and perform the operation as stated.)

5. Wash chalk tray and eraser.

6. Dip second sponge into rinse water. Squeeze out excess water.

MISCELLANEOUS

PROCEDURE

7. Rinse chalkboard and tray.

8. Allow chalkboard to air dry.

9. Replace eraser and supply of chalk. Wipe up spills.

10. Take equipment to utility room. Wash and dry and return to designated storage area.

VIII. MICROBIOLOGY OF THE HOSPITAL ENVIRONMENT

PURPOSE: To present a true understanding of the importance of maintaining a hospital in a state of protective cleanliness in order to prevent contamination and transmission of disease and infection.

EQUIPMENT:

Basic knowledge of micro-organisms and their control.

DEFINITIONS:

1. **Micro-organisms** are extremely small living plants or animals which are visible only when observed through a microscope. These are scientifically referred to as bacteria, but are commonly called germs or "bugs".

2. **Hospital environment** (environ—something that encircles or surrounds)—therefore, the hospital environment is anything surrounding one in the hospital community (the air, equipment, buildings, walls, ceilings, floors, people, animals).

It is essential that all persons working in the hospital environment have a workable knowledge of bacteria and methods to control their growth. Bacteria occurs in three principle forms and are divided into two principal groups:

1. Round 0 (Coccus)—*see illustrations on next page*.
    a. Cocci—exist singly as small, round, oval shaped bodies.
    b. Diplococci—exist two together or in pairs.
    c. Streptococci—exist in long chains, each organism attached end to end.
    d. Staphlococci—exist in irregular clusters resembling bunches of grapes.

2. Rod-like (Singular—Bacillus, Plural—Bacilli) cylindrical rod-like bacteria cells that usually exist as singular unattached cells. However, the Diphtheria bacilli and the Tubercle bacilli are exceptions.
    a. Tetanus bacilli
    b. Tubercle bacilli—may occur in three cell arrangement giving the impression of a branch.
    c. Diphtheria bacilli—groups of cells lined side by side like match sticks.
    d. Typhoid bacilli

1. Round O *(coccus)*:

COCCI

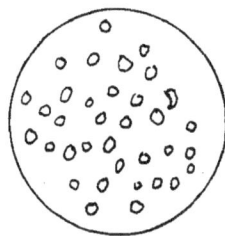

These bacteria exist singly as small, round, oval shaped bodies.

DIPLOCOCCI

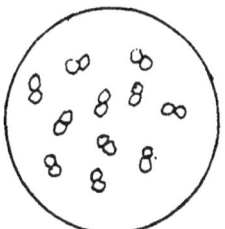

These bacteria are cocci which exist two together or in pairs.

STREPTOCOCCI

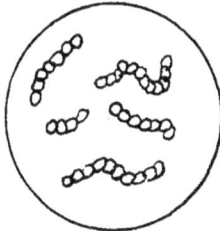

These bacteria are cocci which exist in long chains, each organism attached end to end and to others.

STAPHYLOCOCCI

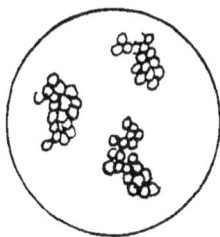

These are cocci which exist in clusters like grapes.

GONOCOCCI.......

PNEUMOCOCCI......

2. BACILLI (rod-like)

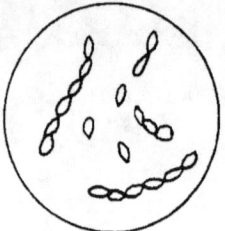

These are the rod-shaped bacteria which may exist either separately or in chains.

TETANUS BACILLI ....
TUBERCLE BACILLI ....
DIPHTHERIA BACILLI ....
TYPHOID BACILLI ....

3. SPIRILLA (coiled)

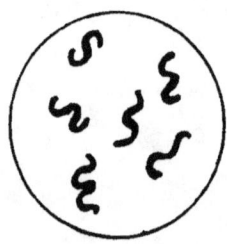

These are spiral shaped organisms which exist separately.

TREPONEMA PALLIDUM (SYPHILIS)

3. Spiral (Singular—Spirillum, Plural—Spirilla) occur predominantly as unattached individual cells. Some are short, tightly coiled rods while others are long and exhibit a series of twist curves.

    a. Treponema Pallidum (Syphillis)

BACTERIA ARE DIVIDED INTO TWO GROUPS:

1. Non-Pathogenic—non-harmful bacteria (for example Fungi—mold, yeast); and

2. Pathogenic—harmful bacteria or bacteria capable of producing disease.

However, any bacteria organism found out of its natural habitat can be pathogenic. The pathogenic bacteria, although in the minority, must receive the greatest amount of attention because these are the bacteria that are implicated in hospital infections. The Housekeeping Department is usually the first place checked to see what procedures and methods are being used when a staphylococci infection occurs.

As previously mentioned, bacteria are not visible to the naked eye. In fact, their size is only approximately 1/25,000 of an inch. They are so tiny that the surface of a head of a pin could accommodate as many as ten million.

Bacteria are everywhere—yet they have no legs, fins, wings, or for that matter, any means of locomotion. They are found in the soil, the air, the water, on utensils and equipment, in our food, and uncleaned surfaces are seeded with them. Their media of transportation is air, water, insects, animals, and people. In fact, any moving object carries bacteria. But most infectious diseases are transported by people, causing serious problems of cross-infection. Bacteria then becomes a health problem.

In many respects, bacteria are like humans. They require oxygen (there are a few that can thrive without oxygen and still others that can thrive under either condition), food, moisture (water), and the right temperature to thrive. Take either away and they will die or remain inactive. They thrive best in temperatures ranging from approximately 70° to approximately 110° Fahrenheit.

If environmental condition is right (food, moisture and temperature), bacteria will reproduce rapidly. Bacteria reproduce by a process called "fission," or merely splitting in two. Only one bacterium is necessary for reproduction (for example, one will split and form two, two will split and form four, and so on). If they keep reproducing (some take 30 minutes, others may take up to six hours), within a period of twenty-four hours, the one original cell could have about 16,000,000 descendants. Where one disease causing organism may not cause an illness, 16,000,000 certainly could.

The importance of controlling their reproduction is obvious. Since an unclean surface is usually seeded with bacteria, and sanitation procedures reduce the bacteria population (since all cleaning normally removes some organic matter), cleanliness is therefore the principal method for attacking them. For where there is a clean surface, bacteria either die or remain dormant. This can be brought about by physical agents and chemical substances.

CONTROL BY PHYSICAL AGENTS OR CONDITIONS:

1. **Mechanical**—surface is scrubbed or flushed with water. If cleaning is properly performed, the majority of bacteria will be removed.

2. **Temperature**—moisture, steam, boiling water, dry or hot air sterilization, incineration, and freezing or extreme cold.

Temperatures of 161° Fahrenheit or above for 15 seconds will kill most disease causing bacteria (as a safety factor, 170° Fahrenheit through 180° Fahrenheit for 15 seconds are recommended for sanitizing purposes). At freezing temperatures the reproduction process almost completely stops. However, these low temperatures generally reduce the number of organisms, but do not kill all of them—they just render them "static" or "inactive".

There is a group of bacteria called the "spore formers", that when conditions are not favorable, change their form (certain types of the Rod-shaped bacteria, for example genera Bacillus and Clostridium) into small ovals or spheres (capsules) that are highly resistant to physical and chemical agents. Mature spore lay dormant until conditions for growth are suitable, then it develops into a thriving bacterium again. To destroy spores, a temperature of 250° Fahrenheit for 10 to 15 minutes with direct exposure to saturated steam is necessary.

CONTROL BY CHEMICAL AGENTS:
(For inanimate objects)

DEFINITIONS:
1. **Disinfectant**—a chemical agent that kills the growing, but not necessarily the spore forms of disease producing bacteria. Disinfection is the act of destroying the infectious agents.

2. **Sanitizer**—a chemical agent that reduces the microbial population to a safe level as judged by Public Health requirements (which usually kills 99.9% of the growing bacteria).

3. **Germicide *(Microbicide)***—a chemical agent that kills the growing forms but not necessarily the spore forms of bacteria—are commonly used for all kinds of germs and in any place. (A Phenolic base germicide is used in all clinical areas and a Quaternary Ammonium Compound is used in laboratories, kitchens, administrative, and other selective areas.)

4. **Bactericide or Bactericidal**—any chemical agent that kills bacteria.

5. **Sporicidal, Fungicidal, Viricidal**—all refer to chemical agents that kill spores, fungi, and viruses respectively.

6. **Bacteriostat**—any chemical agent that retards or inhibits the growth of bacteria.

7. **Antimicrobial**—a chemical agent that interferes with or inhibits the growth of bacteria.

Common chemical agents in use are: Alcohol, Cholorine, Iodine, and Iodophores, Quaternary Ammonium Compounds, Formaldehyde, Phenols, and related compounds.

IX. CHEMISTRY OF DETERGENT

The word "detergent" has been used with increasing frequency, possibly because it has been necessary to create a definite line of demarcation between the old time "washing powders", and the newer products of chemistry.

A detergent is defined as a cleansing agent. A cleansing agent is applied to equipment or other surface, and cleanses by separating and carrying off surface soil.

The selection of detergents on a scientific basis is quite complex, and as yet, no satisfactory method of evaluating them in simple terms has been devised. At present, we may say that the selection of a detergent is an unscientific procedure, and that the following factors influence their selection and efficiency:

1. Hardness and pH (relative acid-alkaline balance) of the water.

2. Equipment to be used. For example, excessive causticity is objectionable for hand cleaning methods, and excessive foaming is objectionable in mechnical cleaning operations.

3. Temperature. Different detergents do not function efficiently at the same temperature.

4. Time. Detergent action is a *chemical* action, and chemical reactions require time for completion. Detergents give best results when the proper *contact* time with the surface to be cleaned is allowed.

5. Concentration. The optimum concentration varies with different detergents. Also, the effect or reduction in concentration is different with different detergents. It is important that the *proper concentration* be maintained in the wash solution.

Inasmuch as water is the first consideration in efficient cleaning, it naturally follows that the chemical composition of the water used must be of major concern. It should be recognized that the objective of detergents is to properly condition water for the removal of soil from surfaces. Proper water softening, therefore, is a primary demand in a good detergent.

Above and beyond the necessity of water conditioning, an efficient detergent must perform a number of specific functions. No one chemical compound will satisfy the requirements of an effective detergent, so a blend of compounds must be prepared.

The application of cleaners is largely dependent on the type and condition of the soil, together with the type and condition of the surface from which the soils is to be removed. Thus, when we consider a single type of soil on a specific surface, the problem of cleaning becomes relatively simple, but when one considers the mixture of soils often encountered, it can be seen that the problem becomes more complex.

BASED ON ALL THESE FACTORS, THE BALANCED CLEANER WORKS IN ALL THESE WAYS:

1. By conditioning the water so there is no additional soil added to surfaces and so that the effectiveness of the cleaner is not reduced by solids ("hardness") in the water.

2. By penetrating the soil or wetting it with the water.

3. By dissolving as much of the soil as is possible by the use of controlled acid or alkali.

4. By dispersion or emulsification of the remaining soil.

5. By holding the soil in suspension until it is flushed away.

FUNCTIONS OF CLEANER INGREDIENTS:

In order to understand sanitation chemistry better, it is necessary to know the functions or properties of cleaner ingredients. These are defined as follows:

DEFINITIONS:

1. **Emulsification**—the mechnical action of breaking up fats and oils into very small particles which are uniformly mixed with the water used.

2. **Saponification**—the chemical reaction between an alkali and an animal or vegetable fat resulting in a soap.

3. **Wetting**—the action of water contacting all surfaces of soil or equipment.

4. **Penetration**—the action of a liquid entering into porous materials or into crevices, joints, or seams.

5. **Deflocculation or Dispersion**—the action of breaking up aggregates or flocs into individual particles.

6. **Suspension**—the action which holds up insoluble particles in a solution.

7. **Peptizing**—the physical formation of colloidal solutions from soils which may be only partially soluble.

8. **Rinsing**—the condition of a solution or suspension which enables it to be flushed from a surface easily and completely.

9. **Sequestration**—the removal or inactivation of water hardness constituents by the formation of a soluble complex or chelate.

10. **Water Softening**—the removal or inactivation of the hardness of water (i.e. Trisodium and alkalies soften water by precipitating the hardness).

11. **Dissolving**—a chemical reaction which produces water soluble products from water insoluble soil (i.e. Alkaline deposits—an acid application will convert the Alkaline deposits into a water soluble product).

CLEANER INGREDIENTS:

There are five groups of materials generally used to accomplish the functions of cleaning:

1. **The Alkalies**—for example, Sodium Hydroxide (NaOH) (Caustic Soda Lye); Sodium Carbonate (Na_2CO_3) (Soda Ash) Sodium Bicarbonate ($NaHCO_3$) (Baking Soda).

2. **The Phosphates**—for example, Trisodium Phosphate ($Na_3PO_4 \cdot 12H_2O$) ("T.S.P."); Tetrasodium Pyrophosphate ($Na_4P_2O_7$) ("Pyro").

3. **The Wetting Agents**
   a. Anionic—Sodium salts or sulfates or sulfonates of oils or alcohol made from oils.

b. Non-ionic—ethers, esters, or alcohols.
c. Cat-ionic—Quaternary Ammonium Compounds.

4. **The Organic Acids**—for example, Acetic Acid (CH_3OOH) (Vinegar); Hydroxyacetic Acid ($HOCH_2COOH$) (Glycolic Acid); Lactic Acid ($CH_3CHOHCOOH$) (Hydroxyproprionic Acid).

5. **The Chelation Agents**—similar to the polyphosphates—Trisodium. However, the Chelates are stable to heat and compatible with the Quaternary Ammonium Compounds.

BASIC NURSING PROCEDURES: FUNDAMENTAL NURSING CARE OF THE PATIENT

TABLE OF CONTENTS

		Page
1.	Morning Care	1
2.	Oral Hygiene	2
3.	Special Mouth Care	3
4.	Care of Dentures	5
5.	Bed Bath	6
6.	Making an Unoccupied Bed	8
7.	Making an Occupied Bed	12
8.	Serving Diets from Food Cart	16
9.	Central Tray Service	18
10.	Care of Ice Machine and Handling of Ice, Bedside Pitchers and Glasses	19
11.	Feeding the Helpless Patient	21
12.	Evening Care	22
13.	Care of the Seriously Ill Patient	23

BASIC NURSING PROCEDURES: FUNDAMENTAL NURSING CARE OF THE PATIENT

1. MORNING CARE

PURPOSE

To refresh and prepare patient for breakfast.

EQUIPMENT

Basin of warm water
Towel, washcloth and soap
Toothbrush and dentifrice/mouthwash
Curved basin
Glass of water
Comb

PROCEDURE

1. Clear bedside stand or overbed table for food tray.
2. Offer bedpan and urinal.
3. Wash patient's face and hands.
4. Give oral hygiene.
5. Place patient in a comfortable position for breakfast.
6. Comb hair.

POINTS TO EMPHASIZE

1. Morning care is given before breakfast by night corpsman.
2. Assist handicapped, aged or patients on complete bed rest.

CARE OF EQUIPMENT

Wash, dry and replace equipment.

2. ORAL HYGIENE

PURPOSE

To keep mouth clean.
To refresh patient.
To prevent infection and complications in the oral cavity.
To stimulate appetite.

EQUIPMENT

Glass of water
Curved basin
Toothbrush and dentifrice - electric toothbrush if available
Mouth wash
Towel
Drinking tubes as necessary

PROCEDURE

1. A patient who is able to help himself:
   a. Place patient in comfortable position.
   b. Arrange equipment on bedside table within his reach.

2. A patient who needs assistance:
   a. Place patient in comfortable position.
   b. Place towel under his chin and over bedding.
   c. Moisten brush, apply dentifrice and hand to the patient.
   d. Hold curved basin under his chin while he cleanses his teeth and mouth.
   e. Remove basin. Wipe lips and chin with towel.

POINTS TO EMPHASIZE

Oral hygiene is particularly important for patients
   a. who are not taking food and fluid by mouth
   b. with nasogastric tubes
   c. with productive coughs
   d. who are receiving oxygen therapy

CARE OF EQUIPMENT

Wash equipment with soap and hot water, rinse, dry and put away.

3. SPECIAL MOUTH CARE

PURPOSE

To cleanse and refresh mouth.
To prevent infection.

EQUIPMENT

Electric toothbrush if available
Tray with:
- Mineral oil or cold cream
- Lemon-glycerine applicators
- Paper bag
- Drinking tubes or straws
- Applicators and gauze sponges
- Curved basin
- Paper wipes
- Bulb syringe

Cleansing agents

- Tooth paste
- Equal parts of hydrogen peroxide and water
- Mouthwash

Glass of water
Suction machine for unconscious patient

PROCEDURE

1. Tell patient what you are going to do.
2. Turn patient's head to one side.
3. Brush teeth and gums.
4. When it is not possible to brush teeth and gums, moisten applicator with a cleansing agent and use for cleaning oral cavity and teeth.
5. Assist patient to rinse mouth with water.
6. If patient is unable to use drinking tube, gently irrigate the mouth with a syringe directing the flow of water to side of mouth.
7. Apply lubricant to lips.

For Unconscious Patient

Use suction machine.

SPECIAL MOUTH CARE (Continued)

POINTS TO EMPHASIZE
1. Extreme care should be exercised to prevent injury to the gums.
2. Position patient carefully to prevent aspiration of fluids.
3. Caution patient not to swallow mouthwash.

CARE OF EQUIPMENT

Dispose of applicator and soiled gauze. Clean equipment and restock tray.

4. CARE OF DENTURES

PURPOSE

To aid in keeping mouth in good condition.
To cleanse the teeth.

EQUIPMENT

Container for dentures
Toothbrush and dentifrice
Glass of water
Mouthwash
Curved basin
Towel
Paper towels

PROCEDURE

1. Have patient rinse mouth with mouthwash.
2. Remove dentures. Place them in container.
3. Have patient brush tongue and gums with mouth-wash.
4. Place a basin under tap in sink and place paper towels in basin. Fill basin with cold water.
5. Hold dentures over basin and under cold running water. Wash with brush and dentifrice.
6. Place dentures in container of cold water. Take to patient's bedside.
7. Replace wet dentures.

POINTS TO EMPHASIZE

1. Handle dentures carefully to prevent breakage.
2. When not in use, dentures should be placed in covered container of cold water and placed in top drawer of locker.
3. Give special attention to the inner surfaces of clips used to hold bridge work or partial plates in place.

CARE OF EQUIPMENT

Wash equipment, rinse, dry and put away.

5. BED BATH

PURPOSE

To cleanse the skin.
To stimulate the circulation.
To observe the patient mentally and physically.
To aid in elimination.

EQUIPMENT

Linen and pajamas as required
Half filled basin of water
Bar of soap
Rubbing alcohol/skin lotion
Bedpan and urinal with cover
Bed screens

PROCEDURE

1. Tell patient what you are going to do.
2. Screen patient.
3. Offer bedpan and urinal.
4. Shave patient or allow patient to shave himself.
5. Lower backrest and knee rest if physical condition permits.
6. Loosen top bedding at foot and sides of bed.
7. Remove pillow and place on chair.
8. Remove and fold bedspread and blanket. Place on back of chair.
9. Remove pajamas and place on chair.
10. Assist patient to near side of bed.
11. Bathe the patient:

    a. Eyes:
       (1) Do not use soap.
       (2) Clean from inner to outer corner of eye.

    b. Face, neck and ears.
    c. Far arm.
    d. Place hand in basin and clean nails.
    e. Near arm.
    f. Place hand in basin and clean nails.
    g. Chest.
    h. Abdomen.

BED BATH (Continued)

PROCEDURE (Continued)

12.
- i. Far leg, foot and nails. Place foot in basin when possible.
- j. Near leg, foot and nails. Place foot in basin when possible.
- k. Change water. l. Back and buttocks.
- m. Genitals and rectal area.

13. Give back rub.
14. Put on pajamas.
15. Comb hair.
16. Make bed.
17. Adjust bed to patient's comfort unless contrain-dicated.

POINTS TO EMPHASIZE

1. Give bed baths daily and P.R.N.
2. Give oral hygiene before bath.
3. Avoid drafts which might cause chilling.
4. Use bath towel under all parts to aid in keeping the bed linen as dry as possible.
5. Change bath water after washing lower extremities and as necessary.
6. Be sure all soap film is rinsed from body to prevent skin irritation.
7. Keep patient well draped at all times.
8. Observe and chart the condition of the skin in regard to lesions, rashes and reddened areas.
9. Pillow should be removed unless contraindicated to give patient a change of position.
10. Assist handicapped patients with shaving.
11. Always move or turn patient toward you.

CARE OF EQUIPMENT

1. Remove soiled linen and place in hamper.
2. Wash equipment, rinse, dry and put away.

6. MAKING AN UNOCCUPIED BED

PURPOSE

To provide a clean, comfortable bed.
To provide a neat appearance to the ward.

EQUIPMENT

Two sheets
Plastic mattress cover
Blanket
Plastic pillow cover
Pillowcase
Protective draw sheet or disposable pads, if indicated

PROCEDURE

1. Place mattress cover on mattress. Where necessary and available, plastic mattress covers are used.
2. Place center fold of sheet in center of bed, narrow hem even with foot of bed.
3. Fold excess sheet under the mattress at head of bed.
4. Miter corner.
    a. Pick up hanging sheet 12 inches from head of bed.
    b. Tuck lower corner under mattress.
    c. Bring triangle down over side of bed.
    d. Tuck sheet under mattress.
5. Pull bottom sheet tight and tuck under side of mattress.
6. If draw sheets are indicated, place in center of bed as illustrated. Tuck excess under mattress.
    a. Linen draw sheet is made by folding a regular bed sheet in half - hem to hem.
7. Place center fold of second sheet in center of bed, with hem even with the top of mattress.
8. Tuck excess under foot of mattress.
9. Center fold blanket in middle of bed 6 inches from top of mattress.
10. Fold excess under foot of mattress.
11. Make mitered corner.

MAKING AN UNOCCUPIED BED (Continued)

PROCEDURE (Continued)

12. Place bedspread on bed, center fold in middle of bed even with the top of the mattress. Fold under blanket.
13. Fold cuff of top sheet over bedspread at head of bed.
14. Tuck excess spread under foot of mattress.
15. Miter corner at foot of mattress.
16. Go to other side of bed and follow steps 3 to 15.
17. Place plastic cover on pillow.
18. Place pillow case on pillow.
19. Place pillow on bed with seams at head of bed, open end away from the entrance to the ward.

POINTS TO EMPHASIZE

1. Woolen blankets are to be used only when cotton blankets are not available.
2. Never use woolen blankets when oxygen therapy is in use.
3. Use protective draw sheet or protective pads when indicated.

10

MITERED CORNER

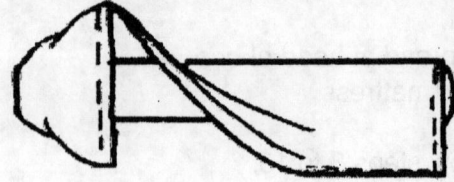
Pick up hanging sheet 12 inches from head of bed.

Tuck lower corner under mattress.

Bring triangle down over side of bed.

Tuck sheet under mattress.

COMPLETING FOUNDATION
APPLY DRAW SHEETS

1. PLACE RUBBER DRAW SHEET IN CENTER OF BED

2. TUCK EXCESS RUBBER DRAW SHEET IN ON NEAR SIDE OF MATTRESS

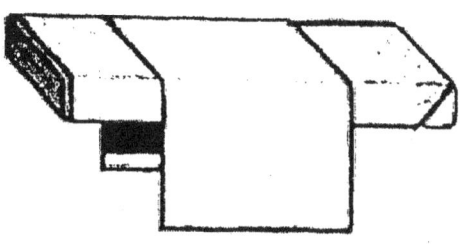

3. PLACE COTTON DRAW SHEET OVER RUBBER DRAW SHEET

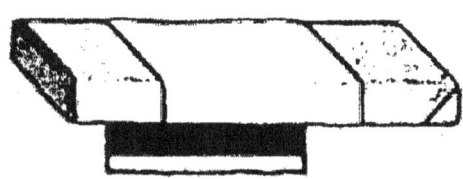

4. TUCK EXCESS COTTON DRAW SHEET IN ON NEAR SIDE OF MATTRESS

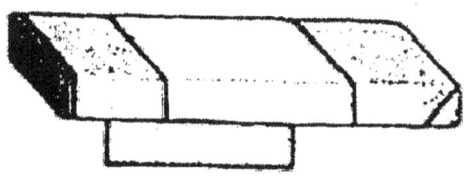

5. TUCK EXCESS RUBBER DRAW SHEET IN ON OPPOSITE SIDE OF MATTRESS

6. TUCK EXCESS COTTON DRAW SHEET IN ON OPPOSITE SIDE OF MATTRESS

7. MAKING AN OCCUPIED BED

PURPOSE

To provide clean linen with least exertion to patient.
To refresh patient.
To prevent pressure sores.

EQUIPMENT

Two sheets
Pillowcase
Blanket
Protective draw sheet or disposable pads, if indicated
Hamper

PROCEDURE

1. Place chair at foot of bed.
2. Push bedside locker away from bed.
3. Pull mattress to head of bed.
4. Loosen all bedding.
5. Remove pillow and place on chair.
6. Remove bedspread by folding from top to bottom, pick up in center and place on back of chair.
7. Remove blanket in same manner.
8. Turn patient to one side of the bed.
9. If cotton draw sheet is used, roll draw sheet close to patient's back.
10. Turn back protective sheet over patient.
11. Roll bottom sheet close to patient's back.
12. Straighten mattress cover as necessary.
13. Place clean sheet on bed with the center fold in the middle and narrow hem even with foot of bed.
14. Tuck in excess at head of bed. Miter corner and tuck in at side.
15. Bring down protective sheet; straighten and tuck in.
16. Make draw sheet by folding a sheet from hem to hem with smooth side out.
17. Place on bed with fold toward head of bed. Tuck in.

MAKING AN OCCUPIED BED (Continued)

PROCEDURE (Continued)

18. Roll patient over to completed side of bed.
19. Go to other side of the bed.
20. Remove soiled sheets and place in hamper.
21. Check soiled linen for personal articles.
22. Turn back draw sheets over patient.
23. Pull bottom sheet tight and smooth.
24. Pull protective sheet and draw sheet tight and smooth.
25. Bring patient to center of bed.
26. Place top sheet over patient, wide hem even with top of mattress.
27. Ask patient to hold clean top sheet.
28. Remove soiled top sheet. Place in hamper.
29. Place blanket 6 inches from top of mattress.
30. Make pleat in sheet and blanket over patient's toes.
31. Tuck in excess at foot of bed and miter corners.
32. Place bedspread on bed even with top of mattress. Fold under blanket.
33. Fold sheet over bedspread and blanket at head of bed.
34. Tuck in excess bedspread at foot of bed. Miter corners. Allow triangle to hang loosely.
35. Put clean pillowcase on pillow. Place under patient's head with closed end toward entrance to ward.
36. Adjust bed as desired by patient.
37. Straighten unit. Leave bedside stand within reach of patient.

POINTS TO EMPHASIZE

1. Always turn patient toward you to prevent possibility of injury and/or falls.
2. Make sure that foundation sheets are smooth and dry.

MAKING AN OCCUPIED BED

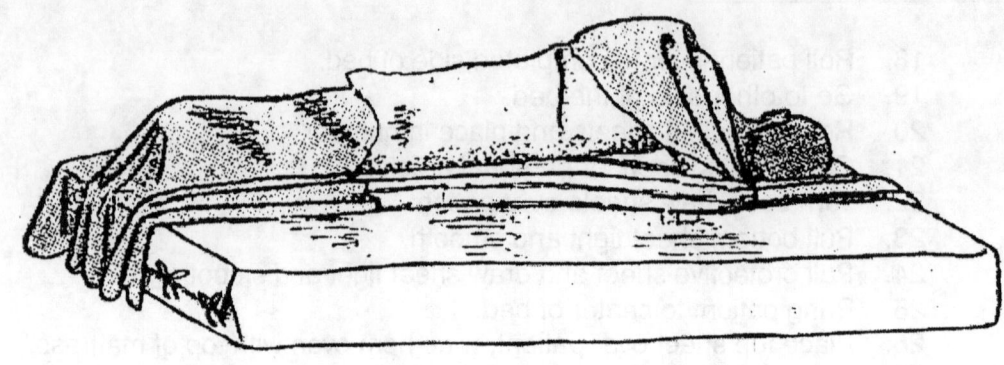

TURN PATIENT TOWARD YOU
FAN FOLD SOILED LINEN
AGAINST PATIENTS BACK

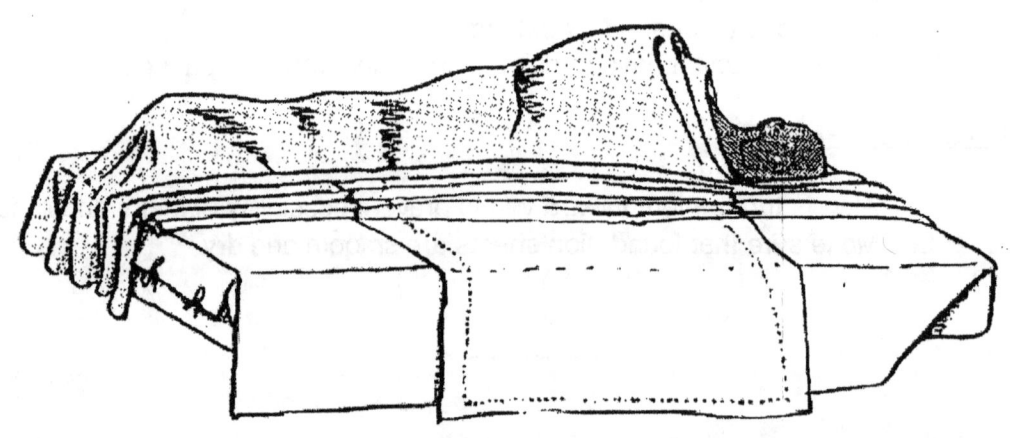

MAKE UP ONE HALF THE BED
BOTTOM SHEET, THEN
RUBBER DRAW SHEET

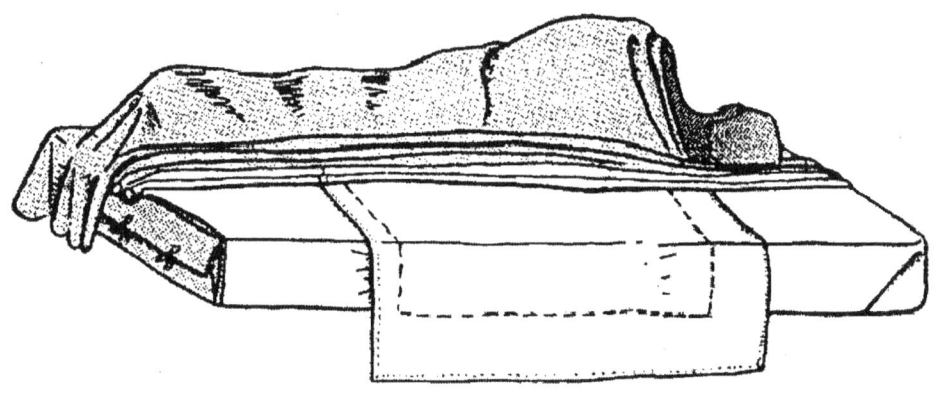

ADD COTTON DRAW SHEET

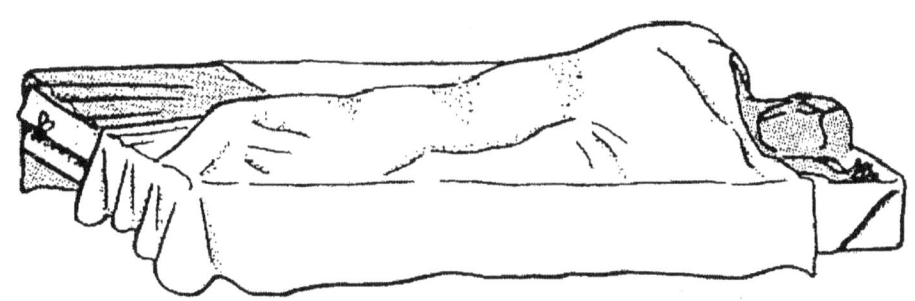

TURN PATIENT ONTO CLEAN LINEN
MAKE OPPOSITE SIDE OF BED

8. SERVING DIETS FROM FOOD CART

PURPOSE

To provide an attractively served food tray for a patient in a hospital where central food tray service is not available.

EQUIPMENT

Cart with food
Cart with trays, dishes, silver, and serving utensils

PROCEDURE

1. Clear the patient's bedside or overbed table.
2. Place table within patient's reach.
3. Place patient in a comfortable position.
4. Wash hands. Wheel food and tray carts to the unit.
5. Place beverage, salad, soup and dessert on the tray.
6. Fill glasses, cups and bowls three fourths full.
7. Serve small portions of hot food in an attractive manner.
8. Check diet list for type of diet each patient is to receive.
9. Carry tray and place it in a convenient position for the patient. Help the patient with the food if necessary.
10. After patient has finished, note how much he has eaten. Collect tray and return to main galley.

POINTS TO EMPHASIZE

1. The ward should be quiet and in readiness for meals.
2. Serve hot food hot and cold food cold.
3. Ice cream, sherbert and jello are kept in the refrigerator until ready to serve.
4. Do not hurry patient.
5. Do not smoke while working with food.
6. Refer to Special Diet Manual for special diet information.
7. Check visible file to determine if patient may have regular diet.
8. Make rounds to check that every patient has been served and received the correct diet.

SERVING DIETS FROM FOOD CART (Continued)

CARE OF EQUIPMENT WHERE MAIN GALLEY DOES NOT HAVE DISH WASHING FACILITIES

1. Scrape and stack dishes:
   a. Solid food into garbage can.
   b. Liquids into drain.
2. Clean and stack trays.
3. Wash dishes with hot soapy water. Stack in dish sterilizer.
4. Follow instructions on sterilizer. Temperature of final rinse water 180° F. Allow to air dry. Put away.
5. Place trays on cart with tray cover, silver and napkins. Salt, pepper, sugar go on all trays except Special Diets.
6. Clean food cart. Return to main galley.

9. CENTRAL TRAY SERVICE

PURPOSE

To provide attractively served food to the patient in an efficient manner.

PROCEDURE

1. Check list of patients who are not permitted food or fluids by mouth.
2. Clear bedside or overbed table.
3. Place table within reach of patient.
4. Place patient in comfortable position.
5. Wash hands. Wheel cart with trays to unit.
6. Take tray from cart and check to see if it is complete.
7. Read tray card.
8. See that tray is served to patient listed on the selective menus or the Special Diet Request that is placed on each tray.
9. Call each patient by name or check his identification band. Place his tray within easy reach.
10. Feed patient or assist him as necessary such as buttering his bread, cutting his meat, etc. Allow patient to do as much for himself as possible.
11. Make rounds to check that each patient entitled to a tray has been fed. The Diet List may be used as a check off list.
12. After the patient has finished eating, collect tray immediately and return to cart. Make a note of food eaten and record on Intake and Output Sheet as indicated.
13. Report all complaints about food to Food Service.

POINTS TO EMPHASIZE

1. Serve trays promptly.
2. Do not hurry patient.
3. Make rounds to check that all patients have been fed.

10. CARE OF ICE MACHINE AND HANDLING OF ICE, BEDSIDE PITCHERS, AND GLASSES

PURPOSE

To prevent ice machines from becoming a source of infection due to cross-contamination.

EQUIPMENT

To clean and disinfect ice machine:
- Clean gloves, disposable
- 4x4 sponges
- Scouring powder
- Sodium hypochlorite
- Clean 1 gallon container
- Clean ice scoop

PROCEDURE

1. Disconnect ice machine from electrical outlet.
2. Wash hands.
3. Use ice scoop to dispose of any existing ice. Pour tap water into ice storage compartment to melt any remaining ice.
4. Put on gloves and remove scale and other debris with 4x4 sponges and scouring powder.
5. Rinse thoroughly with tap water.
6. Place 1/2 ounce of sodium hypocholrite in 1 gallon of water.
7. Using 4 x 4's wipe all accessible areas of interior with sodium hypochlorite solution. Pay particualr attention to ice chute.
8. Repeat step #7.
9. Allow solution to remain in machine for 30 minutes.
10. Rinse thoroughly with clean tap water three times.
11. Clean the exterior of the ice machine.
12. Connect ice machine to electrical outlet.

POINTS TO EMPHASIZE

1. Keep exterior of machine clean between weekly disinfecting of interior.
2. Limit access to ice machine to nursing service personnel.
3. Always keep door closed when not removing ice.
4. Locate ice machine in a "clean" area of the ward or hospital.
5. If ice must be transported, containers should be clean and covered.
6. Use a scoop or tongs when handling ice. Never handle ice with bare hands.
7. Never store the scoop in the ice when not in use.

CARE OF ICE MACHINE AND HANDLING OF
ICE, BEDSIDE PITCHERS, AND GLASSES (Continued)

POINTS TO EMPHASIZE (Continued)

8. The scoop or tongs must be sanitized at least daily.
9. Each patient should have his own bedside water pitcher with cover.
10. Glasses used for drinking water should be sent to the kitchen for exchange of clean glasses on a routine basis.
11. Culture ice machines according to local hospital policy and record in ice culture log.

CARE OF EQUIPMENT

1. Discard disposable equipment.
2. Replace cleaning gear.

11. FEEDING THE HELPLESS PATIENT

PURPOSE

To promote adequate nutrition of the helpless patient.
To encourage self-help when condition permits.

PROCEDURE

1. Place the patient in a sitting position unless otherwise ordered.
2. Place a towel across the patient's chest. Tuck a napkin under his chin.
3. Place tray on overbed table or bedside stand.
4. Give the patient a piece of buttered bread if he is able to hold it.
5. Feed the patient in the order in which he likes to be fed.
6. Offer liquids during the meal. Have patient use a drinking tube if necessary.
7. Give a small amount of food at one time. Allow the patient to chew and swallow food before offering him more. Do not rush your patient.
8. If patient is inclined to talk, talk with him.
9. Note amount of food he has taken. Record amount of fluid if on measured intake and output.
10. Remove tray. Leave patient comfortable.

POINTS TO EMPHASIZE

1. As you are feeding a blind patient tell him what you are offering and whether it is hot or cold.
2. Encourage a blind patient to begin feeding himself as soon as he is able and when indicated.
3. When encouraging a blind patient to feed himself, arrange tray the same way each time. Place foods on plate in the same clockwise direction and fill glasses and cups one-half full to avoid spilling.
4. If patient has difficulty in swallowing, have oral suction machine at bedside.

12. EVENING CARE

PURPOSE

To relax and prepare patient for the night.
To observe the patient's condition.

EQUIPMENT

Basin of warm water
Towel, washcloth and soap
Toothbrush, and dentifrice/mouthwash
Curved basin
Glass of water
Rubbing alcohol/skin lotion
Comb

PROCEDURE

1. Offer bedpan and urinal.
2. Give oral hygiene.
3. Wash patient's face and hands.
4. Wash back. Give back rub. Comb hair.
5. Straighten and tighten bottom sheets.
6. Freshen pillows.
7. Place extra blanket at foot of bed if weather is cool.
8. Make provision for ventilation of unit.
9. Clean and straighten unit and remove excess gear.

POINTS TO EMPHASIZE

1. Indicated for all bed patients and those on limited activity.
2. Change soiled linen as necessary.
3. Patient may assist with care as condition permits.
4. Ask the patient if soap may be used on the face.
5. Screen patients who require the use of bedpan.

13. CARE OF THE SERIOUSLY ILL PATIENT

PURPOSE

To provide optimum care and close observation of the seriously ill patient.
To keep the patient mentally and physically comfortable.

EQUIPMENT

Special mouth care tray
Rubbing alcohol/skin lotion
Bed linen as necessary
Pillow and/or supporting appliances
Special equipment as needed:

- I.V. Standard
- Suction machine
- Oxygen
- Drainage bottles
- Intake and Output work sheet

PROCEDURE

1. Place patient where he can be easily and <u>closely</u> observed.
2. Keep room quiet, clean and clear of excess gear.
3. Bathe patient daily and P.R.N.
4. Maintain good oral hygiene every 2-4 hours.
5. Wash, rub back and change position every 2 hours unless contraindicated.
6. Speak to patient in a calm, natural tone of voice even if he appears to be unconscious.
7. Report any sudden change in condition.
8. Keep an accurate intake and output record if ordered.
9. Offer fluids if patient is conscious and is able to take them.
10. Record and Report:
    a. Changes in T.P.R. and blood pressure.
    b. State of consciousness.
    c. All observations.

CARE OF THE SERIOUSLY ILL PATIENT (Continued)

POINTS TO EMPHASIZE

1. All patients are seen by a chaplain when they are placed on the Serious or Very Seriously ill list.
2. Be considerate and kind to the patient's relatives.
3. Keep charting up-to-date.
4. Do not discuss patient's condition when the conversation might be overheard by the patient or unauthorized persons.
5. Refer all questions concerning the patient's condition to the doctor or nurse.
6. Be sure all procedures for placing a patient on the SL or VSL have been completed; for exmaple, inventory of personal effects and valuables.

BASIC NURSING PROCEDURES:
TAKING TEMPERATURE, PULSE, AND BLOOD PRESSURE

CONTENTS

		Page
I.	TAKING ORAL TEMPERATURE	
	A. Thermometers Disinfected on Ward	1
	B. Individual Thermometer Technique	4
	C. Taking Temperatures With the Electronic Thermometer	6
II.	TAKING AXILLARY TEMPERATURE	7
III.	TAKING RECTAL TEMPERATURE	8
	A. Thermometers Disinfected on Ward	8
	B. Thermometers Disinfected in Central Supply Room	9
IV.	TAKING PULSE AND RESPIRATION	10
V.	APICAL-RADIAL PULSE	11
VI.	TAKING BLOOD PRESSURE	12
VII.	RECORDING ON THE TEMPERATURE, PULSE, AND RESPIRATION FORM	13
VIII.	RECORDING ON PLOTTING CHART	19

BASIC NURSING PROCEDURES: TAKING TEMPERATURE, PULSE, AND BLOOD PRESSURE

I. TAKING ORAL TEMPERATURE
A. THERMOMETERS DISINFECTED ON WARD

PURPOSE

To determine the patient's body temperature as recorded on a clinical thermometer.

EQUIPMENT
1. Tray containing:
    a. Two containers of disinfecting agent marked #1 and #2
    b. Container of green soap solution
    c. Container of water
    d. Container of clean cotton
    e. Waste container for soiled cotton
    f. Minimum of 6 thermometers, 3 in each container of disinfecting solution
    g. T.P.R. book
    h. Pencil and pen
    i. Watch with second hand

PROCEDURE
1. Take equipment to bedside.
2. Tell the patient what you are going to do.
3. Remove thermometer from container #1.
4. Wipe thermometer (over waste container) with water moistened sponge from stem to bulb using rotary motion. Discard sponge in waste container.
5. Shake down thermometer mercury to 95° F.
6. Place thermometer under patient's tongue. Caution him to keep his lips closed.
7. Distribute other thermometers to second and third patients in same manner.
8. Take third patient's pulse and respiration. Record results in T.P.R. book.
9. Take pulse and respiration of second patient, record, then first patient. Record results in T.P.R. book.
10. Remove thermometer from first patient's mouth after 3 minutes.
11. Wash thermometer (over waste container) with soap-moistened sponge from stem to bulb using rotary motion. Discard sponge in waste container.

PROCEDURE (Continued)

12. Moisten cotton sponge with water and wipe thermometer from stem to bulb in a rotary container. Discard sponge in waste container.
13. Read thermometer. Record results in T.P.R. book.
14. Place thermometer in the <u>original</u> container of disinfecting agent.
15. Repeat the steps 10 through 13 for second and third patients.
16. Disinfect these thermometers for a minimum of 20 minutes (depending on disinfecting agent used).
17. Continue using thermometers from alternate containers until all patient's temperatures have been taken.
18. Record T.P.R.'s on SP 511.

CARE OF EQUIPMENT

1. After each use
    a. Remove waste.
    b. Clean tray.
    c. Reset tray.
    d. Replace solutions (water - soap).
2. Daily
    a. Wash containers in warm, soapy water, rinse and dry.
    b. Change all solutions.
    c. Wash thermometers in cold, soapy water, rinse and place in disinfecting agent.
    d. Refill and reset tray.

POINTS TO EMPHASIZE

1. Wait for 10 minutes before taking temperature of patient who has had hot or cold drink or who has been smoking.
2. Be sure thermometer reads 95 or below before using it.
3. Encircle abnormal vital signs with red pencil in T.P.R. book.
4. Report all abnormal vital signs to Charge Nurse.
5. Describe quality of pulse and respiration in the observation column on Nursing Notes (SF 510).

POINTS TO EMPHASIZE (Continued)
6. After washing thermometer with soap, be sure to rinse well with water before putting it into disinfectant, as bacterial action is nullified in the presence of soap; for example, Zephiran chloride and iodine preparations.
7. Individual thermometers should be used for patients suspected of having a communicable disease.

THERMOMETERS STERILIZED IN CENTRAL SUPPLY ROOM

EQUIPMENT
1. Tray containing:
   a. Container of sterile oral thermometers that are sealed in paper envelopes.
   b. Container of green soap solution.
   c. Container of clean cotton.
   d. Container for waste material.
   e. T.P.R. book.
   f. Pencil.
   g. Watch with second hand.

PROCEDURE
1. Tell the patient what you are going to do.
2. Remove thermometer from envelope.
3. Shake thermometer mercury to 95° F.
4. Place thermometer under patient's tongue. Caution him to keep his lips closed.
5. Take, record and report vital signs as in previous procedure, numbers 7 through 11, pages 25 and 26.

CARE OF EQUIPMENT
1. After each use:
   a. Empty container of waste cotton.
   b. Return container of soiled thermometers to CSR in accordance with local instructions and exchange for an adequate supply of clean thermometers.
   c. Reset tray.
2. Daily:
   a. Wash containers in warm, soapy water, rinse and dry.
   b. Refill and reset tray.

TAKING ORAL TEMPERATURE
B. INDIVIDUAL THERMOMETER TECHNIQUE

PURPOSE

To determine the patient's body temperature as recorded on a clinical thermometer.

EQUIPMENT
1. Individual thermometer for each patient at bedside
2. Plastic thermometer holder with disinfectant solution - protective container of 2 1/2 cc. disposable syringe can be used
3. Adhesive tape
4. Container of clean cotton balls
5. Container for soiled cotton balls
6. T.P.R. book and pen
7. Watch with second hand

PROCEDURE
1. Upon admission, set up thermometer and holder at patient's unit:
   a. Fill thermometer holder (protective container from a 2 1/2 cc. disposable syringe) with disinfectant.
   b. Place thermometer inside container.
   c. Tape container to head of bed or side of bedside locker.
2. When taking temperatures:
   a. Take containers for cotton balls to bedside.
   b. Tell patient what you are going to do.
   c. Remove thermometer from holder.
   d. Wipe thermometer with clean cotton ball. Discard cotton ball in waste container.
   e. Shake down thermometer mercury to 95° F.
   f. Place thermometer under patient's tongue.
   g. Follow above steps to second and third patient,
   h. Take third patient's pulse and respiration. Record results in T.P.R. book.
   i. Take pulse and respiration of second patient, record, then first patient,
   j. Remove thermometer from first patient's mouth after 3 minutes.
   k. Wipe thermometer with clean cotton ball. Discard cotton ball in waste container.
   l. Read thermometer and replace in holder. Record results in T.P.R. book,
   m. Repeat steps j through l for second and third patient.

CARE OF EQUIPMENT
1. After each use:
   a. Discard soiled cotton balls and container.
2. Weekly and when patient is discharged:
   a. Collect thermometers and holders.
   b. Disinfect thermometers as outlined on page 26.
   c. Place in new holders containing disinfectant.
   d. Discard old holders.
   e. Replace thermometers and holders at bedside.

C. TAKING TEMPERATURES WITH THE ELECTRONIC THERMOMETER

PURPOSE
To determine the patient's body temperature with an electronic thermometer which is a beat sending device with an accuracy of a plus or minus of .2 degrees. It utilizes a disposable probe cover and records oral and rectal temperatures within 15 seconds.

EQUIPMENT
1. Base for electronic thermometer
2. Thermometer with oral probe (sensing device)
3. Rectal probes where applicable
4. Disposable probe covers

PROCEDURE
1. Remove probe from base which is connected to electricity.
2. Attach strap of thermometer around shoulder to secure thermometer to side (left side if right handed).
3. Remove probe and insert probe into disposable probe cover.
4. Turn thermometer on by pressing small bar on top.
5. Place covered probe into patient's mouth in the sublingual area and slowly push probe along the base of the tongue as far back as possible without discomfort to the patient.
6. Hold probe in place until indicator on thermometer records a completed thermometer reading.
7. Transfer reading to appropriate records.
8. Eject the disposable probe cover.
9. Press bar on back of thermometer erasing present reading and repeat the above procedure for the next patient.
10. Remove thermometer pack and replace securely in base for recharging thermometer.

POINTS TO EMPHASIZE
1. Grasp probe at reinforced area in the center to decrease breakage.
2. Always keep base plugged into electrical current.
3. Always keep thermometer in base when not in use to keep the battery charged.
4. Use specified probe for rectal temperature and insert probe cover 1/2 inch on adults or 1/4 inch on babies for accurate recordings.
5. For axillary temperatures do not press bar to activate thermometer until the oral probe with cover is in place, then allow 60-90 seconds for recording of temperature. Indicator will not come on.

II. TAKING AXILLARY TEMPERATURE

PURPOSE

To determine a patient's temperature when the oral or rectal route is contraindicated.

EQUIPMENT

Oral thermometer tray
T.P.R. book
Pencil or pen
Watch with a second hand

PROCEDURE

Same as for oral temperature (pages 1 and 2) except:
1. Wipe axilla dry.
2. Place oral thermometer in axilla. Have patient cross arms over chest.
3. Leave thermometer in place for 10 minutes.
4. Write "A" above temperature in T.P.R. book, and T.P.R. graph (SF 511).

III. TAKING RECTAL TEMPERATURE
A. THERMOMETERS DISINFECTED ON WARD

PURPOSE
To determine patient's temperature when the oral method is contraindicated.

EQUIPMENT
1. Tray containing
   a. Two containers of disinfecting agent marked #1 and #2
   b. Container of green soap solution
   c. Container of water
   d. Container of clean cotton sponges
   e. Container for waste cotton sponges
   f. Minimum of 4 thermometers in container #1 of disinfecting agent. (Number of thermometers determined by ward needs).
   g. Tube of water soluble lubricant
   h. T.P.R. book
   i. Pencil and pen
   j. Watch with second hand

PROCEDURE
1. Take equipment to bedside.
2. Tell patient what you are going to do.
3. Remove thermometer from container fl.
4. Wipe thermometer (over waste container) with water moistened sponge from stem to bulb using a rotary motion. Discard sponge in waste container.
5. Shake thermometer mercury to 95° F.
6. Lubricate thermometer with water soluble lubricant.
7. Turn patient on side unless contraindicated.
8. Separate buttocks and gently insert thermometer 1 1/2 inches into the rectum in an upward and forward direction. Insert 1/2 - 3/4 inch in infants and children.
9. Hold thermometer in place for 5 minutes. Count pulse and respiration and record in T.P.R. book.
10. Remove thermometer.
11. Wash thermometer (over waste container) with soap moistened sponge from stem to bulb using rotary motion. Discard sponge in waste container.
12. Moisten cotton sponge with water and wipe thermometer from stem to bulb in a rotary motion. Discard sponge in waste container.
13. Read thermometer and record temperature in T.P.R. book. Place "R" above recording to indicate that it was taken rectally.
14. Return thermometer to glass #2 for sterilization for a minimum of 20 minutes.
15. Leave patient in comfortable position.

16. Record T.P.R.'s on SF 511. Use "R" to indicate rectal temperature.
17. Continue taking additional rectal temperatures in the same manner.

CARE OF EQUIPMENT
1. After each use
   a. Remove waste.
   b. Clean tray.
   c. Transfer thermometers from container 12 to container #1 after 20 minutes has elapsed.
   d. Replace water and soap solution.
   e. Reset tray.
2. Daily
   a. Wash containers in warm, soapy water, rinse and dry.
   b. Change all solutions.
   c. Wash thermometers in cold, soapy water, rinse well and place in disinfectant agent.
   d. Refill and reset tray.

POINTS TO EMPHASIZE
1. Wait 30 minutes before taking temperature on patient who has had an enema.
2. Use only a stub bulb thermometer expressly made for rectal use.
3. Do not leave patient unattended while thermometer is inserted.
4. Report abnormal vital signs to Charge Nurse.
5. Describe the quality of pulse and respirations in observation column on Nursing Notes (SF 510). On wards where many rectal temperatures are taken, (for example, Pediatrics, ICU, etc.), increase the number of thermometers in each container. Continue using thermometers from alternate containers, allowing at least 20 minutes for sterilization, until all patients' temperatures are taken.
6. Be sure to rinse thermometer well before putting it into the disinfectant, as bacterial action is nullified in the presence of soap - for example, Zephiran chloride and iodine preparations.

B. THERMOMETERS DISINFECTED IN CENTRAL SUPPLY ROOM

EQUIPMENT
1. Tray containing
   a. Container of rectal thermometers sealed in paper envelopes
   b. Container of clean cotton sponges
   c. Container of soap solution
   d. Container for waste cotton sponges
   e. Container for used thermometers
   f. Tube of water soluble lubricant

g. T.P.R. book
h. Pencil or pen
i. Watch with second hand

PROCEDURE
1. Remove thermometer from envelope.
2. Take, record and report vital signs as in previous procedure page 30.
3. Return thermometer to container of soap solution for return to C.S.R.

CARE OF EQUIPMENT
1. After each use
   Remove waste
   Clean tray
2. Daily
   Return container of thermometers to C.S.R. in accordance with local instructions and exchange for supply of sterile thermometers.
   Wash containers in warm/ soapy water, rinse and dry.
   Refill and reset tray.

IV. TAKING PULSE AND RESPIRATION

PURPOSE

To determine the character and rate of the pulse and respiration.

EQUIPMENT
Watch with a second hand
Pencil or pen
T. P. R. book

PROCEDURE
1. Tell patient what he is to do.
2. Have the patient lie down or sit in chair. Draw his arm and hand across his chest.
3. Place three fingers over the radial artery on the thumb side of the patient's wrist. Use just enough pressure to feel the pulse beat.
4. Observe the general character of the pulse, then count the number of beats for 30 seconds, multiply by two. If any deviation from normal or irregularity is noted, count for one full minute.
5. With the fingers still on the wrist, count the rise and fall of the chest or upper abdomen for 30 seconds, multiply by 2. If any irregularity or difficulty is noted, count for one full minute.
5. Record in T. P. R. book and report any abnormality.

POINTS TO EMPHASIZE
DO NOT use thumb when taking pulse beat.

V. APICAL-RADIAL PULSE

PURPOSE
To compare the pulse rate of the heart at the apex and the pulse rate in the radial artery.

EQUIPMENT
Stethoscope
Watch with second hand

PROCEDURE
1. Tell patient what you are going to do.
2. Have patient lie quietly in bed.
3. Open pajama coat to expose chest.
4. One person standing on the left side of the bed places a stethoscope over apex of heart (slightly below and to the right of the left nipple) to locate the apical heart beat.
5. Another person standing on the right side of bed locates the radial pulse; hold watch so that it can be seen by both people.
6. Using the same watch and at a signal from the person taking the apical pulse, both people count for one minute.
7. Replace pajama coat; leave patient comfortable.
8. Record in observation column on Nursing Notes (SF 510). Example: Apical 92. Radial 86.

POINTS TO EMPHASIZE
Two corpsmen are necessary to carry out this procedure because the two pulses must be taken at the same time to compare rates.

CARE OF EQUIPMENT
1. Wipe earpieces and diaphragm/bell of stethoscope with alcohol sponges before and after procedure.
2. Return stethoscope to proper place.

VI. TAKING BLOOD PRESSURE

PURPOSE
To determine the pressure which the blood exerts against the walls of the vessels.

EQUIPMENT
Sphygmomanometer
Stethoscope
Pencil and paper
Alcohol sponges

PROCEDURE
1. Tell patient what you are going to do.
2. Place patient in comfortable position sitting or lying down.
3. Place rubber portion of cuff over the brachial artery. Secure either by hooking or wrapping depending on the type of apparatus.
4. Clip indicator to cuff (aneroid) or place apparatus on a level surface (mercury) at about heart level. Make sure the tubing is not kinked and that it does not rub against the apparatus.
5. Locate brachial pulse at bend of elbow.
6. Place stethoscope in ears with ear pieces pointing forward.
7. Hold stethoscope in place over the brachial artery. Inflate cuff until the indicator registers 200 mm. Loosen thumb screw of valve and allow air to escape slowly.
8. Listen for the sounds. Watch the indicator. Note where the first distinct rhythmic sound is heard. This is the Systolic Pressure.
9. Continue releasing air from the cuff. Note where sound changes to dull muffled beat. This is the Diastolic Pressure.
10. Open valve completely. Release all air from cuff.
11. Remove cuff. Record reading.

POINTS TO EMPHASIZE
1. Either arm may be used in taking blood pressure, but in repeating readings, it is important to use the same arm.
2. Some departments in the hospital may define diastolic pressure as the last sound heard.
3. If unsure of reading, completely deflate cuff and repeat procedure.

CARE OF EQUIPMENT
1. Fold and replace cuff.
2. Wipe ear pieces and bell/diaphragm of stethoscope with alcohol sponge before and after procedure. Replace.

VII. RECORDING ON THE TEMPERATURE, PULSE, AND RESPIRATION FORM

PURPOSE
To keep an accurate and up-to-date record of the patient's cardinal or vital signs.

EQUIPMENT
Pen with black or blue-black ink
Standard Form 511, Temperature-Pulse-Respiration
Ruler
Addressograph plate

PROCEDURE
1. Complete identifying data in lower left corner of SF-511.
2. Fill in spaces as indicated in the heading by printing:
   Month
   Date of month.
   Hospital day.
   Postoperative or postpartum day.
   Hours T.P.R's are taken.
3. Using a small dot, record temperature and pulse in spaces corresponding vertically to hour and horizontally to scales on left side of form. Join dots of previous readings by drawing straight lines with ruler.
4. Print respiration rate in space indicated to correspond with date and hour taken.
5. Record blood pressure in space indicated to correspond with date and hour taken.
6. Record height and weight on admission in spaces provided. Repeated weight recordings are made to correspond with date and hour taken.

POINTS TO EMPHASIZE
1. For every four hour and twice a day temperature and pulse, record within dotted lines.
2. For four times a day temperature and pulse, record on dotted lines.
3. Blood pressures required more than twice a day should be graphed on a Plotting Chart (SF 512).
4. Any pecularities of the patient that affects the temperature, pulse, or respiration, i.e.; drop in temperature due to medication; ongoing cooling procedure; and/or absences from ward, may be recorded in ..graphic column at the designated time.
5. Indicate method - if axillary or rectal is used.

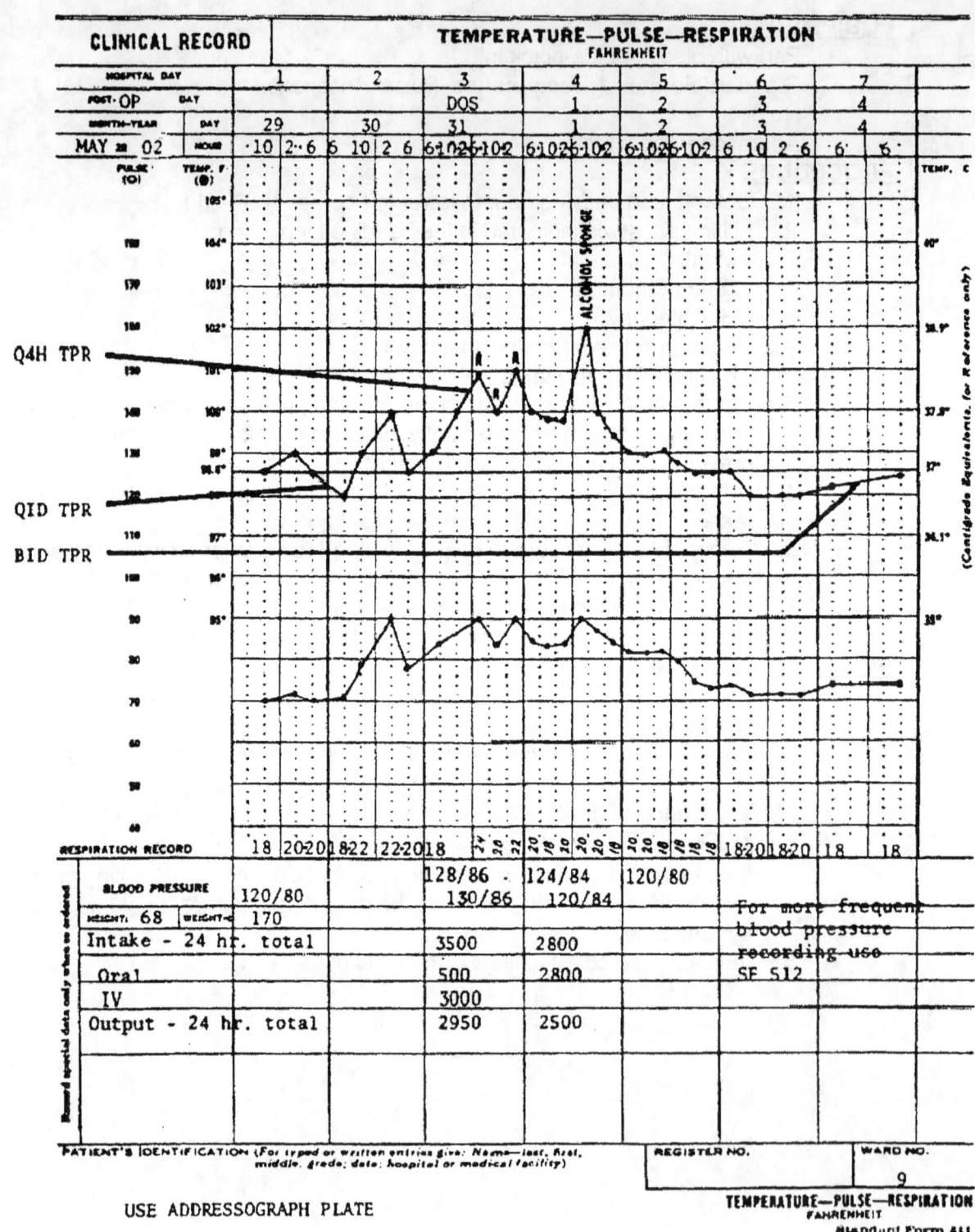

SAMPLE TEMPERATURE - PULSE -RESPIRATION (SF511)

USING THE TEMPERATURE - PULSE - RESPIRATION
GRAPHIC FORM 511

All entries shall be lettered in black or blue-black ink. Ballpoint pens may be used. Each sheet should have identifying data at the foot of each page. These data should be legible, correct and complete.

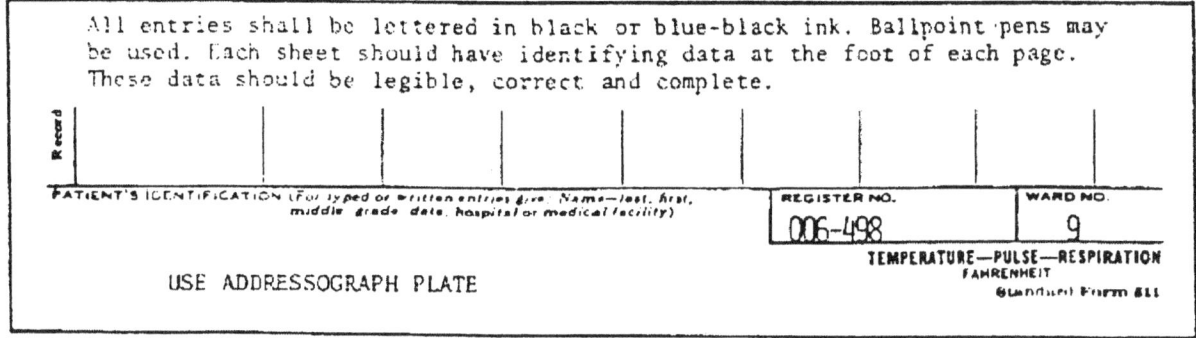

Each sheet is divided into seven major columns, one for each day of the week. The day of admission is the first hospital day.

The month, day of the month, and year appear in the spaces for that purpose. In the sample below, the patient was admitted to the hospital on May 7, 2002.

The day of operation or delivery is lettered "Operation" or "Delivery". The following day is the first postoperative or postdelivery day. For example, if the patient had surgery on his third hospital day, the chart would appear as follows:

CLINICAL RECORD

HOSPITAL DAY		1	
POST- OP DAY			
MONTH-YEAR	DAY	7	
MAY 20 02	HOUR	6	6

PULSE (O)	TEMP. F (●)		
	105°		
180	104°		
170	103°		
160	102°		
150	101°		
140	100°		
130	99°		
	98.6°		●
120	98°		
110	97°	●	
100	96°		
90	95°		
80			●
70		●	
60			
50			
40			
RESPIRATION RECORD		16	18

To chart the temperature and pulse, place a dot on the graph according to the scale on the left in the vertical column that designates the correct time and date. Connect the dot of the previous recording with a solid line.

The respirations are recorded in the vertical column according to the hour.

In the sample at the left the 6 a.m. TPR was 97-72-16. The 6 p.m. TPR was 98.6-76-18.

Each day is divided into two columns, a.m. and p.m.

CLINICAL RECORD		TEMPERATURE—PULSE—RESPIRATION FAHRENHEIT								
HOSPITAL DAY		1	2	3	4	5	6	7		
POST- OP DAY				DOS	1	2	3	4		
MONTH-YEAR MAY 02	DAY	7	8	9	10	11	12	13		
	HOUR	. .	. .	. .	. .	. .	. .	. .		
PULSE (♥)	TEMP. F (●)	: :	: :	: :	: :	: :	: :	: :		TEMP. C
		a.m. p.m.								

The a.m. and p.m. subdivision is further divided by two vertical dotted lines. For every four hour temperature and pulse reading, place the recordings WITHIN the dotted lines.

CLINICAL RECORD		TEMPERATURE—PULSE—RESPIRATION FAHRENHEIT								
HOSPITAL DAY		1	2	3	4	5	6	7		
POST- OP DAY				DOS	1	2	3	4		
MONTH-YEAR MAY 02	DAY	7	8	9	10	11	12	13		
	HOUR	2·6·10 2·6·10	2·6·10 2·6·10	2·6·10 2·6·10	2·6·10 2·6·10	2·6·10 2·6·10	2·6·10 2·6·10	2·6·10 2·6·10		
PULSE (♥)	TEMP. F (●)	: : :	: : :	: : :	: : :	: : :	: : :	: : :		TEMP. C

2 a.m. / 6 a.m. / 10 a.m. / 2 p.m. / 6 p.m. / 10 p.m.

Twice a day temperature and pulse recordings are placed WITHIN the dotted lines in the center of the a.m. and p.m. column.

CLINICAL RECORD		TEMPERATURE—PULSE—RESPIRATION FAHRENHEIT								
HOSPITAL DAY		1	2	3	4	5	6	7		
POST- OP DAY				DOS	1	2	3	4		
MONTH-YEAR MAY 02	DAY	7	8	9	10	11	12	13		
	HOUR	·6· ·6·	·6· ·6·	·6· ·6·	·6· ·6·	·6· ·6·	·6· ·6·	·6· ·6·		
PULSE (○)	TEMP. F (●)	: : :	: : :	: : :	: : :	: : :	: : :	: : :		TEMP.

6 a.m. / 6 p.m.

For four-times-a-day readings, place the recordings ON the dotted lines.

CLINICAL RECORD		TEMPERATURE—PULSE—RESPIRATION FAHRENHEIT								
HOSPITAL DAY		1	2	3	4	5	6	7		
POST- OP DAY				DOS	1	2	3	4		
MONTH-YEAR MAY 02	DAY	7	8	9	10	11	12	13		
	HOUR	6 10 2 6	6 10 2 6	6 10 2 6	6 10 2 6	6 10 2 6	6 10 2 6	6 10 2 6		
PULSE	TEMP. F	. . . .	. . . .	. . . .	. . . .	. . . .	. . . .	. . . .		TEMP. C

6 a.m. / 10 a.m. / 2 p.m. / 6 p.m.

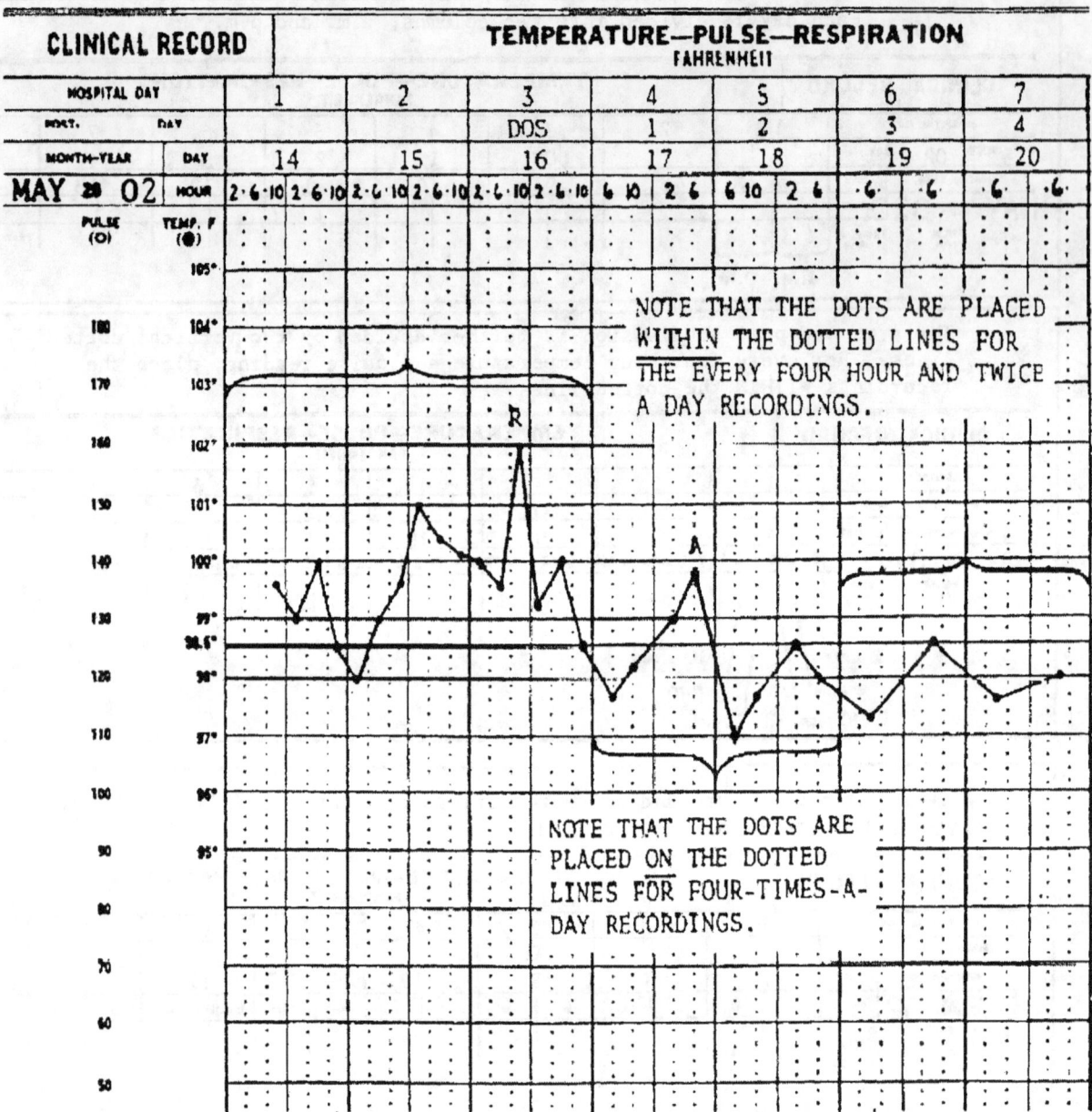

If a temperature is taken by rectum, place an "R" (for rectal) above the dot on the graph.
If a temperature is taken by axilla, place an "A" (for axillary) above the dot on the graph.

VIII. RECORDING ON PLOTTING CHART

PURPOSE

To keep an accurate, visible record of repeated observations of intake-output, weight, blood pressure, etc.

EQUIPMENT

Pen with, black or blue-black ink
Standard Form 512, Plotting Chart
Ruler

PROCEDURE

1. Complete identifying data in lower left corner of chart. (Page 25)
2. Print date and purpose in upper left corner.
3. Calibrate measurements along vertical portion of graph:
    Start scale at bottom working toward top at a definite and uniform rate of progression, as 0-10-20.30.
    Label scale at top to show unit of measure as cc. , lbs. , or mm.
4. Note date time intervals of measure along top horizontal portion of graph.
5. Show meaning of symbols used in a key to the side of graph.

Note: Red pencil may be ued when filling in bar graphs.

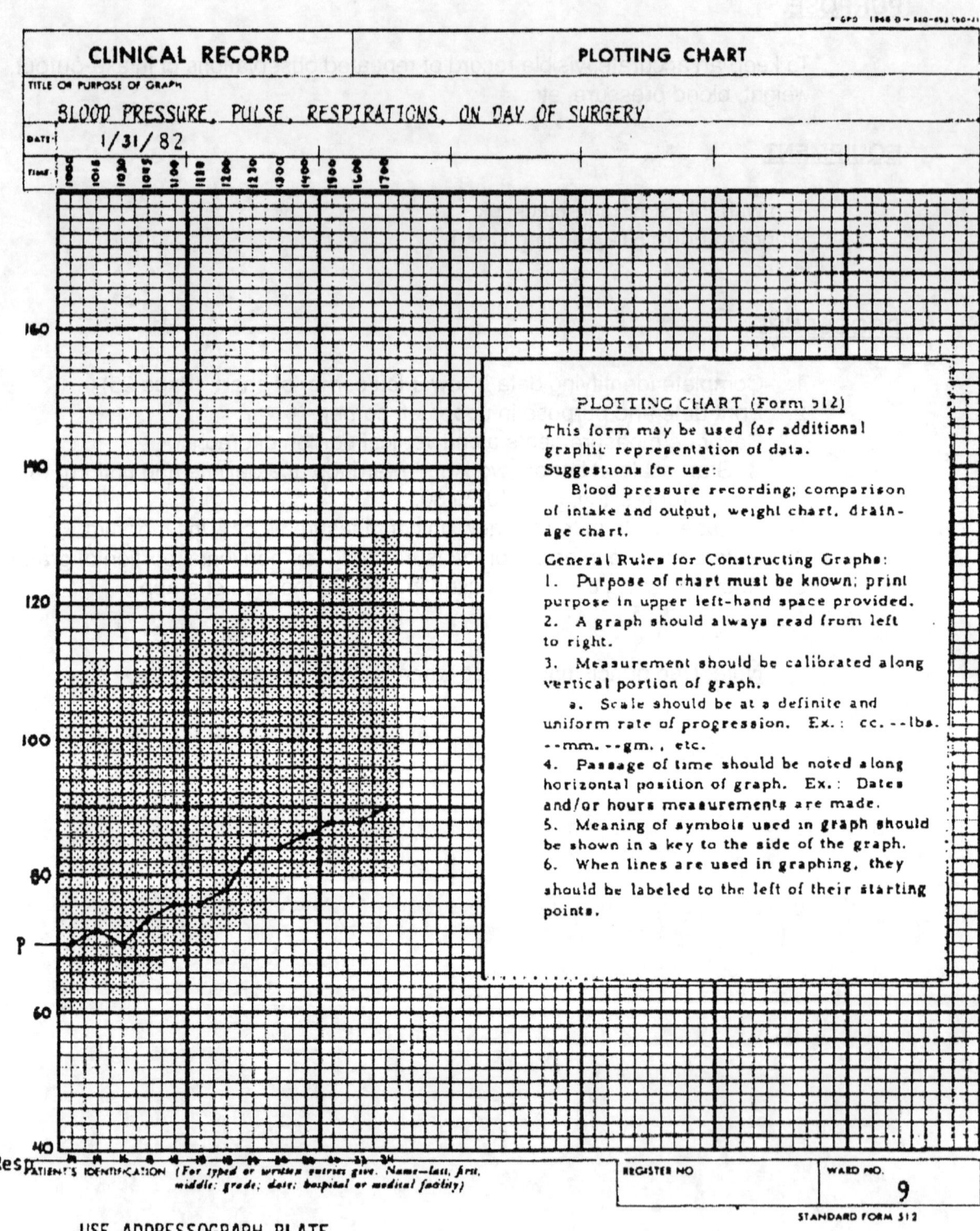

COMMON DIAGNOSTIC NORMS

CONTENTS

		Page
1.	Respiration	1
2.	Pulse-Rate	1
3.	Blood Pressure	1
4.	Blood Metabolism	1
5.	Blood	1
6.	Urine	3
7.	Spinal Fluid	4
8.	Snellen Chart Fractions	4

COMMON DIAGNOSTIC NORMS

1. RESPIRATION: From 16-20 per minute.

2. PULSE-RATE: Men, about 72 per minute.
   Women, about 80 per minute.

3. BLOOD PRESSURE:
   Men: 110-135 (Systolic)   Women: 95-125   (Systolic)
        70-85   (Diastolic)   65-70   (Diastolic)

4. BASAL METABOLISM: Represents the body energy expended to maintain respiration, circulation, etc. Normal rate ranges from plus 10 to minus 10.

5. BLOOD:

   a. Red Blood (Erythrocyte) Count:
   Male adult - 5,000,000 per cu. mm.
   Female adult - 4,500,000 per cu. mm.
   (Increased in polycythemia vera, poisoning by carbon monoxide, in chronic pulmonary artery sclerosis, and in concentration of blood by sweating, vomiting, or diarrhea.)
   (Decreased in pernicious anemia, secondary anemia, and hypochronic anemia.)
   b. White Blood (Leukocyte) Count: 6,000 to 8,000 per cu. mm.
   (Increased with muscular exercise, acute infections, intestinal obstruction, coronary thrombosis, leukemias.)
   (Decreased due to injury to source of blood formation and interference in delivery of cells to bloodstream, typhoid, pernicious anemia, arsenic and benzol poisoning.)
   The total leukocyte group is made up of a number of diverse varieties of white blood cells. Not only the total leukocyte count, but also the relative count of the diverse varieties, is an important aid to diagnosis. In normal blood, from:
   70-72% of the leukocytes are *polymorphonuclear neuirophils.*
   2-4% of the leukocytes are *polymorphonuclear eosinophils.*
   0-.5% of the leukocytes are *basophils,*
   20-25% of the leukocytes are *lymphocytes.*
   2-6% of the leukocytes are *monocytes.*
   c. Blood Platelet (Thrombocyte) Count:
   250,000 per cu. mm. Blood platelets are important in blood coagulation.

   d. Hemoglobin Content:
   May normally vary from 85-100%. A 100% hemoglobin content is equivalent to the presence of 15.6 grams of hemoglobin in 100 c.c. of blood.
   e. Color Index:
   Represents the relative amount of hemoglobin contained in a red blood corpuscle compared with that of a normal individual of the patient's age and sex.
   The normal is 1. To determine the color index, the percentage of hemoglobin is divided by the ratio of red cells in the patient's blood to a norm of 5,000,000. Thus, a hemoglobin content of 60% and a red cell count of 4,000,000 (80% of 5,000,000) produces an abnormal color index of .75.

f. Sedimentation Rate:
   Represents the measurement of the speed with which red cells settle toward the bottom of a containing vessel. The rate is expressed in millimeters per hour, and indicates the total sedimentation of red blood cells at the end of 60 minutes.

Average rate:	4-7 mm. in 1 hour
Slightly abnormal rate:	8-15 mm. in 1 hour
Moderately abnormal rate:	16-40 mm. in 1 hour
Considerably abnormal rate:	41-80 mm. in 1 hour

   (The sedimentation rate is above normal in patients with chronic infections, or in whom there is a disease process involving destruction of tissue, such as coronary thrombosis, etc.)

g. Blood Sugar:
   90-120 mg. per 100 c.c. (Normal)
   In mild diabetics: 150-300 mg. per 100 c.c.
   In severe diabetics: 300-1200 mg. per 100 c.c.

h. Blood Lead:
   0.1 mg. or less in 100 c.c. (Normal). Greatly increased in lead poisoning.

i. Non-Protein Nitrogen:
   Since the function of the kidneys is to remove from the blood certain of the waste products of cellular activity, any degree of accumulation of these waste products in the blood is a measure of renal malfunction. For testing purposes, the substances chosen for measurement are the nitrogen-containing products of protein combustion, their amounts being estimated in terms of the nitrogen they contain. These substances are urea, uric acid, and creatinine, the sum total of which, in addition to any traces of other waste products, being designated as total non-protein nitrogen (NPN).

   The normal limits of NPN in 100 c.c. of blood range from 25-40 mg. Of this total, urea nitrogen normally constitutes 12-15 mg., uric acid 2-4 mg., and creatinine 1-2 mg.

6. URINE:

   a. Urine - Lead:
      0.08 mg. per liter of urine (normal).
      (Increased in lead poisoning.)
   b. Sugar:
      From none to a faint trace (normal).
      From 0.5% upwards (abnormal).
      (Increased in diabetes mellitus.)
   c. Urea:
      Normal excretion ranges from 15-40 grams in 24 hours.
      (Increased in fever and toxic states.)
   d. Uric Acid:
      Normal excretion is variable. (Increased in leukemia and gout.)
   e. Albumin:
      Normal renal cells allow a trace of albumin to pass into the urine, but this trace is so minute that it cannot be detected by ordinary tests.

f. Casts:
   In some abnormal conditions, the kidney tubules become lined with substances which harden and form a mould or oast inside the tubes. These are later washed out by the urine, and may be detected microscopically. They are named either from the substance composing them, or from their appearance. Thus, there are pus casts, epithelial casts from the walls of the tubes, hyaline casts formed from coagulable elements of the blood, etc.
g. Pus Cells:
   These are found in the urine in cases of nephritis or other inflammatory conditions of the urinary tract.
h. Epithelial Cells:
   These are always present in the urine. Their number is greatly multiplied, however, in inflammatory conditions of the urinary tract.
i. Specific Gravity:
   This is the ratio between the weight of a given volume of urine to that of the same volume of water. A normal reading ranges from 1.015 to 1.025. A high specific gravity usually occurs in diabetes mellitus. A low specific gravity is associated with a polyuria.

7. SPINAL FLUID:

   a. Spinal Fluid Pressure (Manometric Reading):
      100-200 mm. of water or 7-15 mm. of mercury (normal).
      (Increased in cerebral edema, cerebral hemorrhage, meningitis, certain brain tumors, or if there is some process blocking the fluid circulation in the spinal column, such as a tumor or herniated nucleus pulposus impinging on the spinal canal.)
   b. Quickenstedt's Sign:
      When the veins in the neck are compressed on one or both sides, there is a rapid rise in the pressure of the cerebrospinal fluid of healthy persons, and this rise quickly disappears when pressure is removed from the neck. But when there is a block of the vertebral canal, the pressure of the cerebrospinal fluid is little or not at all affected by this maneuver.
   c. Cerebrospinal Sugar:
      50-60 mg. per 100 c.c. of spinal fluid (normal).
      (Increased in epidemic encephalitis, diabetes mellitus, and increased intracranial pressure.)
      (Decreased in purulent and tuberculous meningitis.)
   d. Cerebrospinal Protein:
      15-40 mg. per 100 c.c. of spinal fluid (normal).
      (Increased in suppurative meningitis, epileptic seizures, cerebrospinal syphilis, anterior poliomyelitis, brain abscess, and brain tumor.)
   e. Colloidal Gold Test:
      This test is made to determine the presence of cerebrospinal protein.
   f. Cerebrospinal Cell Count:
      0-10 lymphocytes per cu. mm. (normal).
   g. Cerebrospinal Globulin:
      Normally negative. It is positive in various types of meningitis, various types of syphilis of the central nervous system, in poliomyelitis, in brain tumor, and in intracranial hemorrhage.

8. **SNELLEN CHART FRACTIONS AS SCHEDULE LOSS DETERMINANTS:**

   a. Visual acuity is expressed by a Snell Fraction, where the numerator represents the distance, in feet, between the subject and the test chart, and the denominator represents the distance, in feet, at which a normal eye could read a type size which the abnormal eye can read only at 20 feet.
   b. Thus, 20/20 means that an individual placed 20 feet from the test chart clearly sees the size of type that one with normal vision should see at that distance.
   c. 20/60 means that an individual placed 20 feet from the test chart can read only a type size, at a distance of 20 feet, which one of normal vision could read at 60 feet.
   d. Reduction of a Snellen Fraction to its simplest form roughly indicates the amount of vision remaining in an eye. Thus, a visual acuity of 20/60 corrected implies a useful vision of 1/3 or 33 1/3%, and a visual loss of 2/3 or 66 2/3% of the eye.

   Similarly:

Visual Acuity (Corrected)	Percentage Loss of Use of Eye
20/20	No loss
20/25	20%
20/30	33 1/3%
20/40	50%
20/50	60%
20/60	66 2/3%
20/70	70% (app.)
20/80	75%
20/100	100% (since loss of 80% or more constitutes industrial blindness)

www.ingramcontent.com/pod-product-compliance
Lightning Source LLC
Chambersburg PA
CBHW082034300426
44117CB00015B/2481